Sum of Us

Also by Georgina Sturge

Bad Data

Sum of Us

A History of the UK in Data

Georgina Sturge

The
Bridge
Street
Press

THE BRIDGE STREET PRESS

First published in Great Britain in 2025 by The Bridge Street Press

1 3 5 7 9 10 8 6 4 2

Copyright © Georgina Sturge 2025

The moral right of the author has been asserted.

All rights reserved.
No part of this publication may be reproduced, stored in a retrieval system, or transmitted, in any form or by any means, without the prior permission in writing of the publisher, nor be otherwise circulated in any form of binding or cover other than that in which it is published and without a similar condition including this condition being imposed on the subsequent purchaser.

A CIP catalogue record for this book
is available from the British Library.

Hardback ISBN 978-0-349-12902-0
Trade Paperback ISBN 978-0-349-12901-3

Typeset in Bembo by M Rules
Printed and bound in Great Britain by Clays Ltd, Elcograf S.p.A.

Papers used by The Bridge Street Press are from well-managed forests and other responsible sources.

The Bridge Street Press
An imprint of
Little, Brown Book Group
Carmelite House
50 Victoria Embankment
London EC4Y 0DZ

The authorised representative
in the EEA is
Hachette Ireland
8 Castlecourt Centre
Dublin 15, D15 XTP3, Ireland
(email: info@hbgi.ie)

An Hachette UK Company
www.hachette.co.uk

www.littlebrown.co.uk

To all those who feel like they don't count.
Time will reveal you.
Historians will look for you.

Contents

Introduction	9
1 Starting from Zero	21
2 Population Problems	37
3 Vital Signs	53
4 Life on the Line	73
5 Rising Damp	92
6 Working Nine to Five	106
7 One In, One Out	125
8 The Second Sex	142
9 A Downward Slope	164
10 All for One and One for All	184
11 First Born	209
12 Calculating Change	227
13 Divisions	246
14 All Equal	267
15 A New Order of Magnitude	290
Summing Up	311
Appendix	326
Acknowledgements	329
Notes	331
List of Illustrations	365
Index	367

Introduction

It's rare to find a history book which doesn't quote some statistics. Any story will benefit from a moment of zooming out and taking in a bird's-eye view, and numerical data is very good at providing us with that. When it comes to the history of society and the lives of ordinary people, broad counts and averages are sometimes the only kind of evidence we have. Throughout history there are some individual characters that we can find out quite a lot about – kings and queens, saints, archbishops, politicians, artists and adventurers – and we have a good sense of what went on in certain settings featuring the rich and powerful. But that is, of course, because these were the type of people deemed worthy of being written about, or having their portrait painted at a time when to do so was a major undertaking. By contrast, it's often very hard to find out what went on in the lives of most people because the same kind of detailed records are just not there. Statistics at least give us some information about the people as a mass.

But what if data is more than just the trace that a mass of people leaves behind? What if the activity of collecting data (or trying and failing to collect it) has been a player in our history in its own right? Because there is far more to the act of counting people than just tallying them up and then breaking for lunch. As a process it can be disruptive or intrusive. At other times it can be emancipatory. As we shall see through the many stories in this book, it is in fact a force which can turn the wheel of progress in both directions.

We could even go as far as to say that any time we have tried to count ourselves or measure some aspect of our experience, we have been shaping our own story. This book is about those moments when we have started to count and measure ourselves in different ways and the surprises, shocks and fundamental changes which have come as a result.

Statistics condense and preserve a massive amount of information about a time and place, and they reflect what is considered important to record by the people doing the counting. The way in which information is recorded – who it prioritises, who it ignores and how it divides people up into boxes – not only reflects power structures that are already in place but gives them more solidity. It is often through resistance to counting and campaigns to change the way we count that real shifts in power have taken place. What we will find is that the story of data is the story of ourselves and our struggle with ourselves. It is a story of the ebb and flow of consent and objection, mistrust and cooperation, pride and shame.

When we talk about data here, it mainly means statistics or, in other words, information in a numerical form. Numbers are everywhere in modern life, but they haven't always been. Statistics are not a natural resource that we decided to extract one day – they are man-made and there was a moment in history when they were a new 'invention'. It was nothing short of revolutionary when we discovered a way to condense the characteristics and experience of a whole society into tables and charts which could be comprehended with a single glance. And as with all inventions, statistics invited their share of scepticism. Before they were accepted as a way of making sense of our surroundings, for a long time it was considered preposterous, unnecessary and even sinful to countenance the idea of trying to count the whole population. The main narrative of this book begins in the nineteenth century, because that is when the difficulties and objections to counting in general were overcome.

This book is about the UK, but much of it will have relevance to the experience of other countries. Aspects of the UK's history, like the Industrial Revolution, its imperial expansion and the development of its democracy have parallels in other Western European countries over the same period. In our efforts to count ourselves, we have also run into issues that come up time and again, no matter the place or the era. These reflections on what happened in the British context can certainly be applied to other settings and, indeed, will be useful to keep in the back pocket for whatever may happen to us in the future.

Let's also take a moment to clarify what kind of data we are talking about and where it comes from. At the centre of this narrative, propping it up like a spinal column, is the UK census. Every ten years since 1801 (except for 1941), we have made an in-depth stock-take of the population by collecting some information on every individual present in the country – this is what is meant by a census. The census is carried out separately by the statistical authorities in England and Wales, Scotland and in Northern Ireland (and in the whole of Ireland when it was part of the United Kingdom). In this book, we will also bring in some of the colonial censuses which were carried out across the British Empire, although for most of this story we will stay in the UK and, for the most part, on the island of Great Britain.

Although the census is at the core of this tale, this book is not a history of that document (for that there are other excellent, recent books).[1] This is about the relationship between people and the data that represents them, and for that we need to look at all sources of data that exist. A lot of information has been collected over time by government departments, and we also have to consider social surveys, data from inquiries and commissions, and even data from polling and public research. If data was collected on people and it had any kind of influence on public policy or debate, it is relevant here.

In beginning this story, we have to ask the question, 'Why would we want to count ourselves?' There was a time, before the modern era, when the rulers of this country – and any other one like it – had no idea how many people were living there, what their living conditions were like, or what they did for a job or to sustain themselves, other than what came from anecdotal reports. Outside the walls of the royal court and, as time went on, the parliament, there was a general foggy darkness when it came to information on the population and no particular reason to try to fill in the blanks. But our history is not one of monarchs sitting quietly in their castles, respecting each other's boundaries. Nor is it one of governments being happy with their lot and never dreaming of more. Ours is a history of the almost constant threat of invasion from our immediate neighbours and of our own brutal incursions into others' territory. The first efforts to count people at significant scale were to assist in this: they were lists of men who could be conscripted and assets which could be taxed or plundered to finance war. As time went on, people in power realised a more extensive roll call was needed to answer simple questions for policymaking, such as whether the population was growing or shrinking.

By the mid nineteenth century, there had been a huge expansion in the amount of data collected by the state. And what we saw in these new statistics often challenged our perceptions and prejudices. We were shocked by statistics showing the population of towns and cities doubling and quadrupling in size in a matter of years and had to face the fact that the majority of us now lived urban lives. Until 1841, we didn't have any detail about women's occupations, except in some cases if they were domestic servants. When we finally did collect that information in detail, it was found that women made up a third of workers across the whole manufacturing sector, a figure that by 1901 was two thirds. The fact that women kept appearing in paid employment figures, and in growing numbers, made it useless to deny that they played an important role outside of the home. When statistics were first collected on country of birth, we were surprised to find that there were people from virtually every part of the world living in the UK even in the 1850s, and that nearly one in fifty Londoners at that time were foreign-born.

The Victorian era also pushed the frontiers of scientific progress, expanding our understanding of ourselves through science and medicine and transforming our way of life via machines. Through collecting data on people, we turned the lamp of inquiry onto the lives of people and social conditions, and the truth of the dire working and living conditions endured by many people was exposed. Data uncovering the causes of poverty helped put to bed the persistent idea that it was moral or even genetic failings which kept people poor.

In the twentieth century and beyond, collecting new data has continued to bring us down to earth by exposing inequalities. In the 1960s, while men were landing on the moon, statistics showed that in parts of the country up to two thirds of people still didn't have hot water or an indoor toilet.[2] We extended our field of statistical inquiry much further into the realm of the personal. The rise of identity politics and increased concern about social inequalities saw us focusing our counting efforts on people who were on the margins.

Nowadays, governments rely on taking vital statistics of the places they govern – the health of the economy and of the nation, the number and whereabouts of the population and their condition – and use numerical data to justify their decisions and measure successes. We, as laypeople and in our working lives, take it for granted that statistics should exist on pretty much anything we care to investigate. Statistics are treated as the peak form of evidence in many policy areas because we view them as a solid and even neutral (as in apolitical) type of information, whether they really are or not.

Those are some of the reasons we have wanted to count ourselves – so far, so good. But when it comes to putting the ambition to count people into practice, it is rarely a simple and uncontroversial process of making a quick list. The act of counting people can be greatly significant in its own right. At some point, around the nineteenth century, the verb 'to count' went from just being an active process of pointing at things and adding them up to also meaning the reflexive state of having been counted. In other words, 'to count' started to be used as 'to matter'. It makes sense that we would use the same word – why would we go to the trouble if we didn't think it did? The act of enumerating things – and specifically people – is recognition that we find them important and worthy of being noticed. A development since the 1990s is the collecting of data on people's personal characteristics, for the reason that recognising an identity – be that related to sexual orientation, ethnicity or belief – is a means of bestowing dignity, which itself is considered a key element in a fulfilled existence.[3] Going further back in time, we can see how collecting data on the working classes, people living in poverty and on the terrible housing and sanitary conditions of whole swathes of the population not only acknowledged their existence but made it clear something had to change.

But there is a dark side to this. Counting people is only a positive form of recognition if people agree with the way they are being labelled and sorted, and with the reason for their information being collected. Unfortunately, there have been many instances in which this was not the case. In our official statistics, people have been counted as 'lunatics', 'idiots' and 'feeble-minded' with what we can hardly imagine was a thorough medical assessment. They have been labelled as paupers, lower class, semi-criminal, illegitimate, degenerate, aliens, half-breeds and pagans based on someone else's idea of what is acceptable, normal or desirable. The classifications used in counting can encourage a view that some people are lesser than others – sometimes quite literally, to the extent that they are counted as less of a human being. Refusing to count people in the way they would like to be acknowledged can be a formal kind of slap in the face.

Counting can put people in their place within a social hierarchy. Sometimes this is through the subtle suggestion of singling people out as different, sometimes through a quasi-technical process of sorting people into social ranks or classes. There were explicit class hierarchies in the first Roman censuses, where taking stock of the population meant taking a full inventory of each person's wealth and assets and assigning them to a certain social rank. The way in which people's occupations have been classified in modern censuses has often reflected prejudice and dismissiveness towards people working in manual jobs, low-paid work and domestic service.

Data can be used to oppress or tightly control, as demonstrated by the use of counting exercises to establish power in parts of the British Empire. Under Britain's colonial administration in South Africa, data collection was used to formalise categories within a hierarchy of status, determined largely by race, which dictated everything about how a person's life would look. Across the empire, many populations put up fierce opposition to being counted because they rightly recognised it as one of the first steps to total control.[4] In other more recent settings, censuses and population registers have been used as surveillance tools to single people out and persecute them – such as in Nazi-occupied Western Europe. When the bond of trust between statisticians and the people behind the statistics is broken, counting becomes an instrument of force and something to be gravely feared.

But when we are not happy with the way in which we are represented on paper, or if we feel liberties have been taken, we can refuse to be counted. Or at least we can try to refuse, which might sometimes be more realistic. Many of the stories in this book are about acts of protest and power struggles. Boycotting a data collection – in other words, withholding personal data – can be a powerful statement of disagreement or defiance. This was what happened in 1911, when campaigners for women's voting rights refused to fill in the census, arguing that if they didn't count politically, the government had no right to count them.

All of this is a negotiation. Data is a resource for governments, and it comes from individuals who can try to withhold it if they are not getting something fair in exchange. Data collected via the 1939 National Register – a live wartime database on England and Wales's population – was instrumental in the setting-up of the NHS and the welfare state after the Second World War. These had overwhelming public approval, although the Register itself eventually came to be seen as a needless intrusion into people's privacy and too much like the apparatus of a surveillance state. We need only look to the introduction of identity cards in the early

2000s for another example of lost public buy-in for a data collection project.

This negotiation is not unique to the UK. Bolivia's 2022 census was delayed until 2024, with some alleging that this was because the incumbent governing party did not want to face a suspected rise in the population of the major cities.[5] Population size is often used to determine the resourcing of public services and to decide how many seats an area has representing it in parliament, and the suspicion was that the government wanted to keep certain places under-represented because they tended to vote for other parties. The feeling in these areas, that the population was not getting its fair share, was precisely the reason they wanted the census to happen right away and not to be needlessly postponed.[6] Violent protests and strikes went on for several weeks at the end of 2022. Deciding to hold off from counting people can be a political act. Getting the silent treatment from the state – in other words, having the census boycott you – can be quite a statement about your perceived worth.

Which brings us to the reason why statistics matter so much. It is because things tend to solidify in the moulds we create for them. Put differently: when we count something in a particular way, it reflects and reinforces the way we see it. We now use a specific way of categorising ethnicity because that is how our system developed to collect data on it. Are these categories consistent in terms of what they describe about a person's identity? No. And yet people have developed a degree of attachment to them and will almost certainly take offence if they are put within a category not of their choosing.

Labels can quickly become important to the way people see themselves in relation to others. They can enforce difference or division and also be taken up as statements of defiance and pride: Black, gay, English, European. But despite the very real attachment that we feel towards categories that contain us, ways of classifying people are often quite arbitrary. Some of the geographical administrative boundaries within our country make very little sense and yet people often feel a strong sense of kinship and common identity within them. The same is true of our die-hard commitment to football clubs that we chose to support when we were children. Our country even has an arbitrary number to represent its identity: +44, the international dialling code. There is no reason why we should feel attached to it, and yet on some level we are, as it reminds us of home.

Categories and labels also tend to be impermanent. The way we count ourselves reflects how we see ourselves at a given time and that framework defines how we view ourselves in relation to others for as long as it takes for the next one to come along. Statistics are just a version of ourselves 'on paper'. They will always reduce us to a small cluster of characteristics and fail to capture a great many aspects of ourselves that might be more defining. Even in this age of 'big data', the imprint we leave through our online browsing, our social media presence and our spending habits doesn't represent everything about us.

Stories about counting people and taking stock of our surroundings continue to be relevant beyond a specific place and time because we will never perfect our methods. Looking back at when we started to count a previously unrecognised group or aspect of people's experience tells us this: at no point had we figured it out once and for all. At no point had we landed on the perfect survey questions to ask and could just keep sending them out to people for centuries to come. Society changes, our way of life changes, and how we interpret the world and make sense of it changes. Why would the way in which we try to quantify ourselves stay the same? In the future we will have different notions of what counts – meaning what matters – and what we should count, probably involving ways of counting we haven't even thought of yet. And this is because statistics have a shelf life. At some point they start to go off and need to be replaced. The past can teach us about what others have done in such situations and how, hopefully, to avoid our own behaviour becoming a cautionary tale.

Population data is one of the most amazing achievements of our society. Think about a census or a survey, in which millions of individuals simultaneously fill out private information, which is then synthesised into a document describing the entire population. There is no way to get that information except by people agreeing to provide it in their tens of millions. People volunteering their information is a testament to the health of a democracy.

And the information we collect is becoming increasingly personal, with people being asked to be honest in response to rather impersonal surveys about topics they might not even be honest about with the people around them. I'm talking about issues that we are now asked about as a matter of routine, like sexual orientation, gender identity, religious beliefs and mental illness. The more personal the information, the more we rely on people self-reporting and the tighter the relationship between the citizen and state.

We live now in an age where we can't help but shed data everywhere we go, leaving traces of ourselves as if we were radioactive. This has opened up new possibilities for us not to have to volunteer or self-report our data at all but to have it harvested in a passive way, via the digital systems we interact with. This is sometimes framed as a choice (like having the option to disable cookies on a website) but really what is happening is taxation in the form of data for access to the innovations of the modern world. The negotiation between the individual and the collectors and users of data has never been more important.

But that is all a matter for the future. It's time now to go back to where all of this started. It's time to take stock of where we came from and the journey we have been on, with all of its pluses and minuses. This is the story of the good data – or the good that data has done for us.

1
Starting from Zero

On 1 January 1801, it's unlikely that many people in the newly formed United Kingdom of Great Britain and Ireland were thinking about population statistics. Those with an interest in politics might have been musing on the uneasy situation in central Europe, where the French, under the leadership of Napoleon Bonaparte, were still wrestling for control of the Alps. The fashionable types in London and Bath may well have had their minds on other things entirely. For them, France meant only the latest fashions; people were greedy for new bonnets in the Parisian style. In this weather, though, city ladies were more likely to be seen in heavy, voluminous layers of capes and veils, slowly orbiting the parks like fluffed-up waterfowl. For the working classes and the rural population, life was the same scramble as always, although months of near-constant rain had made things even bleaker. The newspapers were dense with advertisements for balsams, syrups and cordials for a full range of winter ailments, some of which would quite likely do more harm than good.

Those who did look closely at a newspaper that day might have noticed the very brief mention of an event which had taken place the day before and which would sow the seeds for a new mode of government in the United Kingdom over the decades and centuries to come.¹ On 31 December 1800, an Act of Parliament for 'taking an account of the population of Great Britain' had passed into law. It meant that for the first time the government had given itself the power to collect a census of the people.

The Population Act of 1800 had been put forward by Charles Abbot, MP and sailed through Parliament completely unopposed. Abbot, who was the Member of Parliament for the small town of Helston in Cornwall, was an uncontroversial figure who would soon become Speaker of the House of Commons. But in advocating for his Population Bill, even in the face of absolutely no disagreement, he was decidedly animated. 'It has long been a matter of surprise and astonishment,' he declared, to a mostly empty chamber, 'that a great, powerful, and enlightened nation like this should have remained hitherto unacquainted with the state of its population.'²

No country could accurately assess how to provide for its population, he argued, without knowing how many mouths there were to feed, or how much land existed for farming. On top of practical concerns about food security, it was just plain embarrassing for Britain that it didn't have an accurate estimate of how many people lived within its borders. According to different educated guesses, the population could have been anywhere between eight and eleven million. By contrast, Sweden, Holland, Spain and the United States had all carried out full censuses of their people as long as fifty years ago and so had reliable figures at both the national and local level. Abbot might not have known it, but Iceland, at that time a Danish colony, had carried out a full census of all its citizens by name nearly one hundred years ago, and in the depths of winter when the sun never rose. France was on the cusp of carrying out a full population census and, obviously, that would not do.

Why had the British not done a census before? Politicians had tried to push for one fifty years previously and had been met with aggressive backlash. The main opponent had been the MP for York, William Thornton. On hearing of the proposal for a census in 1753, Thornton had described himself as 'never more astonished and alarmed since I had the honour to sit in this House'. In dramatic words for what might now seem a relatively tame subject, he continued: 'I did not believe that there had been any set of men, or indeed any individual of the human species so presumptuous and so abandoned, as to make the proposal which we have just heard ... I hold this project to be totally subversive to the last remains of English liberty.'[3]

The concerns about censuses were multi-pronged. The thinking was that they could expose the weakness of our population to enemies abroad (the Spanish and the French). They were also suspected of laying the groundwork for the levying of new taxes, and the long-term fear was that they could be used by a rogue government to carry out targeted forms of oppression. But Thornton offered one more, and particularly curious, argument against them, which was that 'when the Census is once taken, a *Lustrum* will certainly follow'. For those of us who have not been on *University Challenge*, a lustrum was a type of blood sacrifice which the Romans used to carry out after taking a census. Which might sound like something easily avoided, given that Roman rule in Britain had ended in 400 CE.

The Romans had taken censuses very seriously indeed. It is their word, *cēnsēre*, meaning 'to assess', 'to reckon or count' and 'to judge or advise', which gave us the word we use in English today and many similar variations in other languages.

A census-taker in Roman times was called a *cēnsor*, which was also the term for a magistrate or critic. In its linguistic origin, the idea of 'censusing' people was not far from the idea of 'censoring' or restricting them. The activities of making an assessment and enforcing a type of norm were part of the same family of processes. The Romans used censuses as a tool for establishing political and cultural dominance over the vast and varying territory they came to control.

The first Roman censuses were carried out in Rome, likely around 500 BCE. The census may have started out as more of a muster roll for men who were of military age but over time it developed into an elaborate process of enumerating whole households. The role of censor was given to just one or two people, who were responsible for overseeing the exercise across a whole city. This was highly prestigious position, something the author Andrew Whitby has compared to being a kind of emeritus professor of the civil service ranks.[4] According to Whitby, 'the census – and the two censors who performed it – had a place of power and centrality unmatched in any civilisation before or since'.[5]

At the height of the Roman Republic, a census was being carried out every five years and was not just the taking of a tally but a massive sorting exercise. The head of each household in the city would present himself at the Field of Mars, an area the size of a football field specifically designed for census-taking. Each householder would line up before one of the two censors and, when his time came, give a full account of his family situation, including the names and ages of his wife and children, as well as a full inventory of his property and wealth. On the basis of this, he would be sorted into one of the classes in a highly regimented hierarchy which ran from the highest class of senator or knight, through five different classes of commoner, down to the very lowest class, for citizens with little or nothing to their name. This routine was not for social research and certainly not just for the fun of it. Where the censor placed you in terms of class dictated what you could wear, what you were allowed to do, even the extent to which you were bound by the law.

The end of a census round was marked by an animal sacrifice – the *lustrum* – which would have typically involved a bull, a pig and a ram being killed on the altar of Mars. Although unfortunate for the three victims, it was hardly a bloodbath. But Mars was the god of war, and the whole affair was quite literally overshadowed by the suggestion of conflict. A relief that decorated a temple at the Field of Mars depicts Mars himself standing looking on as the animals are led to slaughter.[6] A reminder of human blood-letting in more distant fields was never far away from the taking of a census.

Clearly the Romans had chosen to make their blood sacrifice, so why were English politicians afraid that a similar gory event would happen of its own accord if they were to hold a census? The real root of this fear was stories about counting people in the Bible. There are quite a few biblical stories which feature populations being counted and things going horrifically wrong as a direct result, sometimes even as a punishment from God.

One that had a big influence on how people in the eighteenth century viewed censuses is the Old Testament story of King David, who in around 1000 BCE was the ruler of the patchwork of tribes which formed Judah and Israel. Wanting to assess his own military strength, he had ordered a census, in response to which God became furious and punished David's people with a plague. One version goes as far as to say that David was given the idea for a census by Satan, which is pretty on the nose in terms of suggesting that something is a sin.[7]

There is also an association between censuses and bloodshed in one of the most well-known parts of the Bible, the nativity story. When we encounter Joseph and the heavily pregnant Mary on their way to Bethlehem, it is because they had been called back to Joseph's home town to be counted in a Roman census.[8] What follows in Matthew's Gospel is that King Herod, in an attempt to kill the infant Jesus, ordered the murder of every boy under two years of age in Bethlehem and the surrounding area.[9] Mary and Joseph had already fled – and Jesus clearly survived – but it is a particularly haunting story of a counting exercise ending in mass murder. Further back, in the Old Testament or the Torah, we find that the very origin story of the Jewish people involves them being driven out of Egypt, because the authorities had assessed their numbers and judged them to be too many. Counting so often seemed to be followed by disastrous consequences.

These stories seemed to fuse in the Judeo-Christian cultural imagination, forming the idea that when a census was taken, bloody human disaster would follow. In 1753, William Thornton, MP may not have been thinking of a plague when he wholeheartedly warned Parliament against the idea of a census. But he may have seen a parallel in the more realistic threat of the French, who could have taken the opportunity to punish the British for exposing their inferior numbers.

It is worth noting that, outside Roman and Judeo-Christian tradition, other kinds of census have been carried out for millennia. It is possible that the Sumerians did censuses in around 4000 BCE, a time when writing was yet to be invented. The Inca of Peru also kept non-written records of their population using an elaborate system of knots in string. The Ancient Egyptians at one point appear to have made annual censuses focused on finding out what people did for a living. The Chinese were taking censuses on a population thought to have numbered up to five million from around 300 to 200 BCE, which appear to have been for the purposes of taxation and military-raising, and also more utilitarian purposes such as judging the scale of industries. More recently, making population lists was a way of establishing control in lands conquered by the thirteenth-century Mongol Empire.[10]

Not much was happening in the British Isles around the time that these first buds of census-taking were starting to bloom elsewhere. The Romans are believed to have made lists of the population for the purposes of tax-collecting. Naturally, not everyone would have made it onto these lists. Much of the population, perhaps even the large majority, would have lived in hand-to-mouth conditions with virtually nothing of value to the tax collector. And there were some areas of what is now the United Kingdom that had resisted falling into the Roman grip. Places where, rather than the strictness of a Roman social regime, it had been the unrelenting harshness of nature that dictated a person's fortunes.

One such place was the west of Scotland, a landscape of unnervingly vast hills which give way suddenly to deep lochs and rocky coastlines. Nowadays, if you were to travel north-west from Glasgow and trace your way around Loch Fyne, you would eventually find yourself on the floodplains of the River Add, where you might notice a curious lumpy hill rising suddenly from the boggy land. It is thought that in the fifth or sixth century CE this may not have been a hill but rather an island in the sea, and on top of it sat the fortified settlement of Dunadd, the centre of the Gaelic kingdom of Dál Riata.

Dál Riata encompassed part of the west of Scotland, including the islands of Arran, Islay and Jura, the Kintyre peninsula and part of Northern Ireland. At its heart was the freezing Irish Sea, which united the hardy and sea-faring people of its dominion. Excavations suggest that those who lived at Dunadd Fort, who had surrounded their homestead with four layers of fortifying walls, were crafters of fine metal. It also seems they spent some of their time carrying out censuses.

We know this from a set of tenth-century manuscripts called the *Senchus fer n-Alban*. Believed to be based on information collected during the seventh century, it consists firstly of an extensive and probably mythical genealogy about Dál Riata's kings and, secondly, of a rudimentary household census. One of the purposes appears to have been to assess the kingdom's military capability, since it is stated that for every twenty houses, a settlement must provide two seven-bench boats (and, one assumes, the appropriate number of men) for sea expeditions.[11] Although 'senchus' seems to have generally been translated as 'history' or 'knowledge', it does sound a lot like 'census', doesn't it? But this is most likely a coincidence.

England would soon afterwards experience one of its most famous historical episodes of counting. After the Romans left around 400 CE, various waves of overlapping invasions marked a period of great instability. In 1066, England had the misfortune of being invaded from both the north and the south at the same time, with the result that William of Normandy came out on top after a decisive victory at the Battle of Hastings. A Christian king invading a Christian country, William managed to consolidate his power quickly. What followed were nearly two hundred years of heavy-handed, if not brutal, rule in which feudalism came to be a defining feature of life. To control the people and harness their power, William took a leaf out of the Roman playbook and carried out a kind of census.

The count, which took place across most of England in 1086, generated a list of 13,400 settlements and information on the people living in them. It came to be known as the Domesday Book, a name which reflected its status as a final authority on a person's worth, in the manner of the Day of Judgement. Spooky as the name sounds now, it probably didn't carry the same association with dread or bad omens back then. Although it was a census of sorts, what it really counted were dwellings connected to any potential source of money or resource for the state. Helpfully for genealogists, it also includes the names of householders and landowners, who are mostly but not exclusively male. Beyond this, all it gives us are counts of other people in the household and the animals and farming machinery in their possession. Domesday tells us as much about livestock as it does about anyone who wasn't the head of a relatively productive household – that is, we only get a crude tally of their number, if anything at all.

Geographically, Domesday was also incomplete. In England, the city of London was excluded, as were the northern English counties and the city of Winchester; beyond it, Wales, Scotland and Ireland were all but totally excluded. Nonetheless, it gives us a flavour of life in the pre-modern era and a stark reminder of how utterly untouched by mass industry England was, even around the edges of its fledgling cities.

Domesday was a one-off and its lists were not updated. A data darkness re-descended over the British Isles, broken by sporadic flashes of light here and there over the next five hundred years. What lists existed during the medieval and early modern periods can be summarised as three types: lists of people to tax, lists of people to conscript and lists of who was in the in-crowd versus those who were deemed undesirable.[12]

When it came to taxation, a popular tactic of monarchs was to levy a poll tax on men of a certain social status as and when the need arose. This need was frequently to fund wars. There were around sixteen such levies between 1200 and 1300 and around forty in the hundred years after that, and each would have involved making lists of the unhappy targets for tax. In the sixteenth century, taxation became more sophisticated, wider ranging and, at times, bizarre. There was the 1590 sheep tax, which generated lists of flock-owners; the 1662 hearth tax, which required a list of people in possession of a fireplace; and the 1696 window tax, which was for people with the audacity to expect daylight in their homes. The golden age of creative taxes might have been the late eighteenth century, when in quick succession we had a tax on male servants (1777), a tax on female servants (1785), a tax on hair powder (1795) and a tax on dogs (1796), with records kept of the increasingly put-upon taxpayers. In one notable reverse of this trend, an exercise known as the Poor Census was carried out in 1551 in cities including Norwich and Warwick to plan for the provision of relief to the poor.

Lists of privileged persons crop up here and there in medieval times, such as freemen's rolls or registers, which afforded notable businessmen certain perks within a city. But what was far more common was the making of naughty lists. Following England's break with the Catholic Church during the reign of Henry VIII, lists started to be drawn up of recusants – people refusing to denounce their Catholic faith. Comprehensive lists of 'papists' appear in 1680, 1705 and 1715, which are gold dust for family historians now but were not so convenient for those on them at a time when to be a Catholic was sometimes punishable by death.[13]

And there are breadcrumbs of data scattered all around this period, in the form of lists created for often very specific purposes. In the sixteenth century, Britain was a relative safe haven for Protestants fleeing persecution in Europe. The east of England became a destination for Dutch and Flemish refugees, as did parts of the south-east and even Scotland (the mainland's most northerly tip, John O'Groats, is named after one of these refugees, Jan de Groot).[14] In 1565 and again in 1571, Elizabeth I ordered a count and listing of 'strangers' in the harbour town of Sandwich in Kent, which revealed one third of the population to be Flemish or Dutch.[15] Similar information was gathered on French migrants living in Canterbury, and again it was found that they made up around a third of the population of what was then a fading city around a cathedral that saw fewer and fewer visitors by the year.[16]

It was during the reign of Elizabeth that the authorities started doing something else that would prove immensely useful for our understanding of ourselves in the centuries to come. They began to make comprehensive lists of births and deaths. Parish authorities would keep written records of who had been born – and, crucially, been baptised – and who had died, and as time went on these lists started to be compiled across larger areas. From 1603, weekly counts of the number of people who had died were produced for the whole of London. And along with these deaths, other information was recorded, which reflected an extraordinarily vivid picture of the community back at itself.

These London lists also included the *causes of death*, with the idea being that physicians could keep an eye on the spread of diseases and other maladies. Some of the supposed causes of death might have been more useful than others. There are records of people being 'Affrighted' to death, 'Bit with a mad dog' and 'Kil'd by several accidents', which it's unlikely the doctors could have done much to prevent.[17] These records might not have been as well-known as they are today – and might not have been preserved at all – had they not caught the interest of a wealthy textile merchant and general figure in society called John Graunt.

Graunt took it upon himself to compile these 'bills of mortality' into an annual compendium. Helpfully for us, he also provided an explanation of where reports of cause of death actually came from. Upon the discovery of a death, the ringing of a church bell would summon the local 'searcher', who would carry out a superficial autopsy and note the likely cause. These searchers were, in Graunt's words, 'ancient Matrons' whose methods might have been a little less than scientific.[18] A verdict of 'consumption' seemed often to be based on finding the corpse 'lean and worn away'. 'We intend not only to be *Deaths heads* to put men in mind of their *Mortality*, but also ... to point out the most dangerous waies that lead us into it,' Graunt offered his no doubt perturbed reader.[19] And yes, the tragic report of two people 'Kil'd, one from a fall from a tree, one from a fall from a ship at Stepney' serves as cautionary tale, but it's unclear what measures people were supposed to take to avoid dying from 'Sore legge' or just 'Suddenly'.[20]

It is thanks to Graunt's morbid tallies that we know that around sixty-nine thousand people died in 1665 alone from a pestilence that had already cut a path across Europe: the bubonic plague. Throughout a hot summer, the plague spread across London with a savagery which left the capital in stunned silence, with red crosses drawn eerily across thousands of doors. The diarist Samuel Pepys quoted Graunt's death toll figures in writing about his experience of the time, and from the tallies we can now estimate that, in total, the plague may have killed around a quarter of London's population.[21]

It is because of John Graunt too that we have an idea of what the total population of London was at that time. He was ghoulishly fascinated with death – Pepys, who was also a friend of his, described him in the pub one night, 'telling pretty stories of people that have killed themselves, or been accessory to it, in revenge ... and mischief to other people' – but he was also nagged by curiosity about the number of the living.[22] At a similar gathering in 1661, he had been shaken to hear a fellow 'man of great experience' claim that London's population was as high as six or seven million. 'Until this provocation, I had been frighted, with that mis-understood Example of *David*, from attempting any computation of the People of this populous place,' he confessed.[23] But not being able to let it go, he did go on to make an estimate of the London population, which involved taking birth and death rates and studying the number of dwellings that could reasonably sit within the city's walls. His best estimate was that London in the early 1660s was home to around four hundred thousand people.[24] It must only be a coincidence that a plague of biblical proportions struck the city just a few years after Graunt made this assessment. Right?

A friend and collaborator of Graunt was the high society figure William Petty. Petty had been serving on a merchant ship at the age of fourteen when he broke his leg in an accident and was abandoned onshore in Normandy. He was saved by a community of Jesuit monks, who he ended up living with for several years, receiving a fine education. He was clearly gifted at making the best for himself out of any situation. Following this bizarre origin story, Petty presented himself back in London and swiftly rose to the high rank of colonial administrator in Cromwell's occupied Ireland. While there, he oversaw a partial Irish census which likely laid the groundwork for a poll tax. He also supervised a survey of land that had been seized by the English, during which he bought a great deal of it for himself, at a steal, which would supply him with rental income for the rest of his life.[25]

It is perhaps because so many influential people had a dual life, in business and administration, that the principles of running a shop started to transfer onto how people thought about running the state. Graunt had referred to his population estimates as 'shop arithmetic' – quite literally figures on the back of an envelope – but Petty took this one step further and coined the term 'political arithmetic'. This was the notion of making decisions based on hard figures. A merchant wouldn't dream of transacting without knowing how much stock was in the warehouse; why should the country do any differently?

The idea was also rooted in a type of hard-line empiricism. This was the foundation stone of a movement that would grow over the next century into what is sometimes called the Second Scientific Revolution. When the Royal Society was founded in the mid seventeenth century, with William Petty involved, its motto was *Nullius in verba*: 'take nobody's word for it'. It was a meeting of minds attracted by the idea of speaking only 'in terms of Number, Weight or Measure'; to use only 'arguments of sense' and to reject all kind of embellishment, speculation or dramatic flair. John Graunt may not have got the memo before he decorated his bills of mortality with cheerful-looking skeletons and hourglasses with wings.[26]

MEMENTO MORI

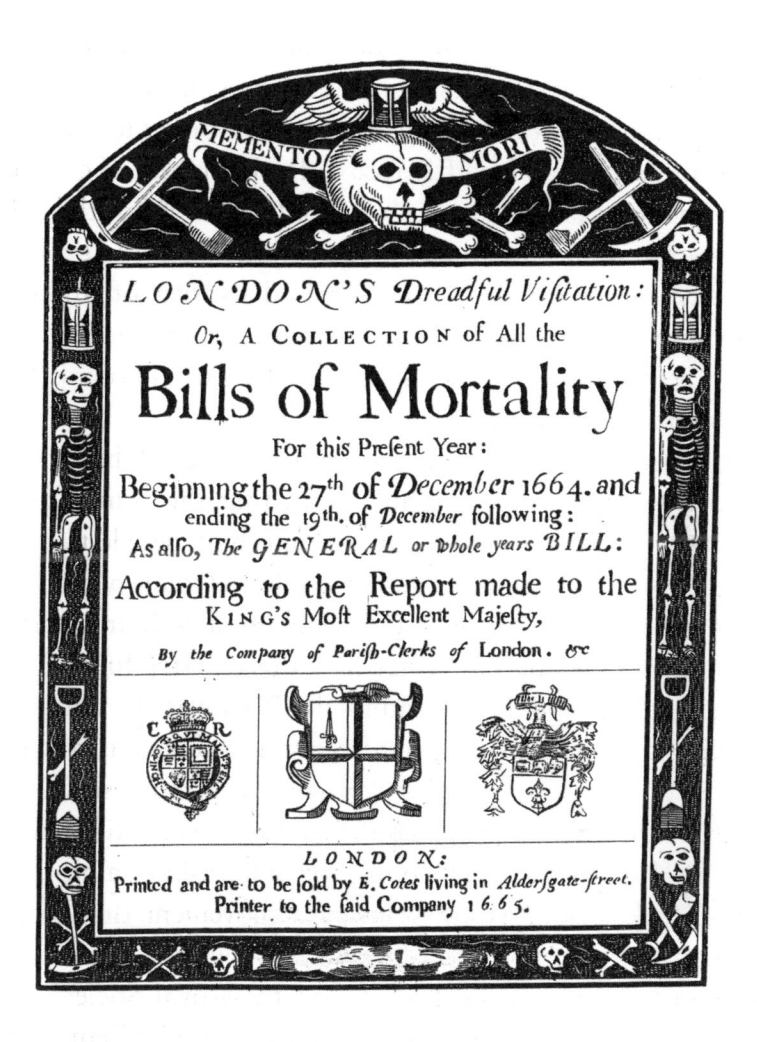

LONDON'S *Dreadful Visitation*:
Or, A COLLECTION of All the
Bills of Mortality
For this Present Year:
Beginning the 27th of *December* 1664. and
ending the 19th. of *December* following:
As also, The GENERAL or *whole years* BILL:
According to the Report made to the
KING'S Moft Excellent Majefty,
By the Company of *Parish-Clerks* of London. &c

LONDON:
Printed and are to be fold by E. *Cotes* living in *Alderfgate-ftreet*.
Printer to the faid Company 1 6 6 5.

Ideas of political arithmetic survived in the public consciousness long after Petty and Graunt's deaths. But data on the population remained severely fragmented. In 1739, a historian, William Maitland, used the jumble of parish records available to stitch together 'with considerable pains' an estimate of the number of houses in London.[27] A similar exercise was carried out in Bristol in 1751, by the scientist John Browning who, when not surveying the population, was conducting disturbing experiments on how electricity worked by giving electric shocks to potted plants.[28] These endeavours seem to have been mainly motivated by curiosity – both the counting exercises and the electrical experiments – but they took place within an atmosphere of rumbling concern about Britain's military capabilities. As we will see in the next chapter, because no one had yet made a tally of the whole population, we couldn't even be sure whether it was growing or shrinking.

By the end of the eighteenth century, the consensus was there: we needed to start counting ourselves, both for the sake of national security and for the good of science.

2
Population Problems

In the eighteenth century, the people of Britain developed a serious taste for gin. Such was the so-called Gin Craze that Parliament passed five major Acts, in 1729, 1736, 1743, 1747 and 1751, to try to stem the torrent of dangerously low-quality liquor being produced by a host of new distilleries. The sheer quantity being consumed was alarming, as was the extent of public drunkenness. The epidemic of binge-drinking, and the disapproving attitude high society held towards it, are encapsulated in William Hogarth's illustration *Gin Lane*. A baby tumbles from its mother's arms as she lolls half-naked next to an emaciated corpse, its gin goblet still in hand. A companion piece, *Beer Street*, shows milder scenes of people made idle and fat – though undeniably jolly – by their over-indulgence in a milder form of booze.

If they were intended to be chastening to drinkers they had a much greater impact in whipping up moral panic among the upper classes about the behaviour of the poor. A particular horror, as in *Gin Lane*, was the idea that mothers would get drunk and neglect their children. Stories abounded of mothers killing their children to sell their clothes for gin and lying oblivious in an alcoholic stupor while their children burned to death.* To this day you'll sometimes hear gin referred to as 'mother's ruin', although generally now in jest. If mothers – and fathers, for that matter – were ignoring their parental duties, in slavery to drink, then what was to become of the children? There was genuine fear that a generation of poorer children would simply die of starvation and neglect.

One onlooker was the Reverend Dr Richard Price, a philosopher and deep thinker who had radical ideas about civil liberties and was a friend of the likes of Mary Wollstonecraft and Benjamin Franklin. Despite his intellectual strength in many domains, Price had one theory which he stuck to with a force that was, as it turned out, entirely misguided. He was convinced that the population of England was shrinking.

Where this idea came from, we can't be sure. It's possible that all the talk of 'mother's ruin' had genuinely convinced some people, Price among them, that child mortality was on the rise and fertility on the decline. But having started out with this idea, as historian Roger Hutchinson puts it, he 'proceeded to convert the assumption into fact'.[1] Using methods which were dubious and refutable even at the time, Price claimed in 1772 that the population of Britain had declined by nearly a *quarter* since the start of the century. He estimated the population of the British Isles, including Ireland, to be around four and a half million – down, supposedly, from six million. Only thirty years later a much more reliable method would indicate that Price's figure had probably been less than a third of the real total.[2]

We need not go into Price's method. Suffice to say it

---

* One such real real-life horror story was of Judith Defour, who strangled her baby to death and left it in a field in Bethnal Green and then, with an accomplice named 'Sukey', sold the baby's clothes for gin. Defour was sentenced to death at the Old Bailey in February 1734.

involved the notorious 1696 window tax and did not account for the fact that decline in tax revenue was the result of people bricking up their windows to avoid it rather than dying from gin. But his pamphlets had caused a stir. People were rightly alarmed by the suggestion that the population was in decline, particularly when the opposite was true of the thriving enemy across the Channel. It prompted more calls for statistics on the population, and in 1788 a whole raft of towns and villages across the country took it upon themselves to carry out local censuses. What it also inspired were alternative and equally dramatic theories that the population was, in fact, rapidly and uncontrollably *growing*.

The Reverend Thomas Malthus lived a life that you wouldn't expect to inspire predictions of the impending collapse of humanity. He was a priest at a small church on the edge of the Surrey hills, a life which cannot have been anything other than picturesque. Yet in 1798 he published an *Essay on the Principle of Population*, in which he warned that England faced an existential threat from its rising population within a matter of years. Such was the force of this prediction that 'Malthusian disaster' is used to this day to describe a catastrophic problem of over-population.

His theory was that unless restricted by external factors, a population grows at a natural and universal rate. Using evidence from population censuses in North America, Malthus concluded that this was a doubling every twenty-five years. A larger population means more mouths to feed, and when comparing this with the considerably slower rate of growth in the food supply, Malthus encountered his 'spectre'. At the point that the population overtook the supply of resources, it would naturally be 'checked' by famine, war, plague or its own self-destruction through vice (the antics on Gin Lane providing one such example). He was a Home Counties prophet of doom, second only to Nostradamus in terms of making the most terrifying predictions.

But Malthus was wrong on several counts, and, to his credit, he did water down his predictions in several updates of his *Essay*. One mistake was to use the population growth rate in the New World as the universal pace. Clearly the growth rate in a new country which was actively trying to expand its frontiers – not to mention one which sustained itself through the labour of imported slaves – was not quite on a par with that in the cities of England. Over the long term, Malthus also could not have foreseen what a difference the cleaning up of the ghastly conditions in these cities and the eradication of disease would make to child survival rates and hence to family-planning decisions.

Looking on with bewilderment was a young journalist and amateur statistician, John Rickman. At the age of just twenty-one, Rickman had written a paper called 'Thoughts on the Utility and Facility of a General Enumeration of the People of the British Empire', which argued for a British census as a matter of necessity. In 1798, a version was published in a national magazine, and Rickman was taken on by Charles Abbot, MP, who we met at the beginning of Chapter 1 and who would entrust him with drafting the text of his Population Bill.[3] Rickman was clear-eyed about the need for population data. The French Republic was becoming a real threat and if counting the population was something that the French did, that was even more of a reason for us to do the same.

It was likely a combination of shock at the competing apocalyptic scenarios presented by Price and Malthus and the undeniably rational arguments of Rickman that ultimately saw the Population Act across the finish line in 1800. But although this was a landmark in attempting an accurate tally of the full population, the survey which took place bore little resemblance to what we would call a census now. It was not what would be called a modern census, mainly for the reason that it only collected one record per household, rather than per person.

As the chosen date of the enumeration approached – 1 March 1801 – John Rickman was appointed to manage and oversee the whole operation from a headquarters in Westminster. Tens of thousands of forms were printed and sent out to the equivalent of local authorities today, where they were handed out to clerks tasked with filling in the information for a specific parish. Each clerk had to complete a form stating the number of inhabited and uninhabited houses in their parish, how many families were living there, how many individual men and women and their household occupation. This was then packaged up with local statistics on births, marriages and deaths, and sent back to London for compilation.

There's no doubt it was an ambitious exercise at a time when the only way of getting a message, let alone a census form, to any part of the country was to deliver it in person, along roads which were for the most part unpaved. While the country's canal network was already at an impressive size by 1801, its peak in terms of scale and speed was still decades away. The UK had a grand total of three miles of public railway, in West Yorkshire, and its carriages were horse-drawn. The fastest form of transport was the mail coach, a new innovation which could travel from Bristol to London in sixteen hours, a journey that had previously taken thirty-eight hours under the previous system of post boys on horseback. Given that most of the country was still only accessible by horse – and some of it only on foot – we can only imagine how nearly impossible the challenge must have seemed.

These practical problems proved a bit too much for the exercise. Rickman despaired that summer about writing 'hundreds of letters to little purpose' and working 'about nine weeks without being able to say that anything is done'.[4] When the census report was laid before Parliament in June 1801, in terms of completeness it resembled a Swiss cheese. Only thirteen of the fifty-one counties and shires in England could be said to be complete. The returns from Wales and the Welsh border had suffered greatly from non-response. Monmouth, Hereford and Gloucester were only around a third to half complete. Just two returns had been sent from the county of Cardigan in Wales and none at all from Caernarfon.[5] While most of the Scottish overseers had diligently submitted their forms, there had been no response whatsoever from some of the small islands. It may not have helped that neither the instructions nor the forms were printed in Welsh or Gaelic. But by laboriously papering over all the holes with other scraps of parish records, Rickman and his staff were able to arrive at a confident estimate that the population of Great Britain in March 1801 was around 10,901,200 people.

In some ways, the layout of England between Domesday and the Victorian era was surprisingly similar. The 13,400 settlements in 1086 had become 14,000 by the time the 1801 census rolled around.[6] The south of the country was still divided into hundreds, a Saxon designation, and the north and Midlands into wapentakes, which had their root in the Danelaw. The administrative units across the rural parts of England had been unchanged for well over a thousand years.

London had clearly changed beyond recognition, though, as had the new industrial cities in the north. What is known as Merseyside today was in 1086 a marshy coastline where small rural communities lived off the land and sea. By 1801

Liverpool was a teeming metropolis capable of sending steam-powered boats across the Atlantic.

As well as the problem of getting some people to respond to the census at all, there had been some confusion about how to fill out the form. Enumerators had dithered over whether to record flats within a building as separate houses or as one large multi-family dwelling. There was uncertainty as to whether to record occupations for wives, children and servants, or to record them all as part of one generic 'third class', with the latter approach being the intended one.[7]

Yet the exercise was successful enough, and its results well-enough received that another census was booked in for 1811. While changes were made to the form, the errors didn't necessarily decrease and coverage was still patchy.* But Rickman was a dedicated technocrat and treated the census as a challenge to exceed the previous achievement every ten years. By the 1820s he was Clerk Assistant in the House of Commons and living on the Parliamentary estate, at a time that witnessed the only assassination of a British prime minister and the destruction of the entire Palace of Westminster in a fire.[8] His own house in New Palace Yard survived the blaze, and for years he and his family lived in the immediate shadow of a colossal blackened ruin.

Despite this, Rickman steered through the 1821 and 1831 censuses, although not without further teething problems. The practice of recording occupations at the family level was deemed to have 'entirely failed', given the rarity of the 'single-breadwinner household' and enumerators had been left haunted by the 'recurring and often unanswerable doubt as to

---

* The 1811 and 1821 censuses tried to reduce confusion about occupations by asking only for the occupation at the family or household level. This only created more confusion, since many households consisted of several breadwinners, including women in many cases.

what is to be deemed a family'.[9] But what did become clear, by 1831, was that the population was increasing at a fairly astonishing, although not quite Malthusian, rate. In thirty years, the population of Great Britain had risen by around five and a half million people, or by more than half.[10]

If you're in London in the wintertime and it isn't raining – please, humour me – one activity is to go ice-skating on the temporary rink that pops up every year in the central courtyard of Somerset House, on the north bank of the river. The setting is an impressive neoclassical building of white stone, whose columns and large windows resemble those of Buckingham Palace. The edges of its courtyard feature unnerving sheer drops, which allow you to see down through the windows of two floors of basements, which now hold offices and meeting rooms. When Somerset House was first built, those dank lower levels were only a wall away from the waters of the Thames, which came right up to the building so that boats could come in and out via several large tunnels. It's the site of a palace where Elizabeth Tudor lived in the years before she became queen. And it's the place that was chosen in 1837 to house the newly created and first official statistics bureau for the United Kingdom, the General Register Office. The first head of the GRO, a role known as the Registrar General, was the appropriately named Thomas Lister.

In 1836, Parliament passed the Civil Registration Act, which meant all births, marriages and deaths had to be formally registered. Previously, as we've seen, the majority of births and deaths were already being recorded, at least at the parish level. The problem was that these events tended to be recorded by religious authorities, and anyone dissenting (or being shunned) could find themselves excluded. The Church had been ordering national-level lists of papists as recently as 1780.[11]

If a person didn't appear in official records, it could cause them major problems if they ever had to go to court.[12] Try arguing an inheritance case when there is no legal record of the birth of the heir or the death of the deceased. The government had started to recognise that while showing disapproval of these audacious births and marriages was one thing, it was not beneficial to society as a whole to have lots of people walking around with no legal identity.[13] Places of worship other than churches were permitted to host birth, marriage and death ceremonies, and their proceedings became official record.

It was a victory for dissenters, a group which at that time would have included Catholics, Quakers, Baptists, atheists and followers of other religions. For example, by the 1830s it was fairly common in the docks of London and Liverpool to come across *lascars*, who were sailors recruited largely from what is now Bangladesh and who practised Islam. Britain was multicultural and always had been, no matter the minuscule size of some of these subcultures. From a statistician's perspective, any gap in the data compromised the whole. In the first three months after it became possible to register other places of worship to host marriages, around one thousand such places were registered.[14] In the year ending June 1838, around four thousand marriages were recorded as taking place outside the 'established church', which suggested that around one in twenty-five marriages had previously gone unregistered.[15]

It wasn't long before the statisticians realised this new central database could be used to examine an increasingly pressing issue of the day: inequality. It was noted that marriage registration records would often be submitted with an X or other mark in place of a person's name. This, the statisticians realised, indicated that the person had not learnt to write their own name. Analysis of all the marriage records submitted in 1839 showed that one in three men and half of women in England and Wales were illiterate. The use of marks was highest in Bedfordshire, where it seemed that two thirds of women and over half of men could not read or write.[16] The age-at-death statistics also revealed shocking disparities between different parts of the country. In Devon, one in five people were living past the age of seventy, compared with just one in twenty in Manchester and Salford. In Liverpool in 1840, a quarter of children were not making it past their first birthday.[17]

In 1840, the architect of the census himself became just another statistic. Like nine out of ten of the other people who had passed away that year in London, John Rickman did not live past the age of seventy.[18] Shortly before his death, he had been working on plans for what would come to be considered the UK's first 'real' census, which was carried out in 1841. For the first time, the census was going to record information about not just the generally male head of a household but every single person within it, including their name, age, occupation and place of birth. It would take thirty-five thousand enumerators to gather the information for England and Wales alone but this effort would more than pay off. The 1841 census is year zero for much of historical family research.

The rule on these individual-level records is that they can be completely opened up to the public after a certain length of time. At present, this is one hundred years after the census was taken, on the basis that almost all the people who feature in it will by then be deceased.[19] The incredible detail of the 1841 returns means we can find out exactly what the structure of a household was like. We can also find people by name, which is made easier than ever now that the records have been digitised and made available online. On Devonshire Terrace in Marylebone, London, we find twenty-nine-year-old Charles Dickens living with his wife and three children, along with five servants. In a small village balancing on the edge of the Pennines, we encounter the reverend's daughter Emily Brontë, who may already at that time have been working on her gloriously unsettling novel *Wuthering Heights*, and in the vicarage in Daresbury, Cheshire, lives nine-year-old Charles Dodgson, who would later write *Alice in Wonderland* under the pen name Lewis Carroll. Queen Victoria appears in the census, named simply as 'The Queen', and living in domestic bliss in Buckingham Palace with her husband Albert, a baby daughter and ninety-six servants.

An entry from Yorkshire shows a household which might seem unusual for having had a female head and no adult males. Sarah Crapper lived in the village of Thorne with her three young children, their female servant Betsey Arnold and their fifteen-year-old lodger John Bingham, who was an apprentice bookmaker. Eight-year-old Elizabeth Green also lived at the address, although who she belonged to is a mystery. We now know that Sarah wasn't the lone head of this household – her sailor husband Charles was away at sea when the enumerators called. The only reason we know this is because her young son Thomas would later become famous as the inventor of the flushing toilet and his biographers would fill in more of the detail.[20]

At the time, of course, the public couldn't see all the details other people had submitted to the census; they had to make do with the aggregate figures which were released after two years of counting in 1843. These showed that the population was still growing at an exceedingly fast rate, but that there were signs of it slowing down.[21] The *Illustrated London News*, which printed a special edition to mark the release of the 1841 census results, noted that if the rate of increase continued, it would mean a doubling of the population by 1850: 'Double the number of families will exist,' the newspaper declared, '[who] must be supplied with subsistence; but there will also be double the number of men to create subsistence and capital ... to man her fleets, to defend her inviolate hearths, to work the mines and manufactories, to extend the commerce, to open new regions of colonization; and double the number of minds to discover new truths, to confer the benefits and to enjoy the felicity of which human nature is susceptible.'[22] It also pointed to the fact that a Malthusian apocalypse had not come to pass as proof that 'moral restraint ... [was] in practical operation'. Gin-fuelled debauchery seemed to be on the wane.

Responsibility for the census had, by this point, passed into the hands of the GRO and the business of undertaking it was turning into a relatively well-oiled machine that could be cranked into life every ten years. The 1851 census was organised in a much more professional manner than its predecessors and its results were published in half the time from a decade previously. The year 1851 was also the occasion of possibly the single most important social and cultural event of the century, the Great Exhibition. For five months straight, visitors from all across the country and abroad filed through a gargantuan greenhouse known as the Crystal Palace which had been installed in Hyde Park. So huge that fully grown trees and several floors of exhibits could fit inside, it showcased the latest in mechanical innovation alongside various 'curiosities' collected by dubious means from all around the world.

The Registrar General, who was then George Graham, a former army officer and brother of the Home Secretary, had the brainwave of trying to give a sense of scale to the latest census statistics by appealing to the imaginations of the many people who had seen the Great Exhibition first hand: 'Of 100,000 persons a general notion can be formed by all who witnessed this spectacle at the Crystal Palace [as it is] somewhat less than the greatest number (109,915) that ever entered it in one day,' he wrote in his 1851 census report. It followed that because the population of Great Britain was then around 21.1 million, they could 'at the rate of a hundred thousand a day ... have passed through the Building in 211 days'.[23] The additional number of people living in Great Britain in 1851, as compared with 1801, would alone have taken 102 days to file through the Great Exhibition.

In among this mass of humanity, the statistics shone a light for the first time on some populations whose circumstances were considered outside 'the norm'. The 1851 census showed that of the fifty thousand children born in the south-east of England in 1850, around one in fifteen had been born out of wedlock.[24] In 1851, around twenty-one thousand people were living in 149 'lunatic asylums' across Great Britain, and at least eighteen thousand were sleeping in barns or in the open air in tents. The official census report describes the brazen effort of a 'tribe of gipseys [who] struck their tents and passed into another parish to escape enumeration'.[25] The 1841 census had recorded around forty thousand people in England and Wales who were 'foreign-born', about one thousand of whom had been born in UK colonies. By 1851, this had increased to over fifty thousand foreign-born non-British nationals and nearly thirty-four thousand people who had been born in British colonies.[26] There were as many as one hundred thousand foreign nationals living in Great Britain as a whole, or around one in every two hundred people.

This deluge of new population data came at a time when Britain was in a self-admiring mood. Gone was the fear that our embarrassingly small population would be laughed at by the French. Decades of regular stock-taking had revealed that it was growing at a lusty rate and was even outpacing its neighbour countries. The civil service had been inspired by what could be achieved by standardising the collection of data and collating it for the country as a whole. The state was much more visible in people's lives than before, but its outposts across the country, including records and register offices, were tolerated for the most part as a non-threatening, almost secular presence. For politicians, population data had already become an essential form of fuel – or at least the engine oil – for the machinery of government. 'Political arithmetic' had morphed into something more like a science of statecraft, and Britain was even starting to be considered a major player in this domain.[27]

This was in Great Britain itself, mind you: a very different situation was playing out in the UK's colonies and in Ireland. When the results of the 1851 Irish census were published in 1856, they told a woeful story. If the population were to have grown at the usual rate, the census-takers noted, it would have been around nine million in 1851. Instead, it numbered only six and a half million. Of the missing, it was estimated at the time that around two and a half million had died from famine and disease, although historians now tend to put the figure at around one million.[28] The potato crop had failed partially in 1845, extensively in 1846 and almost entirely in each year after that until 1850. Emergency food was not provided and so people either starved, stole or, in some extreme cases, resorted to cannibalism. The famine was accompanied by waves of fever, dysentery, influenza, cholera and even smallpox.

The remainder of the missing had emigrated, at a rate of up to a quarter of a million people per year during the direst period of hunger.[29] England and Wales were obvious destinations, with many Irish families taking up residence along the west coast of the British Isles. Analysis of the 1851 census returns for Glamorgan found that three Irish names (Patrick, Dennis and Cornelius) had entered the top fifty most common men's names and two (Bridget and Ellen) were now among the top fifty for women.[30]

A great many sought a more decisive break and headed for America. We know from the census of New York that by 1855 the Irish made up around 470,000 out of 2,222,000 in the state, or more than a fifth of its population.[31] But although the New World offered freedom and, crucially, survival, many Irish still found themselves on the lowest rung. Of the nearly one hundred thousand New Yorkers who were recorded in the 1855 census as not being able to read or write, 62 per cent had come from Ireland.[32]

Statistics, it turned out, could not help but paint an evocative picture in spite of their drily functional purpose. The census, which had started out in the minds of politicians as a simple counting exercise at the end of the eighteenth century, had become a hotly anticipated chapter in a book that was growing richer and more textured with every ten-yearly addition. Just as the silhouette image was being replaced with the wonder of daguerreotype photography as a way of capturing people's likenesses, a new level of realistic detail was blooming on the pages of statistical reports. The reality of people's lives was becoming public, and so too was the scale of some serious public problems.

3

Vital Signs

It promised to be another beastly hot day in central London on Friday 8 September 1854. The morning sunshine was just starting to break through the smoky haze over Broad Street, as a small group of workmen strode up to the public water pump. A dog barked somewhere and gulls shrieked overhead, but otherwise the Soho street was eerily quiet and still. Within a couple of minutes, the workmen had removed the handle from the pump and were carrying it away. In doing so they may very well have saved lives. And the reason they'd been commissioned to carry out this act of public sabotage was all to do with statistics.

Around ten days earlier, a tailor who lived at 40 Broad Street had suddenly fallen ill. He had been seized with repeated bouts of diarrhoea, followed by stomach cramps, muscle spasms and exhaustion. He probably would have had the horrifying realisation of what was afflicting him before it cut his life short just two days later. News of an epidemic of cholera was sweeping the country as quickly as the disease itself. Cholera outbreaks were common in England at the time, and pandemics had also happened within most people's lifetime. An 1833 cholera epidemic took the lives of around twenty thousand people, and another between 1848 and 1849 had claimed fifty thousand in England and Wales alone.[1] But this outbreak on Broad Street would prove to be particularly localised and deadly, not to mention uniquely preserved in the public memory. In the twenty-four hours after the tailor's death, around two hundred residents of the surrounding area would die, fifty of them on Broad Street alone.[2]

Cholera as a disease was not well understood. Although it was around this time that the cholera bacterium was discovered, most doctors would not learn of its existence or the proven methods to treat it until the 1880s.[4] So-called cures being widely advertised and administered by doctors included opium and castor oil, which in their own right would have wreaked biblical havoc on the bowels while not helping to stop the infection at all.[5] And for sufferers, the disease itself was already an absolute horror. Starting with explosive bouts of diarrhoea, things deteriorated very quickly. Bowel evacuations became near continuous and after a while consisted of misty, translucent 'rice water'. It was as if the body was trying to rid itself of all its fluid. The body shrivelled and shrank, and the face and lips turned blue and waxy until all that remained was a stricken, leathery corpse. The worst part was that throughout the death spiral, it was said that the mind stayed completely alert: a horrified front-row witness to the body's live shrivelling. At the onset of cholera symptoms, half of sufferers would be dead within twenty-four hours.[6]

In total, at least 618 people would perish in the Broad Street outbreak of 1854. This was around one in twenty-three people living in the affected area, which largely consisted of the parish of St James's in Soho. On Broad Street itself, 10 per cent of residents would die, with at least one death in thirty-five out of its forty-nine households. This would include 'no less than 21 instances of husband and wife dying within a few days of each other' and, in one case, both parents and their four children.[7] So ferocious was the pace of the outbreak that residents had wondered if it was a revisitation of the Black Death, stirred up by the disturbance of a nearby plague pit.

Doctors and public health officials in the 1850s couldn't definitively say how the disease was spread. A dominant theory for disease transmission in general was that it was primarily airborne, travelling as a 'miasma' or fine cloud of particles. Cholera is, in fact, waterborne, but this truth would only be accepted – and not without considerable backlash – thanks to the efforts of one Dr John Snow.

John Snow walked into Broad Street late on Sunday 3 September 1854. Heavy rainfall followed by several days of intense heat had the gully-holes, which provided partial covering to the drains, steaming with 'foul, nauseating and noxious vapours'.[8] The hot, sour run-off water from the Broad Street Brewery, along with waste from cowsheds, grease-boiling houses and slaughterhouses, contributed to the reek. It would have been easy to conclude that some evil miasma was spreading disease on the basis of smell alone.

Snow lived on the better side of the tracks, or rather, west of Regent Street, which acted as a partition between Soho and the smarter neighbourhoods. Being both a doctor and keenly interested in problems of public health, he was not afraid to venture into the heart of the outbreak. He also had a theory that he had been trying to test out in south London, by looking at cholera prevalence in areas covered by different water companies. The Broad Street case offered a much more localised kind of experiment. An idea started to germinate in his mind.

Snow's eye was drawn to the pump on Broad Street, immediately in front of number 40 where the first patient had been taken ill. Tap water was not even on the horizon for most households in Soho and bottled 'mineral' water was an unaffordable luxury. Residents generally had one option for hydration and that was to fetch water from a communal pump. Broad Street had suffered particularly heavy casualties in the outbreak: could the pump have been the source? Snow paid a visit to the General Register Office, where he quickly requested and obtained details of deaths registered in the area, by individual address, over the last few days.* He started to sketch out a rough map of the deaths by street and, although they undeniably seemed to radiate out from Broad Street and the pump, there were a great many one-off deaths on more distant streets that were otherwise untouched.

Water from the Broad Street pump was considered especially delicious. The well tapped directly into a tributary which filtered over a gravel bed, meaning it was relatively unpolluted. People had been known to spurn closer pumps in St James's parish and pump their water from Broad Street. This complicated Snow's investigation. If it had been the case that each street had a pump and its residents were forbidden from using any other, identifying the super-spreader pump would have been a simple matter of comparing the week's deaths street by street. The fact that people were willing to pick a determined path for up to a quarter of a mile through streets heaped high with all manner of detritus for the sweet Broad Street nectar made things far more complicated. Snow realised he would have to go house to house to find out which pump people were accustomed to use.

---

* There was relatively little data protection in place at the time and Snow was able to obtain personal records very quickly, simply for his own personal research. It should be noted, though, that he was a friend of William Farr, chief statistician at the GRO, and quite a famous figure in his own right, having personally administered the then experimental drug chloroform to Queen Victoria while she was in labour only the year before.

It was in doing this that a clear picture started to emerge. Across the affected area, sixty-one out of seventy-three persons who died during the first two days had been habitual drinkers of Broad Street water. This was communicated to Snow by the survivors. The proprietor of a coffee-house informed him that, as of 6 September, nine of her customers were dead. She served Broad Street pump water at dinner, and it was also a key ingredient in her coffee. Meanwhile, a workhouse containing around five hundred people had only experienced five deaths and Broad Street Brewery, which employed seventy men, had no casualties at all. As it turned out, both had access to their own well.[9]

And then there was the smoking gun. The Eley brothers, who had a factory on Broad Street, had recently helped their mother move to Hampstead in north London, where the air was decidedly fresher.[10] But the widow was still so partial to the Broad Street water that her sons used to bring her a bottle whenever they came to visit. Unfortunately, one such visit had occurred on the previous Thursday, and by the end of the week she was dead, along with a visiting niece with whom she had shared the water. There was no way this was a coincidence. It didn't really get much better than Hampstead in terms of air quality in 1850s London and many a Soho resident, including Karl Marx and his family, used to escape there at weekends. It didn't make sense that a miasma of cholera had floated up to Hampstead and struck down two victims like lightning. It had to be the water. Snow's notes also contain the story of an army officer living in St John's Wood – another clean and leafy suburb – who 'came to dine in Wardour Street, where he drank the water from Broad Street pump at dinner. He was attacked with Cholera and died in a few hours.'[11]

Snow took his findings to the Board of Guardians of St

James's Parish, who were responsible for public health. Their tactic so far had been to essentially douse the whole area in bleach, which under many circumstances would probably have done the trick. Not, however, if the source of infection was underground within the well, as Snow was now claiming. He presented his statistics and stories, including the zinger involving the Widow Eley of Hampstead. It wasn't quite 'you know nothing, John Snow', but the board members were initially sceptical. He persisted, presenting them with the brewery and the workhouse. In the end, they agreed to take precautionary measures and remove the handle of the pump.

One reason this story survives and is well known today is that it was also the background to a famous early piece of data visualisation. After the outbreak had subsided and the initial danger to life was suppressed, Snow took some time to look again at the statistics and to see whether there was something in them that would definitively prove his waterborne theory. He created a now-famous map, which was presented to the Epidemiological Society in December 1854. It shows a simplified layout of the streets of Soho, with black bars drawn on the location of houses whose residents who had died. The height of the bars indicates the number of deaths at a single address, giving the impression of shadows lying across the map as if from skyscrapers of the dead. What jumps out immediately is the centre of Broad Street – an Empire State Building of death. It should be noted that the design itself was not Snow's original idea – it was based on the work of Edmund Cooper, who had been commissioned to study whether the very same outbreak had originated from the disturbed plague pit – but that makes it no less visually striking.

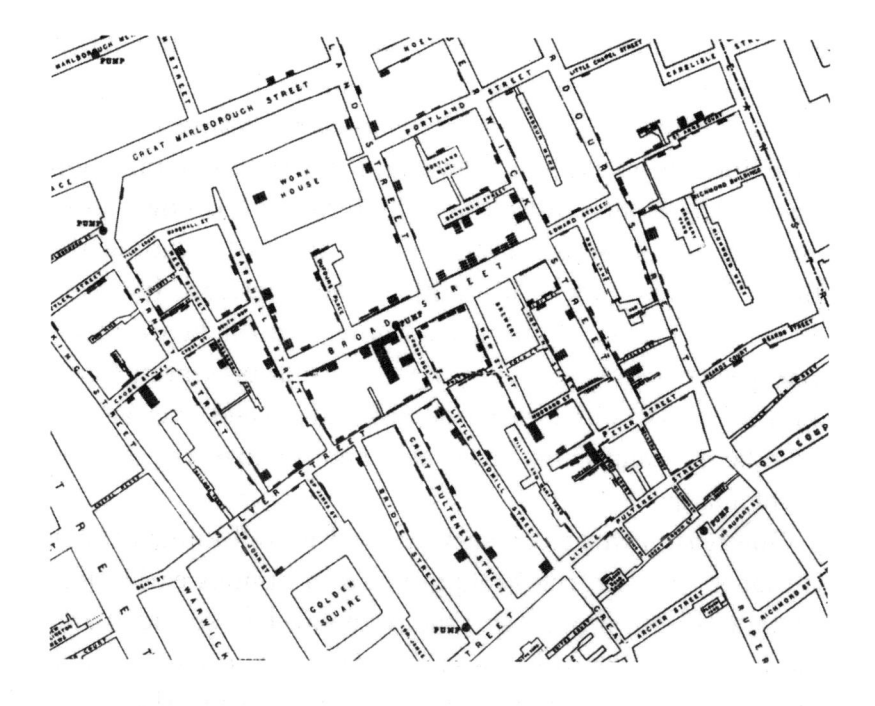

One person who had seen this map and heard of Snow's intervention was the Reverend Henry Whitehead, a clergyman at the local St Luke's Church. From the first day of the outbreak, he had attended the houses in Broad Street and the surrounding area, watching with dismay as the parishioners dropped like flies. Whitehead had an inquiring mind as well as the drive to improve the conditions of the poor, and yet he too was sceptical when he heard of Snow's waterborne theory. After all, the Reverend himself had drunk from the Broad Street pump at the height of the outbreak and had seen patients recover after drinking its water in large quantities. In the months following, he repeated Snow's exercise of going door to door and collected even more detailed accounts from the survivors as to when and where they had fetched their water in the run-up to the fateful events. It was true, as John Snow had identified, that there were a great many more deaths among the Broad Street water drinkers, but what he and Snow couldn't resolve was why some people who drank the same water had been absolutely fine.

Suddenly Whitehead's eye fell on the case of the five-month-old daughter of the Lewis family at 40 Broad Street, who had died on 2 September 'after an attack of Diarrhoea four days previous to death'.[12] This sounded very much like a death from cholera, with symptoms that would have started on 28 August. The tailor at 40 Broad Street wasn't patient zero after all, it was the baby girl living on the ground floor of the same house.

Broad Street was an overcrowded area, where it was not unusual to find whole families living in a kitchen or even in a basement.[13] The Lewis family were typical of these circumstances, living in one or two rooms on the ground floor of 40 Broad Street. Plumbing was non-existent and a typical recourse was to empty human waste onto the floor of the cellar, where it would supposedly seep down a drain. In practice, these drains were regularly clogged and those who could afford it would employ 'night soil men' to periodically shovel away the build-up of filth.

On Whitehead's tip-off, a surveyor was called in to examine the Lewis cellar, returning with a report of 'abominations, unmolested by water, which I forbear to recite'.[14] The drain was entirely blocked and the bubbling swamp of human waste which had sloshed for years against the back of the cellar had caused the brick wall there to disintegrate. It was into this foul soup that Mrs Lewis had discarded the water used to clean her baby's nappies. The surveyor concluded that decay had 'brought the brick work into the condition of a sieve, and through which the house drainage water must have percolated for a considerable period'.[15] The infected slop had seeped through into the well shaft of the Bond Street pump less than a metre beyond. The reason some people had drunk the water and survived was all to do with the timing of when the residents of number 40 had hurled a fresh bucketload of their cholera evacuations against that cellar wall.

It was a pivotal moment in proving the power of statistics to *investigate*. It was also a prime early example of a scientific, 'deductive' process being applied to social research. John Snow had gathered the initial statistical data, then formed a hypothesis as to the outbreak's cause and carried out further data collection to test it. It's also significant that what cracked the case was the work of someone who was not a traditionally qualified social researcher but a clergyman embedded in the local community. As the official Cholera Inquiry Committee report on the outbreak noted, it was Reverend Whitehead's 'previous knowledge of the district both before and during the epidemic, owing to his position as Curate of St Luke's, Berwick Street' which 'gave him unusual advantages' and allowed for 'a most minute and painstaking investigation'.[16] It was a new role for statistics, which until then had been mostly associated with the loftier businesses of political arithmetic, population management and statecraft. Statistics now became a tool that could be employed in the streets, which could and should require sleeves to be rolled up and hands made dirty.

What followed was an era of unprecedented involvement by statisticians in the nitty-gritty, which meant the development of what we might now think of as social research skills. John Snow worked in a completely unofficial capacity, asking personal questions of people who might have lost a close family member mere hours earlier in harrowing circumstances. The fact that he was able to get a response from most people he talked to is a testament to his sensitivity as an investigator. Others clearly didn't have the same level of tact. The Cholera Inquiry Committee report sheepishly admits that an attempt to collect information by delivering an 'Inquiry return' form to residents who were mostly illiterate and no doubt in a state of high anxiety 'did not produce the anticipated results'.[17] But the success of Snow's method also tells us something about the power of social conditioning. Poor people in their very worst hour were still willing to submit to intrusive questioning from a stranger at the door simply because they recognised his appearance and manner as that of a gentleman.

Over at the General Register Office, chief statistician William Farr was deeply engrossed in his weekly figures on births, marriages and deaths – although it has to be said, mostly the deaths. Farr searched the statistics almost obsessively for answers to the riddle of an untimely end. 'Life is mystery; and it ceases sometimes inexplicably,' he wrote in an official annual report, adding 'yet many causes of death are evident', as if these provided rungs to cling to in the darkness.[18] Farr's own first wife had died of tuberculosis only months before he started work at the GRO, and one of his big preoccupations was with the causes of disease.

The miasma theory of disease transmission was still widespread at the time among those working in public health. It held complete sway over the President of London's General Board of Health, Edwin Chadwick, who went as far as to declare that 'all smell is disease'.[19] Because Chadwick was so convinced that vapours from cesspools were the source of disease, he laboured to eradicate individual ones like the cellar swamp at 40 Broad Street and instead have all raw waste drain into the Thames. It was not foreseen as a problem that a large proportion of the city's inhabitants also had their drinking water supplied directly from the river. Waterborne disease was not seen as a threat – until the statistics started to show cases of cholera rising in line with more toilet facilities being directly hooked up to the Thames. The cellar drain at 40 Broad Street was also intended to function this way. Had it not been clogged, the disease could have infected people over a much larger radius.

It's worth noting that other disease epidemics also triggered a wave of statistical and medical interest, most notably scarlet fever, typhus and typhoid fever. Scarlet fever, or scarlatina as it was first known, is an infectious disease mainly affecting children. Today it is easily treatable with antibiotics but in the mid nineteenth century it was frequently fatal, with around thirty thousand people dying from it in 1863 and the same again in 1864. Two thirds of its victims were under five years old.

Medicine had long realised that certain diseases were infectious or, in the terminology of the day, zymotic. What was not understood was the mechanism of transmission. 'We may conceive the different kinds of zymotic matter distributed in clouds over the country, sometimes stretching over the whole atmosphere of the island, sometimes brooding over isolated but generally dense populations in unfavourable sanitary conditions,' was a typical view.[20] Because of the belief that disease particles could be swept over a vast distance, Victorian statistical reports usually start with a description of the weather. In the year of the Broad Street cholera outbreak, Farr's statistical report makes lengthy note of the wind speed and weight of the air.[21] In 1857, we find it suggested that 'the high temperature and the stagnancy of the air over cities are both calculated to favour the prevalence of the diarrhoeas'.[22] Even as late as 1876, Farr was endorsing a medical study which claimed to prove that 'the east wind in Spring is the enemy it was suspected to be'.[23]

The annual statistics also tell us a lot about deaths caused by acts of violence. But while John Graunt had, in days gone by, diligently reported deaths by violence and bizarre accidents just for the record, the Victorian statisticians saw themselves as detectives. In Howden, Yorkshire, it came to the attention of a clergyman that the number of official registered deaths in his parish was a lot higher than the number of the deceased who had recently been buried. It was discovered that the registrar had been faking death certificates to claim small sums of money.[24] Other similar cases of fraud were routinely uncovered.

The examination of death certificates also played a role in the extraordinary case of the 1846–51 'Essex poisonings', in which it was alleged that a coven-like group of women had murdered male family members and children with arsenic in order to claim life insurance. Part of the case against the supposed kingpin of the scheme, Mary May of Chelmsford, who was convicted of murder and hanged, was that the information on the death certificate of one of her victims didn't match up with other witness testimony as to his manner of death.[25]

This wouldn't be the last time statistics were used as a tool in criminal investigation. One of the most persuasive and striking pieces of evidence in the 1999 trial of Dr Harold Shipman – a GP convicted of murdering fifteen of his patients but believed to have killed at least 218 of them between 1975 and 1988 – was a graph showing the time of death on certificates he had signed. Where deaths were quite evenly spread throughout the day and night on certificates signed by other GPs, those signed by Shipman showed a huge spike around 2 and 3 p.m., the time he would visit his elderly patients at home.[26] This pattern was far from the only piece of evidence used to convict Shipman but it was a persuasive part of the case.

Back in the nineteenth century, the morbid fixation with causes of death was always focused on prevention. 'Death is inevitable, but why is life cut short?' pondered William Farr. 'The laws of life involve the laws of death; and every forward step of the biologist will open new fields in vital statistics.'[27] The quest was always to establish how a disease was spread and why it affected some people more than others, and many times both were a confounding medical mystery.

One thing that was becoming clear was that people living in squalid conditions were condemned to suffer the hardest. Farr despaired at the fact that large swathes of the country lacked enough medical professionals, leaving quacks to rush in with their nonsense cures.[28] As medical research progressed, it came to be routinely acknowledged that zymotic disease, including scarlatina and cholera, could indeed spread through water – as well as possibly through air.[29] And it was undeniably clear that, whether borne by air or water, disease clearly flourished in overcrowded and unsanitary settings. Farr's statistical research led him to conclude that 'typhoid fever is sustained by the increasing contamination of the waters, and typhus by the increased density of the population'.[30] Sir Charles Hastings, a respected surgeon and founding member of the British Medical Association, went as far as to publicly declare that 'however beautiful their situation and imposing their architecture – nay, *whatever their expenditure on sanitary measures* – such cities are but whited sepulchres, hiding under their fair exterior the rottenness of corruption and death'.[31] Reactive measures like spraying bleach on infected neighbourhoods were not enough: public health measures needed to go far bigger.

William Farr was in regular correspondence with a friend

and fellow statistical investigator into the causes and prevention of disease, Florence Nightingale. Born to a wealthy family, she had grown up in the stately home Embley Park, where her father's guests had included John Rickman, architect of the first censuses, and steampunk icon Charles Babbage, the inventor of the first computer. Although not considered fitting for a lady of her position, Nightingale became a nurse and was posted to the Scutari barracks military hospital in Turkey in 1854, where she tended to casualties of the Crimean War. Her collaboration with Farr was all about demonstrating a link between unsanitary conditions in hospitals and preventable death from disease. Scutari was dilapidated and generally a very poor choice of venue for a hospital, as well as being overcrowded and lacking in supplies. After the war, it turned out to have been the hospital with by far the highest number of deaths.[32]

In spite of – or perhaps because of – these appalling conditions, a popular mythology spread around Nightingale, sweeping the nation back home almost overnight. She was depicted in reports as an 'administering angel' and the 'lady with the lamp'. At times she was seen as the ideal of healing, feminine grace; at others, a nobly suffering and steadfast Joan of Arc. It is scarcely possible to overstate the extent of her fame: it was on a par with that of Princess Diana in the 1980s. There was an explosion of Florence Nightingale memorabilia and her likeness hung everywhere like icons of a saint. Florence was barely recorded as a name in England prior to Nightingale's celebrity – she herself was named after the Italian city where she had been born – but from 1855 onwards it became so popular that Florence was still the second most popular baby girls' name in the early twentieth century.*[33] William Farr named one of his daughters Florence as a tribute.

---

* As of 2021, it was back in the top ten girls' names in England and Wales.

Nightingale, like most, took it for granted that disease was, to some extent, communicated through miasma or, in other words, foul smells. A lot of the disease-control methods she advocated – like increasing air circulation on wards and keeping floors, bedding and instruments clean – were effective, but not for the reasons she thought. Conveniently, many of the measures taken to eradicate smells were also effective in removing the actual transmitter of disease: germs. Then again, Nightingale had not received a full medical education and was certainly no scientist; she was not really seeking to understand *why* disease was prevented, but rather *how*. She collected statistics on disease and mortality in Scutari and other hospitals and was able to demonstrate that after a deep clean and the introduction of sanitary measures there was an immediate fall in the number of deaths. But a one-off clean-up was not enough, and Nightingale used her statistics as the backbone of a campaign for sanitation reform that went all the way to the top.

This included devising her now-famous diagrams – sometimes referred to as 'coxcombs', sometimes as the 'Nightingale rose' – which resemble the blade of a circular saw.[34] They depict the number of deaths of the army in the east (that is, in Crimea) from wounds, from other causes, and from preventable disease. By design, these diagrams over-emphasise the volume of death from preventable disease, so that the reader instantly identifies the problem. They also undeniably communicate the huge drop-off in deaths of all kinds following sanitation measures being improved. Until then, the British hospitals themselves were the most effective weapon of war on Russia's side. The scale of needless death, Nightingale calculated, was equivalent to taking 1,100 healthy men per year out onto Salisbury Plain and shooting them.[35] She requested that a copy of her data visualisations be sent to Queen Victoria, noting 'she may look at it because it has pictures'.[36]

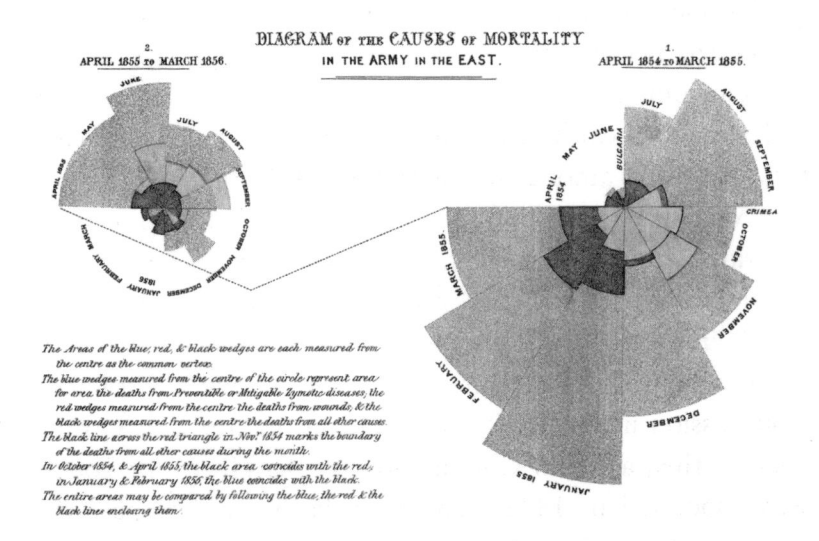

That Nightingale came up with these data visualisations as a way of catching a reader's attention shows she understood more about the value of good communication than many a trained statistician. In fact, it was because she was an outsider to the statistical elite that she recognised what they did not. This was, as she wrote to her friend Sidney Herbert, head of a Royal Commission on Army Medical and Sanitary Reforms, because 'none but scientific men even look at the appendices of a Report' and so policy change could not be brought about by numbers alone. Statistics had to tell an obvious story, and one that the 'vulgar public', as she termed them, could easily grasp.[37] It was activism through data. And it was highly successful. The research was used by Herbert's royal commission in 1857 and by a later Royal Commission on India, which had the wider remit of recommending improvements to sanitation in that country as a whole, as it was referred to frequently in Parliamentary business. It helped, of course, in terms of getting her diagrams onto the desks of the right people, that Nightingale was from a rich and well-connected family and, by this point, an international celebrity. She was never allowed to present her findings in person, however, on account of being a woman.

The public health achievements of the late nineteenth century are easily among the most impactful in British history. The Vaccination Acts of 1853, 1867 and 1871 would prove pivotal in eradicating preventable diseases such as smallpox. Edwin Chadwick – he of 'all smell is disease' – was also hugely influential in shining a light on the unsanitary conditions in slums, through surveys carried out by the Poor Law Commission in the 1830s and 1840s at his request. On the back of this, a Royal Commission on the Health of Towns was appointed in 1843, prompting Parliament to pass the milestone Public Health Act in 1848. This recognised that it was the government's responsibility to fix the appalling conditions in towns and cities. It was also acknowledgement that the people living in such places had the right to be protected by the state from infectious disease.

In June 1858, London was oppressed by what came to be referred to as the Great Stink. Thanks to the Board of Health's tireless work to ensure that all of the city's human, animal, vegetable and mineral waste flowed directly and unfiltered into the Thames, the river had reached a state of the utmost putrefaction. Ninety million gallons of raw sewage flowing into the river each day had coagulated on the riverbed and the surface of the water steamed with rot.[38] The stench was abominable. Nor did it escape the notice of Members of Parliament, who resorted to conducting their sessions behind curtains steeped in chloride of lime. This insufferable cocktail of bleach fumes and sulphur was a more effective accelerant for change than any statistics had proven to be. Ross Mangles, MP for Guildford, led the charge, complaining that responsibility for the precious river should never have been placed in the hands of the bureaucratic Metropolitan Board of Works, whose only action on the Stink had been the proposal for an investigatory boat trip, which understandably had not yet taken place.[39] The man in charge of ventilation for the House of Commons chamber was driven to write to the Speaker to warn 'that he can be no longer responsible for the health of the House; that the stench has made most rapid advance within two days; that up to Tuesday he got fresh air draughts from the Star Chamber Court; but that when night came the poisonous enemy took possession of the Court, and so beat him outright'.[40] By July, the House had agreed to provide an initial £2.5 million to start construction on a new sewer system for the whole of London.[41]

The result was not just any sewer system but a staggeringly vast, complex and frankly beautiful construction which is now regarded as one the Seven Wonders of the Industrial World. Its visionary chief engineer, Joseph Bazalgette, oversaw the project, which would use 318 million bricks, 670,000 cubic metres of concrete and extra-strength granite shipped from Cornwall to build 82 miles of new super sewers and 1,100 miles of drains. It even changed the landscape, with land being reclaimed from the river on its northern shore, which narrowed its flow.[42] The idea was to carry waste far out east beyond the city and release it where it would wash it out to sea on the estuary tide. In true Victorian fashion, the architects took pride in design as well as functionality. A pumping station at Abbey Mills in an otherwise dank part of east London is something akin to the Palace of Versailles.

It was therefore unsettling when in 1866 cholera struck again with a vengeance in Bromley-by-Bow, killing at least five thousand people before it was brought under control.

When confronted, Bazalgette had to admit that this was the one remaining part of town where his sewerage network was not yet operational. This time, the chief statistical investigator of the outbreak was William Farr. John Snow had died in June 1858 at the age of forty-five, just as the Great Stink was hotting up. He would not see the great sewers being constructed, nor would he witness the clear vindication of his waterborne theory of disease. After the sewers became fully operational in 1870, London never saw another mass outbreak of cholera again, and typhus and typhoid fever were also largely kept at bay. By 1890, there were only eighty-three deaths from cholera recorded across a city whose population had grown by two million over the past twenty years, and now stood at around five and a half million.[43]

The massive feat of engineering which was the construction of London's sewers could not for one moment have escaped the attention of the statisticians in Somerset House. The new sewer was being constructed directly in front of their building. Where once the increasingly fetid waters of the Thames had washed right up to the building's edge and into the tunnels underneath, the river would now be separated off by the Thames Embankment. This pleasant tree-lined boulevard became – and remains – a major thoroughfare for commuters. It also now forms an iconic segment of the London Marathon. The casual pedestrian strolling along it would never guess that they're standing on a gargantuan Victorian-era sewage pipe, although they surely couldn't miss the apparatus of the brand-new Thames super sewer which runs in a parallel down the riverbank.

If the thought of all this has left you in need of a cool beverage and a sit down, then I know just the place. A short walk from the Embankment into the centre of Soho will take you to what is now Broadwick Street. There stands a replica of the famous and ill-fated water pump, roughly on the site of where it would have been in 1854. A short distance away is a pub where you can find some much-needed refreshment: it's called the John Snow.

4
Life on the Line

The pace of change in the nineteenth century was like nothing that has come before or since. Not only had the population of Great Britain doubled between 1800 and 1850 but there had also been an almost complete change in many people's way of life. The late twentieth century comes close in terms of the speed with which new technologies transformed our lives, but even it may not match the Industrial Revolution for sheer physical upheaval.

Across the north of England, the West Midlands and Greater London, the physical and human landscape was transforming at an extraordinary clip. The population of Liverpool was five times larger in 1851 than in 1801; that of Manchester had tripled in the same time and was approaching half a million people.[1] Parts of the north-west of England also changed beyond recognition, thanks to the boom in textile production. In 1775, Great Britain had imported around 5 million pounds (in weight) of cotton to supply cottage industries and a small number of early adopters of the spinning jenny, a machine that made easy work of spinning raw fibre into thread. By the 1840s, 600 million pounds of cotton were being imported to feed the ravenous jaws of jennies in their tens of thousands. The modern factory had been born. The real centre of this activity was the county of Lancashire, which in 1851 had a population of just over two million people, spread across rapidly swelling cities including Liverpool, Manchester, Bolton, Rochdale, Oldham and Preston.

The parallel inventions of iron and steam power also meant a revolution in transport. By the 1840s, Great Britain had an impressive four thousand miles of canals, at which point rail took over as a faster and more passenger-friendly mode of travel. Thousands of miles of railway were built in a matter of decades, including the world's first underground railway connecting Paddington and Farringdon in London. Yes, the first tube line ran on steam and was powered by coal.

The Victorians and their predecessors were scrupulous counters of the material inputs and outputs to all this activity. Collecting numerical data was essential to the many individual projects as well as the overall national one to improve efficiency and maximise production. Innovation moved at a blistering pace, with industries being utterly transformed by new mechanical inventions in a matter of years or even months. By the mid nineteenth century, Britain was importing £34 million worth of raw materials from its colonies each year and exporting £37 million of goods back to them.[2] The UK's key industries were four times as productive as half a century earlier and it was in Britain that many of the riddles of mechanical production were being solved through experimentation and creative design.[3] Unbelievably, it was as early as the 1820s that Charles Babbage proposed his intricate design for the Difference Engine, a steam-powered calculating device now recognised as the first computer, which was so far ahead of its time that the components did not yet exist for it to be built. There was one area, however, where Britain was lagging behind. It knew very little, and truly understood much less, about the lives of most of its eighteen million inhabitants (twenty-five million when including Ireland).

And despite Britain's greatness on the world stage, social problems at home had not gone away. Disease was flourishing precisely because of the overcrowded urban conditions industrialisation had encouraged. The Great Stink had made clear to politicians that the issue of sanitation was everybody's problem, whether they lived in the reeking slums of Whitechapel or cowered behind chlorine-soaked curtains in Westminster.

As is often the case, it was outsiders who could see Britain's social problems most plainly. The French intellectual Léon Faucher spent time in England as a journalist and his frank commentary on life there resonated with his British readers. 'Our glory and our shame jostle in the same vast city [of London],' a reviewer reflected on Faucher's *Revue des deux mondes*, published in 1846. 'With wealth unequalled we have poverty unparalleled. [Monsieur] Faucher has been too long amongst us and too shrewd an observer to suffer our shame to escape unnoticed. Painful and severe are many of his remarks but they have occurred before to every thoughtful Englishman, who has deplored the evils of our social state, and our inability to remove by human enactments the wretchedness that stains our pre-eminence and greatness.'[4]

Another outsider whose shrewd take would attract wide attention was Friedrich Engels – or Frederick Engels, as he was marketed to the English.* Engels came to Manchester as a twenty-two-year-old in 1842, sent to work at his father's textile factory in order to learn the art of business and ostensibly to quash the radical notions that were already forming in his head. The move had the opposite effect. Being from the

---

* How we can't be trusted to pronounce 'Friedrich', I don't know.

owner's family, Engels was certainly not handling bobbins himself, but he was keenly observing the conditions of factory workers from a close distance, and he was radicalised even further by what he saw.

His book *The Condition of the Working Class in England*, published in German in 1845 and in English in 1885 (although the gist of the message had filtered across from Europe long before), was a searing account of the inhumane conditions endured by many of the workers fuelling British greatness. Evocative descriptions of the rank, squalid and soiled dwellings – and even entire neighbourhoods – inhabited by the poor are enough to turn a reader's stomach. As a critical insider, Engels also described daily sufferings, injuries and deformities that were the common result of factory work – realities which would rarely have been presented in such a stark and public manner before. Engels is better known nowadays for co-authoring *The Communist Manifesto*, which warned that the inevitable result of these conditions would be revolution.

Henry Mayhew was no outsider, although he was someone who struggled to find his footing in life. A journalist and one-time editor of popular satirical magazine *Punch*, Mayhew was a familiar character in the London literary scene but without much success to his name. In the late 1840s his wife had left him after he had run the family into bankruptcy, and he was in need of a big break. This came in the form of his great work of social investigation, *London Labour and the London Poor*, which was first serialised in the *Morning Chronicle* newspaper in 1849 and later published as a book. Mayhew had been tasked by the *Chronicle* with providing an account of the conditions of the poorest in London, to satisfy the curiosity of its more middle-class readers, and he had thoroughly understood the assignment. His work includes rich descriptions of the working lives of the poor and the conditions in which they lived. We meet street-sellers, casual labourers, small-scale traders, street sweepers, domestic workers, and chimney sweeps. Reading Mayhew's account, we really do feel like we meet these characters, thanks to lengthy accounts which are recounted seemingly verbatim, with the subject's own turns of phrase. It was a pioneering work in capturing the voices and the relatively unfiltered views of the working classes, many of whom could not read or write and virtually none of whom would have had a channel to be heard by the middle and upper classes in ordinary life.

One description is of a girl selling watercress who, 'although only eight years of age, had entirely lost all childish ways'. Dressed in cotton dress and threadbare shawl, with carpet slippers for shoes, she would be up before dawn to harvest watercress before shuffling the streets of Farringdon and Clerkenwell for as many hours as it took to sell it. 'When I gets home, after selling creases [cress] I puts the room to rights,' we hear her recount. 'I ain't got no father, he's a father-in-law [...] he's very good to me. No; I don't mean by that that he says nice things to me, for he never hardly speaks.' In cold weather it hurts her hands to pick the cress and to wash it under the freezing water pump, by the light of a lamp. 'I don't have no dinner. Mother gives me two slices of bread-and-butter and a cup of tea for breakfast, and then I go till tea, and has the same.'[5] From Friday to Saturday night she stokes the fire at the home of a Jewish family observing the Sabbath, where she gets her only hot meals and proper nourishment for the week. She reflects on how kind they have been to her, giving her the only toys she possesses: 'a knife and fork, and two little chairs', bereft of either doll's house or doll. When Mayhew asks her about playing games and going to the park, she looks at him with amazement.[6]

Unlike the watercress girl, many of the individuals Mayhew

speaks to are homeless and utterly destitute. On a winter's night he visits a very rare example of a homeless shelter – the Asylum for the Houseless Poor in Cripplegate – where the needy come at night for half a pound of bread and a place to sleep. The beds are merely spaces on the floor, partitioned from one another with wooden planks and filled with hay and with a leather sheet for a blanket. The rows of swaddled, hollow-cheeked sleepers resemble a catacomb of mummies in makeshift sarcophagi. An out-of-work painter describes to Mayhew how he previously slept rough for three weeks, surviving on discarded crusts and sleeping in straw: 'the cold made me almost dead with sleep; and when obliged to move I couldn't walk at first, I could only crawl along'.[7] A great many of the homeless are Irish, including orphaned children who had fled famine only to find cold comfort with the 'streets for a stepmother'.[8]

Mayhew's style was new because it expressed sympathy – and evoked it in the reader – without condescension. It was popular and inspired a host of similar studies with names like *Sketches in London*, *Sanitary Ramblings* and *The Rookeries of London* – rookeries being a name for the ramshackle slums which were little more than grimy nests for the most disadvantaged.[9] The style was a great deal more objective and realistic but no less vivid – you might even say entertaining – than the portrayal of cheeky and loveable street children in Dickens's *Oliver Twist*. It was also a type of investigation which was methodical and relatively unvarnished by the observer's own reflections. Even though it didn't involve much in the way of statistical data – Mayhew has even been described as 'anti-statistical' – he was nonetheless trying to be scientific.[10]

The Victorians were obsessed with science. The most influential book of the era was Darwin's *On the Origin of Species*, published in 1859, closely followed, some would argue, by the now forgotten *History of Civilization in England* by Henry Thomas Buckle, which claimed to be a 'science of history'.[11] On the one hand science caught the public's imagination through discovery and invention. On the other, it provided a sense of order in a frantic, fast-changing world that would otherwise have seemed on the precipice of chaos. Because, as historian Lawrence Goldman puts it, 'science was in vogue', its methods were gradually adopted by the people trying to study social issues and the lives of the people. As early as 1838, George Porter published a compilation of statistical data, *The Progress of the Nation*, that examined social issues alongside economic ones. John Ramsay McCulloch's *Statistical Account of the British Empire* in 1837 had been another impressive effort to take the pulse of the many diverse societies under Britain's yoke.

Parliament soon got in on the act of amassing large amounts of empirical evidence to assess social problems. Since Tudor times, the system for dealing with relief of poverty in England and Wales had always been a bit of a pot luck. Parishes were each responsible for helping people in their vicinity, and the funding for relief came from donations to the Church and taxation of the local community. This system was known as the Poor Laws, and by the 1830s it had been stretched to breaking point, as the many people uprooted by industrialisation found themselves shunted from parish to parish with the excuse of 'not my problem'. In 1831, the Overseers of the Poor distributed £6.8 million in relief – the equivalent to half a billion pounds in today's money – and in a woefully haphazard fashion.[12] Parliament's response was to convene a royal commission to look into the Poor Law, which was one of the first to painstakingly look for data on the problems it suspected were there. It amassed evidence from over three thousand parishes (although notably not featuring any evidence from the poor themselves) and examined a complete set of statistics on poor relief going back to 1813. One of the participants in the commission was sanitation reformer Edwin Chadwick.

Unfortunately, the recommendations of this commission would turn out to be the wrong thing entirely, despite apparently being guided by evidence. Under the new Poor Law system, there was to be virtually no form of relief for people in the community; instead, the destitute would be expected to report to a new institution called the workhouse. These prison-like structures appeared almost overnight all over the country like spiders in a web and were feared and loathed by many. Being sent to the workhouse often meant being separated from family, which was traumatic as well as impractical for households trying to get back on their feet. Packing people into comfortless places where they were expected to work for no pay turned out not to promote self-sufficiency – and, looking back, it's hard to imagine how it ever would have done.

Regardless, royal commissions were quickly adopted as the new model of evidence-based policymaking. By the 1850s, an average of eight royal commissions were appointed per year, the immediate aim being to 'fertilise public debate with relevant facts'.[13] This thirst for data came from a new standard politicians were setting themselves, in the words of Robert Peel, not to 'legislate on speculation and conjecture, and on assumptions which rest on no satisfactory data'.[14] Between 1801 and 1851, the amount of technical material published by Parliament went from seven volumes per year to seventy. This was a glut of supposedly empirical evidence. It was political arithmetic on steroids.

If science worked by observation – by codifying and classifying and dividing until distinct parts were identified that made sense of the whole – why should there not be an equivalent discipline of 'social science'? An early adopter of this term was the philosopher and, later in life, Member of Parliament John Stuart Mill, who argued that the political and the social were two different fields of enquiry. Social research could be scientific, as the Statistical Society of London noted in an 1838 report, as long as its practitioners were operating only using 'facts, accurately observed and methodically classified'.[15]

Classification was the name of the game. Social researchers – and policymakers – needed to be able to put people into distinct buckets in order to say anything with generality, and yet close-up observation like that carried out by Mayhew showed that lives were fundamentally messy and stubbornly resistant to pattern. Mayhew, who had 'seen the world of London below the surface, as it were', found himself with a 'craving to contemplate it far above it' and agreed to be taken up above London in a hot-air balloon piloted by the famous aviator Charles Green. Swinging in the flimsy basket, Mayhew watched as 'the immense mass of vice and avarice and cunning, of noble aspirations and humble heroism, blent into one black spot'.[16] Seen from too distant a perspective, it turned out all nuance was lost. Could there not be something in between these warts-and-all portraits and the impersonal bird's-eye view of official statistics?

Thirty years later, in the 1880s, there would be a man who could take up this challenge: the researcher, businessman and social reformer Charles Booth. Booth had inherited a very successful shipping business, which afforded him the status to have public opinions on all matters and the capital to do pretty much whatever he liked. What he liked was to study the lives of the poorest in society and to propose remedies. He also liked to quibble publicly with other social campaigners, including the leader of Britain's first fledgling socialist party about whether or not 25 per cent of London's population lived in poverty.[17] Unable to let it go, Booth used his own money, influence and time to commission a survey of life in Tower Hamlets, the known epicentre of London poverty in the 1880s. This expanded into a survey across almost the whole of the city, the findings of which eventually filled seventeen volumes. It is striking that Booth pressed ahead with this considerable task without anyone really asking for it. It's hard to picture a solo business figure today undertaking such a piece of work simply out of curiosity or even a sense of social duty.

Booth's research style was to combine a detailed ground-level study of his subjects with a scientific approach to classifying them. His starting point was to try to estimate the size of the problem which was poverty. To do so he employed local policemen, School Board officials and freelance researchers to go door to door across London and record information on a household's income, its expenditure, how many people were living there, their occupations and any other information of note. The notebooks, many of which were preserved, provide rich although clearly subjective commentary on the 'character' of a street. The residents of Langford Road in Fulham, for example, are described as 'drunken, lazy, vicious, rough' and said to be responsible for a 'monthly average of one to two policemen injured on this street'. The provider of this insight was a Sergeant Stroud of the local force.[18]

Having gathered this information, Booth's next task was to assign a classification to a street or, at times, an individual dwelling. In his first classification, for east London, eight classes were identified:

A. The lowest class of occasional labourers, loafers and semi-criminals
B. Casual earnings – 'very poor'

C. Intermittent earnings
D. Small regular earnings (together with C, 'the poor')
E. Regular standard earnings – above the line of poverty
F. Higher class labour
G. Lower middle class
H. Upper middle class

The cut-off point for 'poor' (classes C and D) was earnings of around eighteen to twenty-one shillings per week for a moderately sized family. This wasn't based on anything particularly scientific – as Booth described it, 'my "poor" may be described as living under a struggle to obtain the necessaries of life and make both ends meet; while the "very poor" live in a state of chronic want'.[19] About 12.5 per cent of east London's inhabitants in 1889 were put in class A ('very poor') and a further 23 per cent in Class B ('poor'). Classes C and D were later combined, and class A downgraded even further to 'Lowest class. Vicious, semi-criminal.' Booth commissioned maps in which streets were colour-coded according to his schema and they very effectively capture how, even today, the end of one street in London and the beginning of another can be like a crossing between two different worlds.

Let's make one thing clear, though: this was not what we would now call an objective, scientific exercise. Booth was neither a scientist nor trained social researcher, and his classification method often seems to have been based more on observations of a street's cleanliness and the manners of its inhabitants than on a detailed appraisal of their income and expenditure. Observations of 'bare-headed women', Irish people and Jews feature often in the notes for streets coded into lower classes. A back alley in Bromley-by-Bow comes with the note 'both sides should be [colour-coded] black; notorious brothels and have been so for years'.[20] But the alley in question is surrounded entirely by streets coded purple, pink and red – that is, mixed to middle class. Do we know for a fact that the inhabitants of these brothels weren't earning more than eighteen shillings a week? It seems doubtful that they were asked. The results of Booth's poverty study give us, in essence, a census of social class.

Watching Booth's vast study take shape in the 1890s was Seebohm Rowntree, a young would-be social researcher living in York. Rowntree's father Joseph had inspired ideas of social reform in his son, having used his position as head of the family chocolate factory to try to improve the conditions for his workers. Rowntree junior, like most people at the time, was unsurprised to see parts of Booth's London map suggesting urban dens of deprivation. But strolling the streets of York, one could see similar inequalities: the height of wealth and the fullest fathoms of poverty. Rowntree wanted to see if he could apply a similar classification technique to York, which he assessed was fairly typical of a small city or town. His method would be far more scientific and, given that he was studying a 'typical' case rather than the uniquely monstrous outlier of London, he intended his findings to be generalisable to the country as a whole. It was far more convincingly a true work of social science.

Rowntree carried out his own household census of the city of York, in which his enumerators asked questions which were arguably far more intrusive than had been used for censuses up to that point. He wanted a full, itemised breakdown of income and expenditure, along with a potted family history and details of present occupations. As with Booth's study, we also have well-preserved observation notes. One household of two elderly brothers is described in the following terms: 'Both receive parish relief. Untidy and filthy house. Floor of kitchen full of holes, and dangerous for old men. The house shares one closet [toilet] with three other houses and one water-tap with twenty-one others. Rent 2s [shillings].'[21] While there is some consistency to what is described – the condition of the house, a description of the family's circumstances, the price of rent – certain embellishments suggest a reproachful tone. An out-of-work polisher with two children and a wife who takes in laundry receives this commentary: '[He] is an invalid and capable of little work. One child, cripple. Man not deserving; has spent all large earnings on drink. Fellow workmen have made several collections for him. All speak badly of him.'[22]

Like Booth, Rowntree constructed a poverty line, above and below which to classify the York inhabitants. To do this he took the innovative approach of figuring out how many calories and, realistically, which types of food a person would need to eat in order to sustain a worker's lifestyle. This was deemed to be a very repetitive diet which rarely deviated from bread, margarine, porridge, potatoes, cheese, gruel and vegetable broth. Three times a week, meat should be eaten, in the form of 'boiled bacon'. A teaspoon of treacle in one's porridge on Wednesdays and Fridays was deemed an acceptable extravagance and children should have a daily allowance of sugar in the morning, to perk them up for the day. Tea was expected to be had once a week on Sundays, and alcohol does not feature as a necessity at all. The cost of this nourishment, along with the cost of other meticulously itemised necessary expenses, was calculated for different sizes of household. The results are bizarrely similar to Booth's apparent guesswork: eighteen shillings per week for a couple with two children, twenty-one shillings per week for a couple with three.[23]

But Rowntree went one step further. If that was the 'primary' poverty line for sustaining mere existence, he came up with a 'secondary' line which allowed for a little extra expenditure on sundries, 'either useful or wasteful'. Remarkably, this Victorian social scientist was proposing recognition that people could still be 'poor' even if they were not at death's door but had a little extra to spend on clothes, homewares, services or treats. It was not a sign of fecklessness to want such things. Rowntree was acknowledging the working class as decision-makers whose choices were worthy of at least a little respect. Mayhew would have understood it. There were, however, still ways of losing this respect and falling to the category of 'undeserving' poor, chief among them being seen to fritter away the household money on drink.

Out of a population of around seventy-six thousand in York, Rowntree found that around 10 per cent were in primary poverty and 18 per cent in secondary poverty. Wanting to compare these results with the figures for London, he asked Booth to apply the same classification to his study. The resulting estimates suggested that the proportion living in poverty was around 28 per cent in York and 31 per cent in London or, in Rowntree's words, 'practically the same'.[24] This was a revelation. It had been assumed by many people, Rowntree included, that London was an exceptional case breeding its own super-strain of poverty. The 'startling probability' was that '25 to 30 per cent of the town populations of the United Kingdom are living in poverty'.[25] Extrapolated to England and Wales as a whole, it suggested that seven and a half million people were living in urban poverty at the turn of the twentieth century, or more than one in four.[26]

'There is surely need for a greater concentration of thought by the nation upon the well-being of its own people, for no civilisation can be sound or stable which has at its base this mass of stunted human life,' wrote Rowntree, because in their suffering the poor were 'all but voiceless'.[27] But he had given them a voice of sorts. And his statistical figures could not be dismissed as mere speculation because he had well and truly kept receipts.

This new insight into the conditions of the working classes and the poor came as a profound shock to the middle and upper classes, who had been living side by side with them for years. It was not necessarily that the well off had been in denial about just how bad things were (although this was definitely a factor in many cases) but rather that there was so little overlap in the lives of different social strata. There were no supermarkets or high street chains frequented by people from all walks of life. Public transport was not widely used, and schools were segregated by social class. The workers inhabited the early morning hours: milking, packing, unloading, delivering and starting up the fires in ice-cold grates. Later in the day the wealthier would emerge, and by the evening they would be out enjoying 'refined' forms of entertainment for which the working classes had neither the money, energy nor time. The social classes were ships passing in the night. Some of the wealthy struggled hard to believe the descriptions of poor people's lives, having it in mind that such scenes belonged in other countries, such as those Britain had colonised. Many who had wealth and pride to protect were deeply unsettled by the discovery that there could be 'a dark continent that is within easy walking distance of the General Post Office'.[28]

What the studies of Rowntree, Booth and others also achieved was to bring more nuance to – and even dispel – prevailing ideas about the causes of poverty. A prominent strand of Victorian thinking was that personal, moral or even genetic failings were the cause of a bad situation in life. One of the reasons workhouses had been proposed as a solution to poverty was that they would teach the poor a level of discipline which they were assumed to lack. At times it was even theorised that the reason people in poverty experienced higher rates of disease was they were constitutionally weak. The expression of these ideas reached its peak in the work of Francis Galton, who theorised in the 1880s that poverty and disease were the inevitable expression of genetic defects which were passed on generationally by those in the lower social classes. 'Nature prevails enormously over nurture,' he had written, and the mind was left with 'some wonder as to whether nurture can do anything at all'.[29] Galton also co-opted Booth's social classification (which was already rather offensive towards its 'lower' end) into a ranking of people by innate mental ability, from the 'notably superior' to 'undesirables'.[30]

This way of thinking had been hard to push back against because it was also convenient for poverty to be regarded as incurable when the economic model relied on a plentiful supply of workers who asked for the bare minimum. 'The public health administrator was faced with two main problems,' writes the historian Richard Titmuss, 'poverty and drains. But although both were indubitably present only one was recognised as a problem.'[31] Drains received a lot of sympathetic attention because they were not seen as being the architects of their own misfortune.

What Rowntree, in particular, made clear with his detailed study was that there was a clear explanation for most cases of poverty that did not involve the person being genetically predestined to be a bottom-dweller. He found that around 16 per cent of primary poverty was explained by the death of the chief wage earner and 22 per cent by the size of the family being larger than its income could support.*

More strikingly, over 50 per cent of primary poverty was explained by people being in regular work but with wages that were too low for them to afford basic subsistence. We still talk about 'in-work poverty' in the present day. This was the first time it had been laid out in such stark terms – and Rowntree did actually visualise his findings in a series of pie charts – that the wages for full-time work were too low to live on, even before one started to think about 'wasting it' through profligate spending. On the causes of 'secondary poverty',

---

* Booth similarly concludes that 'Marriage is early for social or industrial reasons, and not, as a rule, on account of recklessness, while the number of births follows almost inevitably from physical causes ... no reasonably possible exercise of prudence can be expected to stand against the stream. Not in this direction can we look for a solution of the problem of poverty.'[32]

though, Rowntree concluded 'there can be little doubt ... that the predominant factor is drink'. This likely came as confirmation to advocates of the fairly large temperance movement at the time, of which Rowntree, being a Quaker, was one.

IMMEDIATE CAUSES OF POVERTY

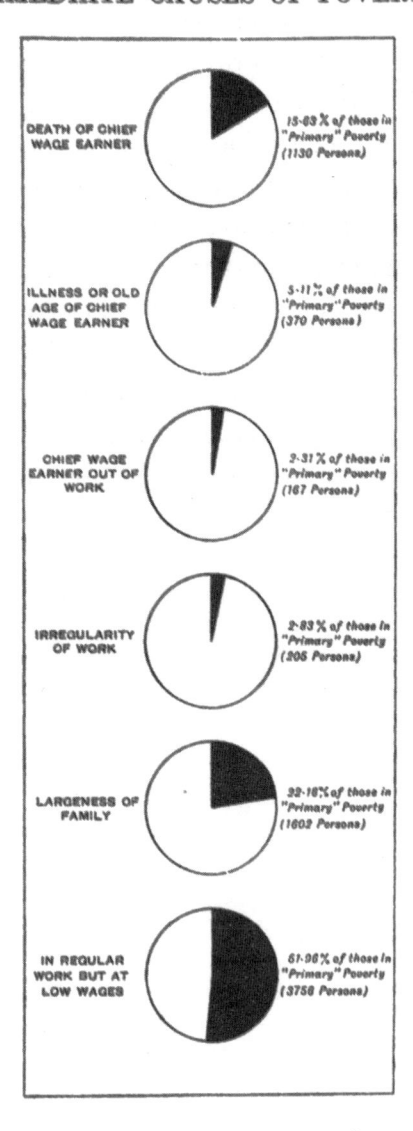

Cause	Percentage
DEATH OF CHIEF WAGE EARNER	15·63% of those in "Primary" Poverty (1130 Persons)
ILLNESS OR OLD AGE OF CHIEF WAGE EARNER	5·11% of those in "Primary" Poverty (370 Persons)
CHIEF WAGE EARNER OUT OF WORK	2·31% of those in "Primary" Poverty (167 Persons)
IRREGULARITY OF WORK	2·83% of those in "Primary" Poverty (205 Persons)
LARGENESS OF FAMILY	22·16% of those in "Primary" Poverty (1602 Persons)
IN REGULAR WORK BUT AT LOW WAGES	51·96% of those in "Primary" Poverty (3756 Persons)

Booth's work on the London poor also added weight to the idea that where poverty was the result of structural factors, what was needed was cold, hard financial assistance, not lectures on morality. These Victorian social surveys ultimately laid the groundwork for the welfare state, which within fifty years would grow into one of the largest and most complete safety nets the world had ever seen.

Many people in the working classes would have been scarcely aware of the light being shone on their suffering and indignity, with their minds on the more pressing matter of survival. That said, those who were conscious of the new scientific interest in their lives seemed to accept or even welcome it, acknowledging that it could be a route towards improvement.[33] The voices of objectors to counting the population, like William Thornton, the MP who had warned of the 'fetters' of statistics that would expose us to 'our enemies at home ... tax-masters', were for the most part echoes from the past. It's often the loudest voices raised in opposition to transparency that will lead you to those with the most to gain from keeping a truth concealed.

5

Rising Damp

At just after one o'clock in the morning on Sunday 24 November 1861, a policeman was doing his rounds on the Royal Mile, the street leading up to Edinburgh Castle in the city's Old Town. All was quiet, although the fish tails, squashed apples and coffee grounds underfoot told of the bustling market place the street had been earlier that evening. The policeman had just turned down an alleyway between two shopfronts when the sound of a commotion drew him back out again. Across the way some kind of squabble was taking place, and the policeman was walking over to investigate when from behind him came an almighty cracking sound. He turned to see the front of the seven-storey tenement building over the alleyway he'd just left bulging outwards, windows popping from their frames. The next instant, the whole thing came thundering down with a deafening dull boom, sending a shower of dust high into the air.[1] As the haze lifted, it became clear that the entire building was simply gone. The high-rise block, twenty metres wide and at least as tall – and home to dozens of sleeping residents – had collapsed in an avalanche of stone.

Firemen were quick on the scene and took down the burners from the gas streetlamps to light up the rubble. They scrambled over the jagged pile, following the groans and wails of trapped residents, and over the course of several hours were able to free around seven or eight of them. Other bodies were recovered lifeless, some of them in a battered and mangled state. Above them tottered the empty shell of the building, the back and side walls of which still stood. Eerily there were still coal fires burning in some of the grates, which now sat exposed high up in the walls while the hands that had stoked them minutes earlier were growing cold.[2]

Throughout that Sunday onlookers stopped to gaze in horror. The sight of those intimate indoor walls that were now on the outside had the profoundest effect on people. A row of neat tins sat undisturbed on a shelf, a walking cane hung on a wall, never to be required again, and in a wardrobe with its door ripped off several gowns fluttered spectrally in the wind. There was even a bird chirping away in a cage, still hanging on a wall high out of reach. The crowd eventually grew so large that soldiers had to be summoned from the castle to control it.

Over several days, more bodies were recovered, including entire families who had perished together in an instant. Mrs MacKenzie on the fifth floor had been killed, survived by her husband who was a policeman on the night shift and who had learned of the catastrophe when her body was brought into the morgue. The final bodies to be recovered, five days after the collapse, were those of the Skirving family who had lived on the first or second floor; they had been pushed five feet below ground.

As rescuers were digging through the torch-lit scene they came across a small foot sticking out from the rubble. Starting to clear the debris around it, they heard a voice call out, 'Heave awa' lads, I'm no' deid yet!' It took several men to saw through a heavy wooden beam and extract twelve-year-old

Joseph McIvor, while he continued his encouraging cries with gusto. There had been some other miraculous escapes. George Gunn, returning from a night out, had by chance stopped to talk to an acquaintance. That two-minute conversation saved his life, as he was just coming into view of the tenement when the whole thing crashed down before his eyes, killing both his parents and two siblings.[3] A dozen or so residents had felt the initial rumblings and managed to escape, including a lodger on the fifth floor who had been warming a bottle of porter by the fireplace to celebrate his birthday. Looking up at the gutted building the next day, he saw his bottle still standing by the grate.[4] The caged bird was also brought down alive by firemen and reunited with its owner.

The morale it took to merrily call out 'I'm no' deid yet!' in the midst of such a setting was not forgotten by the people of the Old Town. A new, smaller block which was built on the site features a stone likeness of a little Joseph McIvor's head and an inscription of the famous phrase. It's known now as the 'Heave awa' Hoose'.*

The tenement collapse was the worst civilian disaster Edinburgh had ever seen. Thirty-five people were killed out of the seventy-seven who had been home that night. It was found that the cause of the collapse was that load-bearing walls had been weakened by having large chunks removed and the building's timber frame was rotten to the core. It was – and probably had been for decades – a death trap. It prompted widespread anger and calls for the improvement of housing standards in the overcrowded city. The structure of the building had been least two hundred, if not four hundred, years old and it was certainly not alone in being so advanced in age. A huge part of the Old Town's architecture was essentially

---

* In the inscription, the phrase was adapted to 'Heave away, chaps', which is clearly not the same but was considered more relatable to English tourists.

medieval and was also poorly maintained, seldom inspected and crammed with far more tenants than originally intended. The poor ventilation and scarcity or non-existence of toilet facilities also made living conditions especially vile. Edwin Chadwick, on a sanitary inspection in the 1840s, had pronounced them 'the most wretched ... of which he had been able to obtain any account, or that he had ever seen'.[5] The city's powers agreed that it was time for something to be done and in 1867 they passed the City Improvement Act, which led to most of the high-rise medieval stock being replaced.

By the mid nineteenth century, the problems of poor-quality housing and overcrowding were being felt in towns and cities all over the UK. The fact was that their populations were expanding at a rate far above that at which a decent standard of housing could be achieved. According to the 1851 census, Great Britain contained 815 settlements formally designated as towns, 580 of which were in England and Wales, and the population was evenly split between town and countryside. By 1861, the number of towns in England and Wales had risen to 781, containing nearly 11 million inhabitants and accounting for over half of the population. Ten years later, there were 938 towns with nearly two thirds of the population, and in Scotland the balance had also tipped, with 57 per cent living in towns and nearly a third living in its principal towns.

By the time of the 1881 census, a new classification into 'urban' and 'rural' areas had been adopted, and ten years on from that the proportion of people living in urban areas had reached a staggering 72 per cent. In one lifetime, the way most people lived had changed from being surrounded by nature and a handful of familiar faces to the forced intimacy of communal living and the comparative anonymity of a town. Liverpool had become Britain's second city, with nearly half a million inhabitants. There were now 103 towns with a population over twenty thousand, which together constituted a population larger than that of the whole of England and Wales in 1801. What was also striking was the speed with which villages and small places were rising up to the importance of large towns. Perhaps nowhere demonstrated this better than Barrow-in-Furness in the north-west, which in 1891 was one of the largest urban areas in the country, with a population of around fifty-two thousand. Its population in 1841, by contrast, is listed as '200(?)' in the official return – a guess, because Barrow-in-Furness wasn't even identified as a distinct area at that time.

As we saw in the previous chapters, the problems associated with overcrowding and squalid living conditions were increasingly being exposed through social research and statistics. Sanitation reports had repeatedly raised overcrowding as an enabler of disease and even depression. And although some of this thinking was influenced by the miasma theory, these proto-social scientists were largely correct. Nowadays we still strive for cleanliness because we know that illness is caused by bacteria, viruses and mould. We also now know that stress can weaken the immune system, and it's hard to imagine a life more stressful than living hand to mouth in a Victorian slum.

Statisticians had tried to get a handle on the actual scale of overcrowding. The first census in 1801 had asked for the number of inhabited and uninhabited houses, from which a fairly accurate estimate of people per dwelling could be derived for much of the country. This tended to work well in England and Wales, where flats or other types of sub-divided building were not particularly common. But in parts of some Scottish towns and cities, blocks of flats like the creaking tenements on Edinburgh's Royal Mile had been the norm for some time. 'Every man's house is his castle' was an axiom which had long been in circulation at this time.[6] And yet, as the population grew and cities and towns failed to expand at an equivalent pace, for many families their castle was little more than a single room carved out within a block housing dozens of others.

Census-takers struggled to know how to record households living in flats because the official instruction from London was to define a 'house' as 'all the space within the external and party-walls of the building'.[7] With this definition insisted on until the 1880s, the official 'overcrowding' figures for Scotland were deemed 'valueless', even by the Scottish Registrar General, who oversaw censuses. There were numerous 'houses' in Edinburgh containing sixteen or eighteen families and around seventy persons. In one instance, a single house contained forty families and 130 people.[8] Glasgow, it seems, quite consistently rebelled against the 'one house' enumeration of a tenement, while Edinburgh went back and forth, returning a count of around ten thousand houses in 1831 and twenty-eight thousand in 1841, while its population only grew by five thousand people.[9] In 1881, when Scottish enumerators adopted their own definition which more accurately captured tenement housing, the number of 'houses' increased to 739,000 from 412,000 a decade earlier.[10]

Given how useless these figures were for measuring overcrowding in Scotland, parts of the north of England and, increasingly, any other town or city centre across the UK, censuses started to also collect information about rooms within a house. The 1871 census of Scotland found that across the country as a whole, one third of families occupied just one room – in Glasgow, this figure was two in five families.[11] In all of Scotland's principal towns, it was only around one in every nine or ten families that had more than two rooms to their home.*

The figures also showed that a small number of families lived in one room *without a window*. In the principal towns, this only applied to around fifty families in total in 1871, but in the Shetland Islands more than five hundred families, or about one in twelve, were living in these conditions. In Ross and Cromarty, in Scotland's north-west, around one in thirty families were occupying one room without a window.[13] These

---

* Aberdeen, Dundee, Edinburgh, Glasgow, Greenock, Leith, Paisley and Perth. Combined population of 1,068,556 people according to the 1871 Scottish census.[12]

were not, however, slum dwellings, the nest-like cupboards for the truly down and out that such a classification was capturing in the cities. Instead, these statistics reflected the fact that many communities in Shetland in the late nineteenth century were still living in what were referred to as 'rude huts without windows, but with an open chimney in the centre, which admitted a certain amount of light and ventilation, and gave exit to smoke'.[14] Shetland looked fairly similar on paper to the cities, in that nine in ten of its inhabitants lived in dwellings of just one or two rooms. But it's a good example of where understanding the context behind statistics can change everything. 'Crude and unsupported theories' were abounding about Shetlanders being the 'worst housed' and therefore 'most unhealthy or most immoral' in Scotland, which the Scottish Registrar General, William Pitt Dundas, roundly dismissed. He insisted that 'so much is the reverse the case that she [Shetland] stands pre-eminent for the healthiness of her population, and also for their morality'.[15] The quality of the living environment was more important in such cases than the plain question of the number of windows – and this wasn't something that the census was very good at picking up.

In the cities, the statistics on rooms per family were producing insights of a different kind. The figures showed that the more rooms a house contained, the more likely it was that families would take in lodgers. In Glasgow and Edinburgh, nearly one quarter of families overall had a lodger. Strikingly, this was true of those who lived in a house with just two rooms, while an even greater proportion – one third – with three or four rooms were likely to rent at least one out. What this reflected was that, in a great many cases, houses and tenement flats were too big. Aside from this being a failure of housing design and supply, it was also warned that immorality was bound to ensue, with all these non-related adults sharing living quarters. A plea went out for housing designed 'to meet the real wants of the class for whom they are intended'.[16]

The census of England and Wales was slower to evolve, and it was not until 1891 that an attempt was made to broaden the definition 'house' to capture individual tenements or flats, which had to have fewer than five rooms. It showed that there were around 5.5 million houses in England and Wales and around 6.1 million distinct dwellings. At a ratio of 1.12 individual dwellings to houses, it meant at least one in eight households in England and Wales was living in a flat. The statisticians also included an estimate of overcrowding, which was defined as there being more than two people per room in a small house or flat.[17] London, unsurprisingly, had quite a high level of overcrowding, with around 20 per cent of the population living as such, but some of the new industrial towns in the north were faring much worse. More than one in three people was living in overcrowded housing in Sunderland and Newcastle upon Tyne and two in five in Gateshead.[18]

Concerns about population density also attracted statistical attention. In England and Wales there were around 390 people per square mile in 1871, although north London had a whopping 47,000. Lancashire had the milder but also notably high population density of around 1,500 people per square mile.[19] When Seebohm Rowntree was working on his study of poverty in York in the late 1890s, he compared its population density to various cities in the United States and was somewhat shocked to find that the density in York was higher than in New York, which had a population forty-five times higher than its namesake.[20] Within York, the most crowded neighbourhoods were on a par with the areas of London that had contained some of the most notorious slums and rookeries: Bethnal Green, Spitalfields, Hoxton and Soho. These neighbourhoods naturally attracted the most attention – and alarm from the upper crust of society – because they were so large and populous. But small pockets of equal deprivation could be found in practically any part of the country.

The clamour for change in the wake of the 1861 Edinburgh tenement collapse was being echoed all around.[21] What people really wanted – and needed – was better quality housing and a lot more of it. But central government and local authorities had no real powers nor the resources to build residential properties. Even if they had, it was not really acknowledged that providing shelter was the state's responsibility.

What had been achieved in the way of housing for the working classes was largely the result of private investment, philanthropy, or a combination of the two. Edinburgh had an early example of this on a pleasant street halfway towards the estuary at Leith, where the Pilrig Model Dwellings Company had constructed terraced workers cottages in 1849. Between the 1840s and 1870s, twenty-eight 'model dwelling' companies were established, along with around two thousand building societies – mutual savings funds to assist people in buying a house. In London, a wealthy American businessman by the name of George Peabody started funding projects to clear slum areas and develop housing estates, with the first of these opening in Spitalfields in 1864. Peabody Trust estates popped up all over London and, along with similar projects by the Improved Industrial Dwellings Company and the Artizans', Labourers' and General Dwellings Company, would re-house 150,000 Londoners or nearly 5 per cent of its population.[22] The Guinness Trust was a similar project started in 1890 by the family behind the iconic stout.

Perhaps the most ambitious private housing projects were the model villages which some large companies built for their workers. The first was New Lanark in the central west of Scotland, which was an entire village constructed around a cotton mill in 1796. It was visionary – and unheard of – at the time to think of providing purpose-built housing for workers rather than expecting them to figure it out for themselves. Dozens of similar model villages sprang up, some of them clearly combining the aim of guaranteeing living standards with the opportunity for a vanity project. Some of the lucky beneficiaries of this were workers at the textile mill in Shipley, near Bradford, belonging to the impressively named Titus Salt. In the 1850s, Salt constructed a picturesque village with neoclassical flourishes, named Saltaire, which would eventually house over four thousand workers and their families in comparative comfort.

Among the most spectacularly odd was Port Sunlight on the Wirral. Situated on the Mersey estuary, which was then a major shipping hub, the development was built by Lord Leverhulme to house workers at the Lever Brothers soap factory. Each small block of flats was built in a different architectural style, from mock Tudor to medieval Flemish, and life there came with a slightly cult-like encouragement to abstain from alcohol and engage in wholesome common activities like tending allotments. It was nonetheless widely celebrated and even inspired a hit West End musical – *The Sunshine Girl* – featuring the catchy number 'When you want a cake of soap to finish off your toilet, we're the folks who boil it'.[23] Bournville, a model village founded by the Cadbury family for workers at their Birmingham chocolate factory, was another place where comfort came with the inconvenience – to some – of not being able to buy alcohol anywhere within its entire square kilometre extent. The Cadbury family were devout Quakers.

Society was generally quite religious at that time, and churches were one of the main types of institution capable of organising campaigns or action at scale. Faith among the middle and upper classes often involved performing acts of charity, and so religion played a big role in the calls for better quality housing. But so too did a kind of distaste and fear felt towards society's poorest, because it was imagined that squalid living conditions allowed or even promoted various kinds of immoral and animalistic behaviour. Social reformer and landlord Octavia Hill's housing projects in west London in the 1860s and 70s were bankrolled by the art critic John Ruskin, who seemingly offered the cash more out of a prudish disapproval of the sight of slums than anything else. Also driving the movement for reform was a sense of shame that Britain was 'no better' than the supposedly savage lands it was colonising. 'May we not find a parallel at our own doors,' asked William Booth, founder of the Salvation Army, 'and discover within a stone's throw of our cathedrals and palaces similar horrors to those which Stanley has found existing in the great Equatorial forest?'[24]

As the nineteenth century progressed, the feeling grew that philanthropy and business were not delivering new and improved housing on the scale that was needed. The annual statistical reports continued to show outbreaks of zymotic disease in urban areas that were often directly explained as being the result of people being 'crowded together dirty in an inadequate supply of fresh air'.[25] Censuses continued to show large proportions of families living in single-room accommodation or taking in lodgers, with all the opportunity for moral corruption which that presented. Some of the housing associations – Peabody among them – had turned out to charge much more expensive rents than the slums they had replaced, which just meant that many tenants moved into substandard lodgings elsewhere. The 1871 census reveals a great many police constables living in the Peabody buildings in Christchurch, Spitalfields, who would likely have been much higher earners than the weavers, rag-dealers and charwomen living in nearby streets.[26]

The authorities needed to do something. Even William Farr, in his statistical reports, became quite political, asking, 'What are the municipal bodies good for if they cannot by administrative measures displace rookeries by healthy habitations, supply the people with water, and with the means of "cleanliness" which stands proverbially "next to godliness"?'[27]

It was in Liverpool that the authorities finally stepped up to answer this call. In the 1840s, around eighty-six thousand people were living in what was certainly some of the worst housing in the country – 'back-to-back' houses in small courts with no drainage system – and a further thirty-eight thousand were living in cellars.[28] A local sanitation campaigner, Dr William Duncan, brought these to the attention of the council, which passed an Act in 1842 to compel landlords to clean up any 'filthy or unwholesome' properties. In 1846, the Liverpool Sanitation Act gave the council the power to create infrastructure for public health. Duncan was appointed as Medical Officer of Health for the city and an early order of business was to close five thousand of the ghastly inhabited cellars.

Twenty years later, when the 1866 Labouring Classes Dwellings Act gave local authorities the right to purchase land and to build and improve housing for the working classes, Liverpool's council were first out of the gate. On Ashfield Street, at the top of an impressive flight of five locks delivering the Leeds and Liverpool Canal down to the northern docks, a residential estate named St Martin's Cottages was built in 1869. It was the very first council housing in the UK and indeed in the whole of Europe. Bearing little resemblance to traditional cottages, the estate consisted of several flat-fronted five-storey blocks of flats not unlike the chunky stone tenements in Glasgow and Edinburgh. They were weatherproof and extremely welcome to the unhoused poor, and they would stand for over a hundred years before being demolished in the 1970s.[29]

It took a while for other parts of the country to follow Liverpool's example, and it was not until the 1890s that building really got going. What had helped was an 1884–5 Royal Commission on the Housing of the Working Classes that was epic even by Victorian standards and which had led to the 1890 Housing of the Working Classes Act. London's first council housing was built in Shoreditch in 1893 after the clearance of a slum and is still very much in use today. The living conditions of the poor had been exposed and the message that they were not going to improve on their own seemed to be finally filtering through. Things were brightening up, although the clouds were not necessarily lifting evenly across the country as a whole.

6

Working Nine to Five

'Milton-Northern! The manufacturing town in Darkshire?'

This is the disbelieving cry of Margaret Hale, the heroine of Elizabeth Gaskell's 1855 novel *North and South*, on being told where her father plans to relocate their southern English family. Long before they approach the fictional northern town, a 'deep lead-coloured cloud' and a 'faint taste and smell of smoke' foretell of their arrival in a land of heavy industry. The colours are greyer, the streets narrower and the houses simpler and smaller, huddled around a 'great oblong many-windowed factory' which squats 'like a hen among her chickens'.[1] The book, which develops into a love story between Margaret and a factory owner, was originally serialised and received wide acclaim, in large part because its themes were so current and its tropes so recognisable. At its centre is the tension between the old world and the new. Modernity – symbolised by the north – means vigour, industry and excitement but a tendency to lack humanity, while tradition – the south – has humanitarian values apparently closer to its heart yet is flawed by snobbery and aversion to change. Both ultimately learn from the other.

Life in England's northern towns and cities was a recurrent subject in the literature of the mid to late Victorian era. So too was the idea of modernity 'going too far' in its obsession with inputs and outputs – you might say with statistics – and people ending up as robots who could be dangerously insensitive towards their fellow man. This is the moral of Charles Dickens's *Hard Times* (1854). In it, Thomas Gradgrind of the fictional Coketown lives by the motto 'Facts alone are wanted in life. Plant nothing else, and root out everything else.' He treats everything, including his children, as a type of mathematical problem to be solved and has no place in his worldview for sentimentality, while his business partner Josiah Bounderby thinks only of riches and power no matter the moral cost. Needless to say, both come a cropper by being too inflexible and utilitarian. As with all caricatures, these depictions capture something recognisably true about the changing world of Victorian Britain.

Towards the end of the eighteenth century, innovations in the textile industry had made it possible, with the aid of machines, to produce much greater quantities of fabric and at higher speeds than human hands had managed before. Steam power and iron combined to make it possible for large numbers of machines to operate in a single space and to produce cloth at a constant rate, around the clock, so long as there were hands to operate them. Unlike anything that had come before it, the manufactory – or simply factory – was born.

There is arguably nowhere that better captures this extraordinary transformation than the city of Bradford. Situated in a green valley in West Yorkshire, and sheltered by the far-off moors, Bradford was once little more than a rural settlement of a dozen or so dwellings. It was listed in the 1086 Domesday Book but without a recorded population, which means it either had no permanent residents at that time or that they found a way to avoid being at home when strangers from the south rolled into the village. By the eighteenth century it had grown into a small market town, with a population of around 6,000 people in the town itself and 13,000 when including the surrounding rural area. The town's fortunes really began to change around the same time, with the new inventions making it quicker to spin and weave wool, which its residents had been doing on a much smaller scale for centuries. Industrialisation attracted money and migrants, and the town swelled to a city of 44,000 inhabitants by 1831 and then to 104,000 by 1851. The pace did not relent, with the city's population more than doubling again by 1871. By that point it contained nearly 260,000 inhabitants, over half of the number living there today, and had overtaken its neighbour Leeds, whose population was by that time going into decline.

In 1871, in the West Riding of Yorkshire – the wider region in which Bradford sits, along with other towns and cities such as Leeds, Halifax and Huddersfield – around one in six people aged fifteen and over was employed in the manufacture of wool or worsted. Bradford was churning out a prodigious quantity of woollen fabric and the place had an affluent feel, attracting the nickname 'Woolopolis'. It was a classic boomtown, indeed perhaps one of the first. A grand neoclassical music hall went up in the town centre, partly financed by the German Jewish wool merchants who had settled there, which would go on to host performers and speakers including Charles Dickens and the Rolling Stones (not at the same time).

Bradford's success was not only thanks to the woolmaking expertise of its original population and its plentiful supply of sheep. What really kicked it into gear was that it was discovered to be sitting on a bed of coal which was close to the surface and relatively easy to mine. The new industrial machines ran on steam power (before this there had been a brief era of mechanism using water power) which required fuel. Coal was highly efficient in this regard, and Bradford's powerhouse wool manufacturers could practically shovel it out of the ground and straight into the factory furnace.

Manchester, which Gaskell's Milton-Northern is based on, had a similar story. By the mid nineteenth century it was the centre of a British cotton industry which had barely existed fifty years earlier, and like Bradford had earned its own nickname, the equally inventive 'Cottonopolis'. By the 1870s, Manchester and its Lancashire surroundings were responsible for around a third of the cotton fabric being produced in the world.

The trope of modern versus traditional – and north versus south – that featured so much in the literature of the time also reflected anxiety that the economy was changing in an uncontrolled and unknown way. It's significant that the northern industrial areas are always described as being dark. They are typically portrayed as existing under a dense cloud of smoke which blots out the sun, and people have to scuttle around barely seeing two metres in front of them. *North and South* is set in the county of 'Darkshire', for crying out loud. Could it be that these descriptions reflect the fact that the reality of what was going on in industrial towns really was obscure to the nation as a whole? For the first half of the nineteenth century there really was very little data.

Naturally, the Gradgrindians in Somerset House were not fans of uncertainty and nor were the politicians down the road in Westminster. Some of the questions that needed to be answered were 'Just how big are these industries getting?', 'How fast are things changing?', 'Who are all these people?', 'What are they doing?', 'Where are they coming from?' and 'Is it sustainable?' Britain had never particularly needed to get a handle on how many people worked in specific industries – bar farming and the military – but suddenly it did.

In the first census, in 1801, enumerators had been asked to record the number of people working in agriculture and the number working in 'trade, manufacturing and handicraft'. This was also the case in 1811 and 1821, except that now they wanted the number of *families* whose chief employment was in these industries. The one takeaway from this data-gathering was that around one third of the population were 'employed in raising subsistence for the other two' or, in other words, around a third of people were from farming families. The problem with this approach was that family members often worked different types of job, so it was not always realistic to categorise each household into one profession.

It was when the first individual-level census was carried out in 1841 that detailed, specific observations were listed for *everyone* in a household. This produced an absolute torrent of data because enumerators had to free-write whatever occupations people declared, and it turned out there were a lot of different job titles out there. In Lancashire, there were 1,255 different occupations relating to the cotton industry alone.[2] This was clearly not what the statisticians had been bargaining for, since only 598 unique occupations had been listed for Great Britain as a whole when they had recorded 'family' occupations in 1831. In the West Riding of Yorkshire, there were 117 unique job titles relating to wool manufacture, including the intriguing billy-piecers and shoddy-teazers. It was also found that the proportion of people employed in agriculture was not one third but just 8 per cent, which was half of the proportion that was employed in manufacturing. It buried the notion that two thirds of us were sitting around waiting for the other third to bring food to the table. Even looking at the proportion of families which contained a farmer, it had now shrunk to one in five.[3] Change was clearly in motion, and we could see that now in black and white.

With each census, the statistician's exasperation with the deluge of unique occupations increased. Arranging thousands of job titles under common headings was occupying 'a large portion of the labour' of the census office and involving 'considerable pains' – and even the shortened list contained four hundred occupations.[4] By 1881, the occupations section was being described as 'the most laborious, the most costly and ... perhaps the least satisfactory part' of the census due to job types being 'sub-divided with great minuteness' into classifications that were incomprehensible to someone without knowledge of industry-specific terms.[5] And from a look at some of these job titles we can see what they mean: beaster, blabber, keel bulley, tingle maker, sand badger; a sprigger, a spragger, an egger and a fluker.[6] To the layperson these might as well be the words to cast an ancient spell. Between eleven and twelve thousand distinct occupations were listed in one census. The same name was also sometimes used for different jobs in different industries or parts of the country. A bank manager was typically a person managing the branch of a bank, but in mining areas it could mean the man supervising the machinery at the mouth of the pit. A muffin-maker was in most cases a baker of English muffins but in the potteries of Staffordshire it was far more likely to refer to someone who had a specific role in the manufacture of chinaware.[7]

Some of the occupations are so specific that only one or two people in the whole country were reported to be doing them. At most a couple of people declared themselves to be a golf ball maker, a golf club maker, an awl maker (an awl being an implement for punching holes in leather), a maccaroni maker (which really does seem to refer to pasta), a rhubarb dealer, a ketchup dealer or a violin bow maker (somebody has to do it). Fork makers, spoon makers and knife makers are all listed separately.[8] Frustrating as it must have been for the statisticians at the time, these detailed occupations are a rich historical record for us now. In the early nineteenth century we can see thousands of people working in jobs that would gradually disappear entirely, as the demand for them ceased to exist: night soil men, scavengers, coral polishers, ivory workers, glass blowers, loom makers, bayonet forgers and leech dealers.[9] In 1851, there were 154 watercress dealers listed, eighteen of whom were females aged under twenty-one. How we would love to know whether one of them was the eight-year-old girl Mayhew had interviewed in London two years earlier.[*]

There were also some instances of occupations being lost in translation, as enumerators would sometimes fail to understand what was being said. Fast-forwarding slightly to a street registry taken in Manchester in 1931, a Matt Busby was listed under the unusual profession of fruit broiler. This was the unhappy result of a thick Glaswegian accent and a baffled enumerator: Busby was in fact one of the first full-time professional footballers to play for Manchester City.[11]

After the considerable pains of gathering all these occupations into broader categories, the statisticians were able to identify towns and cities which specialised in different industries. At the start of the nineteenth century, there had been

---

[*] We can actually search the individual-level records of the 1851 census since they are now accessible to the general public. A possible candidate for the watercress girl is Cornelia Collins, who 'sells watercress' and was living in St Giles district, where Mayhew carried out his research. Her age – fifteen – doesn't fit with Mayhew's description, however. But it might have been exaggerated to enumerators. It's also entirely possible the girl had moved on to selling something else.[10]

around fifteen towns engaged largely in the manufacture of wool, with a combined population of 170,000 people. By mid-century, the same towns contained over half a million people. The cotton towns – Cottonopolis being the largest – grew from fourteen to over twenty in number and their population had quadrupled to around 1.2 million by the 1870s. There is something slightly medieval and romantic about this division of the country into areas for different trades: the copper and tin districts, the potteries, the shoe-making and glove-making towns. We also see a rise in the population of 'watering places', spa towns such as Tunbridge Wells, Cheltenham, Malvern and Harrogate, which became popular getaways for people seeking the 'water cure'.* As the hype for hydrotherapy waned and the tourist industry in these places shrank, some of them began to see their populations decrease again by the century's end.

Women in the early censuses are recorded in a catch-all category described the 'Third and Negative class' or 'the Residue'. This category also included children who weren't working (although a great many of them were), the elderly and infirm, homeless 'vagrants' and people not of sound mind. It is in 1841 that we first get any significant detail about women's paid work, because that was the first census to include an entry for each individual person rather than one for the whole family. The largest single occupation for women and girls was domestic service and the figures revealed that over 900,000 of the 1.2 million people in this profession were female. 'It must be a matter for congratulation that so large a number of females ... should be comprehended in a class in which habits of steady industry, of economy, and of

---

* Hydrotherapy was a fashionable quasi-medical treatment which could involve bathing or being doused in water, being wrapped in wet sheets of varying temperatures, and drinking prodigious quantities of mineral water.

attention to the maintenance of good character are so necessary as that of domestic service,' reads the census report from that year.[12] Apparently it came as a surprise that women could supress their chaotic temperament for long enough to discreetly bring in a tea tray, even though it was already the case that three quarters of servants were female. Perhaps some people in the upper classes were truly surprised: a lot of female servants barely or never crossed paths with their employers because their work took place behind the scenes in the kitchen, the scullery and the nursery, and in the hours before the family awoke.

What was genuinely a revelation was the number and proportion of women working in manual industries, and particularly in manufacturing. Factories had become the norm in large manufacturing industries, which meant there was a larger-than-ever class of women working outside the domestic sphere. In the manufacturing sector, 35 per cent of employees – one in three – was female; in the sub-sector of textile manufacturing, this proportion was 43 per cent.[13] This share would only increase as the century wore on, as male workers were siphoned away from the textile industry to work in metals, mining and other heavy manual occupations. By 1901, nearly two thirds of textile workers in England and Wales were female.[14] Other occupations dominated by female workers were nursing and midwifery, teaching, the manufacture of lace, muslin, linen, gloves and buttons, and other kinds of fiddly work including the making of fireworks.[15] Overall, the 1841 census showed that around one in three adult women had a paid occupation and by 1871 this had become 42 per cent.[16] At the most recent census, in 2021, 55 per cent of adult women said they were 'economically active', which is less of an increase in women joining the labour force over 150 years than over thirty years in the mid-Victorian era.[17]

Recording the occupation of every single person in the household also meant we could see how many children were working and in what kind of jobs. In 1833 the first Factory Act had been passed, which had attempted to limit the working hours of children (and women). Follow-up Acts in 1844 and 1847 restricted these hours down to no more than ten per day or fifty-eight per week and forbade children under the age of eight from working in factories entirely. But we can see that in 1851 there were some occupations which relied on a very young workforce. The manufacture of cotton, linen and silk relied on a workforce one third of which was teenagers and children, and the same was true of the profession of chimney sweep. Children were sought for work in these industries because the handling of materials like thread and beads was quicker with small hands, and chimney sweeping sometimes involved children climbing up inside the chimney flue. Around four in ten domestic servants was a child or teenager, which reflects a common practice of young women working as servants before leaving the profession to get married.

A further Factory Act in 1867 and Elementary Education Acts in the 1870s and 1880s combined to try to prevent children under fourteen from being in full time work and instead to get them to school.[18] It wasn't until 1891 that the last and arguably most major barrier to children being in school was removed by the Fee Grant Act, which effectively made primary school free of charge. But because there was still a demand for small-statured workers in the manufacturing industry, the number of girls in employment continued to increase. By 1871, there were a quarter of a million girls aged under fifteen (and four hundred thousand boys) who were working, including ten thousand under the age of five.[19] By 1891, it was still the case that around one in six employees in the cotton industry was aged between ten and fifteen. There were eighty-five thousand children working in cotton factories: more in absolute numbers than there had been twenty years prior.[20]

These statistical accounts give us a bird's-eye view of the intricate and extensive landscape of jobs and industries in Victorian Britain. We see the potteries from above, steam rising from the domes of their brick kilns; we see ships being built in harbours and a frenzy of loading and unloading at the docks, involving porters, stevedores, tug boys, lockmen and quay-gangers. We see the lights of cotton factories gleaming in the northern valleys, and behind the windows young people working in unfathomable roles as devillers, batters, sliverers and slubberers.[21] By 1900 we see that there are hundreds of thousands of people working on the railways, in omnibuses and trams, and even around six hundred professional motor car drivers.[22] But at this distance we don't get much of a sense of what working life was really like. This was also felt by politicians, statisticians, social researchers and anyone else trying to understand what was happening in the midst of a whirl of activity the like of which had never been seen. For most people, the lives of others outside their social circle were a total mystery. This was long before the days of television and even radio, and a substantial number of people couldn't even read, so there was nothing like the public percolation of different viewpoints and experiences that we take for granted nowadays. But the developments that would change that were already in motion.

Work, for many people, meant performing the same repetitive task for very long hours in uncomfortable conditions. Large factories were noisy and dusty to work in and required concentration over the course of a shift to keep up one's role in the supply chain and avoid getting caught in and mangled by the machinery. In smaller factories and home industry, workers had to frequently interrupt the working day with domestic tasks.

Life for many people in London and other cities was a precarious daily struggle to eke out a meagre living. Mayhew's study of the labour of the London poor is really about the lives of people who worked on the street and so were easy pickings for his investigation. In addition to the watercress girl, Mayhew lists street-sellers of a huge variety of articles: oranges, apples, flowers, seeds, fried fish, pickled whelks, sheep's trotters, baked potatoes, crumpets, cough drops, rhubarb, ginger beer, matches, rat poison, cigars, clothes pegs, dolls, watches and even live squirrels, birds and tortoises.[23] A young street-seller – or costermonger – would leave home in the morning between four and five and sell their wares until around nine, when they would return home for a meagre breakfast. They would then 'remain in the streets until around ten o'clock at night; many having had nothing during all that time but one meal of bread and butter and coffee'.[24] Another occupation was to sell hot pies on the street, which would rake in around five shillings a day and half of that in the winter. Pies could be beef, mutton or eel, or of apples, currants, gooseberries, plums, damsons or cherries depending on the season, and were typically made by the pieman himself. Work would begin at around six in the evening, to catch the after-work crowd, and some would remain out all night. Struggling piemen would resort to hanging around pubs, where a popular game for 'gentlemen "out on the spree"' was to bet against the pieman in a coin toss, having to pay a shilling if they lost and receiving a free pie if they won. 'When they win they will sometimes amuse themselves by throwing the pies at one another, or at me,' reported one forlorn pie seller.[25]

Work could also be unpleasant and dangerous. Mayhew tells of the mud-larks, people scavenging the Thames foreshore at low tide for anything to use or sell, their 'torn up garments stiffened up like boards with dirt of every possible description'.[26] Work as a dustman, nightman, scavenger or sweep, which involved clearing and sifting through refuse of ash, bones, glass shards and human waste, was also particularly dirty and unsafe. The lack of ventilation also made some indoor industries very oppressive to work in. Mayhew found that in a fish-frying shop, 'even when the fish is fresh (as it most frequently is) and the oil pure, the odour is rank' and the clothes of the workers were more 'impregnated with the smell of the fish than were those of any "wet" fish sellers'.[27]

A particularly striking account of working-class life in London comes from the memoirs of Malwida von Meysenbug, a German aristocrat who lived in London in the 1850s. Concerned about poverty and workers' rights, she spent time observing conditions in the East End. 'Poor German families are there by the hundreds,' she wrote. 'The work is stamping raw pelts at a German factory. Imagine a big barrel in a very warm room, filled to the very top with ermine and sable skins. A man climbs into the barrel stark naked and stamps and works with his hands and feet from morning until night. The perspiration pours from his body in streams. This soaks into the skins and gives them their suppleness and durability.'[28] It's hard to imagine a more physically demanding or unpleasant job (or anything that might put a person further off the idea of wearing fur).

The dangers of many professions did not escape the notice of the man who kept the closest eye on the activities of the grim reaper – William Farr. 'The progress of science has created new forces, often fatal,' he lamented, also noting that 'nearly the whole of the increase in violent deaths is due to ... accidents from mechanical violence'.[29] Around seven thousand such deaths were occurring each year in the 1860s, with the mining industry being responsible for a disproportionate number. There were also around three thousand people burning to death, nearly one in five of them children, which was partly the result of clothes catching alight while tending a fireplace.[30] The railways were proving responsible for over twelve hundred deaths per year by the 1870s, many of them of workers on the line.[31] And when it didn't outright kill a person, work still could make them terribly sick. People unknowingly put their health at enormous risk by working with materials such as lead, petrol, coal, radium and arsenic without any protection at all.

In the mid nineteenth century a vibrant pool-table green was very much in fashion. The shade, known as Scheele's green or emerald green, coloured decorative furnishings, artificial leaves and even the icing on fancy cakes. It was also absolutely brimming with arsenic, which would shed itself in a fine dust when disturbed and wreak mayhem on people's health. The homes of the rich and fashionable were essentially poison chambers where vitality was constantly being assaulted by every surface and the air itself. Arsenic was also being used deliberately as a poison at this time – it wasn't that this property was unknown – but the socialite whirling through the night in her green ballgown simply had no idea that she was coated in the same substance that was used to kill rats.

The people, mainly women, producing these green pigmented goods were at even greater exposure, which in 1862 prompted the Ladies' Sanitary Association to blow the whistle about a factory worker who seemed to have died from arsenic poisoning.[32] This led to several inquiries which ultimately confirmed the horrific health risks to workers handling it on a daily basis. A report by Dr William Guy, a professor of forensic medicine at King's College London, unearthed shocking details from a factory making artificial leaves which employed around one hundred young women and where 'suffering was almost universal amongst the workpeople'.[33] After just one day of working there, symptoms would start, including skin rashes, which developed into pustules and ulcers that concentrated in the bends of joints. In several cases 'the affection had been such that the sufferer could not bear to sit down'. A quarter of the women showed the signs of chronic poisoning which included 'excessive thirst, nausea and loss of appetite; sickness and vomiting ... palpitation and shortness of breath; debility, fever, headache, drowsiness, dimness of sight and ... convulsions'. Tragically, though the workers dreaded their occupation, they 'dread[ed] still more the alternative of being without work'.[34]

No occupation took such a toll on people's health or presented such a risk to their lives in such large numbers as mining. In 1841 there were around 120,000 people employed in mining in Great Britain – by 1891 there were nearly 600,000 and by 1901 nearly 750,000. Parts of the country had gone from being uninhabited hillsides to fully functioning towns housing tens of thousands of people, all from the profitability of mining stone, metals and minerals, chief among them coal.

A highly efficient and abundant fuel, coal was powering everything in the UK from machines for spinning and weaving, to steam trains and transatlantic ships, to the new power station at Holborn Viaduct in London which was powering some of the country's very first electric street lighting. In Northumberland and Durham there had been fourteen coal mines in 1753 but by 1843 there were 130, producing five million tonnes of coal each year. By 1891, these mines in the north-east were producing forty million tonnes of coal per year.³⁵ Ystradyfodwg in South Wales, now known as the Rhondda Valley, was listed among the largest urban areas in England and Wales in 1891, having grown from around three thousand inhabitants to eighty-eight thousand over ninety years.³⁶ But working standards in the mines had gone from virtually non-existent to still very poor, and the cost to human health and life was considerable. In 1877 alone, nearly a thousand men died in mines and in 1882 over a thousand died in coal mines alone.³⁷ In the worst mining accident of the Victorian era, 290 men and over two hundred horses were killed in a single huge explosion at Albion Colliery in the Welsh village of Cilfynydd.

Health and safety at work was still an emerging concept as the nineteenth century wound to a close. Parliament had passed numerous Factory Acts since the 1830s, which had created rules for the handling of machinery and had attempted to regulate conditions in some specific industries such as iron and steel mills, and glass and paper factories.³⁸ Enforcement tended to be poor, though, since there was not yet the infrastructure to inspect workplaces on a regular basis.

It was also the dawn of the modern notion of workers' rights. The century had started with quite the opposite development, with a law passed in 1800 that prohibited any form of worker's assembly to try to collectively argue for better conditions. This was down to the fear that English workers would unite as the French had and stage a revolution, and the law stayed in place until the 1820s.³⁹ It was not until 1871 and the Trade Union Act that real allowance was given for workers to organise to negotiate for better conditions and pay, and to formally be allowed to go on strike. The result was an almost instant improvement in pay within industries that were able to self-organise. Public sympathy tended to be on the side of striking workers, since their pay was undeniably low and their working environments clearly beyond the realm of acceptable.

Charles Booth, who had observed striking dock workers in east London, was certainly no socialist, but on the back of his study of London poverty he campaigned vigorously for social support for the working classes, whom he called 'the misbegotten offspring of prosperity'.[40] Booth had also noted during his research that old age was a major factor in driving people into poverty. At the same time as he was working on his study on the London poor, Booth sat on a Royal Commission on the Aged Poor, which took the rare step of inviting testimony from people identified as old-age 'paupers'. He contributed his evidence to a Parliamentary committee on the 'aged deserving poor' and a few years later, in 1909, the first ever UK state pension was introduced.

Changes in the statistics tell us of the rising importance of the working class and the contribution of their labour. In trying to organise the multitude of niche occupations people listed in the census into overall fields of industry, the statisticians had also sorted them into a kind of class hierarchy. When this hierarchy was first introduced in the 1851 census, it contained one class above all others, outside the ranking altogether: the Queen.[41] The statistics show one female in this category, upwards of twenty years of age. The next categories were for members of the government and Parliament, the armed forces and then the 'professions' such as barristers, clergymen and physicians, and which later included artists and professional athletes. Below that were various classes for trade and manufacturing and classes for the production of materials from the animal, vegetable, and mineral kingdoms. The ranking was supposed to be a judgement of the level of 'skill, talent, or intelligence that is exercised' by the worker.[42] Effectively, it was a social class hierarchy. William Farr and his successors at the GRO were playing the role of Roman censors, dividing people up into an elaborate class system based on information they presented at a census.

		GREAT BRITAIN AND ISLANDS IN THE BRITISH SEAS.			
OCCUPATIONS.		Under 20 Years of Age.		20 Years of Age and upwards.	
		Males.	Females.	Males.	Females.
TOTAL		4,764,743	4,937,535	5,458,815	5,998,384
PERSONS OF SPECIFIED OCCUPATIONS AND CONDITIONS		4,750,536	4,704,455	5,404,029	5,924,604
CLASSES.					
Class	THE QUEEN				1
"	I. Persons engaged in the general or local *Government* of the Country	1,486	89	71,191	2,526
"	II. Persons engaged in the *Defence* of the Country.	7,773		88,714	
"	III. Persons in the *Learned Professions* (with their immediate Subordinates), either filling Public Offices, or in private Practice	12,451	51	98,279	1,410
"	IV. Persons engaged in *Literature*, the *Fine Arts*, and the *Sciences*	4,692	8,318	41,618	64,316
"	V. Persons engaged in the *Domestic Offices*, or *Duties of Wives*, *Mothers*, *Mistresses of Families*, *Children*, *Relatives**	3,389,492	3,780,565	21,779	3,227,150
"	VI. Persons engaged in *entertaining*, *clothing*, and *performing personal Offices* for Man	120,504	458,168	512,209	1,329,292
"	VII. Persons who *buy or sell*, *keep*, *let*, or *lend*, *Money*, *Houses*, or *Goods of various Kinds*	20,372	2,690	130,389	56,010
"	VIII. Persons engaged in the *Conveyance* of Men, Animals, Goods, and Messages.	100,345	5,421	285,686	7,479
"	IX. Persons possessing or working the *Land*, and engaged in growing *Grain*, *Fruits*, *Grasses*, *Animals*, and other *Products*	385,193	129,600	1,421,354	454,421
"	X. Persons engaged about *Animals*	12,454	225	86,528	1,055
"	XI. Persons engaged in *Art* and *Mechanic* Productions, in which Matters of various Kinds are employed *in combination*.	131,928	5,288	624,502	11,617
"	XII. Persons working and dealing in *Animal Matters*	91,087	84,383	293,531	162,862
"	XIII. Persons working and dealing in matters derived from the *Vegetable Kingdom*	192,976	185,229	664,859	341,950
"	XIV. Persons working and dealing in *Minerals*	209,970	24,428	677,476	34,130
"	XV. Labourers and others—Branch of Labour undefined	61,320	2,461	322,788	9,217
"	XVI. Persons of *Rank* or *Property* 'not returned under any Office or Occupation	614	1,868	33,681	136,536
"	XVII. Persons supported by the community, and of *no specified Occupation**	17,879	15,667	39,444	84,412
	Other Persons of no stated Occupations or Conditions	14,207	33,080	54,786	73,780

But over the decades, mining rose as an occupation from being the fourteenth class to the ninth (a lower rank being 'better' in terms of prestige).[43] Meanwhile, workers in the textile industries were demoted from class twelve to class eighteen. It may not have meant much in official terms, but where an occupation was ranked certainly would have reflected how these workers were seen in terms of class. And although Victorian society was not as regimented as that of ancient Rome in terms of what class meant for people's rights and restrictions, it still had a bearing on how they were treated by others: what access they had to certain spaces, whether they could weigh into particular conversations, how much their opinions were valued, the extent to which they could rely on credit, how much licence they were given in behaviour, and whether they were trusted to have good intentions.

It's not clear where nurses were supposed to be placed when the occupation hierarchy was devised in 1851. They certainly weren't included within that third-highest rank of professionals with doctors and all other male medical staff. By 1881 however, that was exactly where they were. In fact, it was the first time nurses showed up in the statistics at all, leading to the realisation that 'the Medical profession consist[s] of many more females than males'.[44] It is hard to believe that nurses, with their considerably lower pay, would have ended up there, had it not been for that one very famous Lady with the Lamp, who herself was from an upper-class family.

Being counted was a moment of acknowledgement for people working in important industries and who were in many respects underappreciated. The fact that those in power could look at the statistics and see that it took three quarters of a million men to keep the country's coal mines going gave workers a little bit more leverage. It couldn't be argued that the mining and manufacturing industries were minor operations or that replacements could easily be found if the current workforce decided to walk out. But the idea that statisticians in central London were taking it upon themselves to sort people into a hierarchy in the manner of Roman census-takers showed where the balance of power still lay. And there were others in society who were also finding themselves on the unfavourable end of social classifications of an entirely different kind.

7

One In, One Out

It was approaching Christmas time in 1848 in Macon, Georgia, and the night air was mild and still.[1] Ellen Craft stood on the threshold of her cottage, feeling a tidal wave of dread wash over her. The night was limitless and dark, withholding of comfort. Fear pounding in her ears warned her that what lay ahead was impossible: a journey of one thousand miles through the slave states of the southern United States, where a fugitive, once sniffed out, would be hunted down by bloodhounds and delivered to their bloodthirstier masters. But to stay was to face a living death: a lifetime that belonged to someone else and in which injustice undermined every fleeting joy.

Ellen had been born to a white plantation owner and a mixed-race woman who was his slave, which meant she too was condemned to slavery. A particular indignity was that she was forced to work for her own half-sister. But in William Craft, the slave of another local household, Ellen met a companion for life and the two got married. Ellen was very light-skinned, to the point that she could 'pass' as being of fully European heritage, and the Crafts developed a plan for escape that made use of this advantage. Over the course of weeks beforehand, William bought various items of men's clothing at different shops around town, and both of them secured permission to take leave over Christmas. Finally, on that December night, Ellen changed into the men's clothing and had William cut off her long hair. She was to pretend to be a white man, with William posing as her personal slave. As the time of departure approached, a distressing thought suddenly occurred to Ellen: it was customary for guests to register at hotels and on passenger steamers by writing their names. But neither of the Crafts could write – or read. Ellen had the idea of tying her right arm up in a sling as an excuse for not writing her name when requested and added bandages around her jaw to add to the general look of sickliness and deter other passengers from trying to engage her in conversation.

They set off on a journey that was one of the most daring, risky and scarcely believable to be recorded by escaped slaves. It took three days of continuous travelling, much of it on trains where they would be separated in segregated carriages; Ellen would be alone in the first-class carriage full of 'other' upper-class white men who tried constantly to engage her on how best to deal with runaway slaves. It's impossible to imagine the depth of fear she must have experienced, as a mixed-race illiterate woman and a runaway in the very heart of enemy territory, in a disguise which did in fact attract a lot of attempts at conversation from curious fellow passengers. They took steamboats, and more trains, and carriages, and more steamers, and arrived in Philadelphia in the free United States on Christmas Eve. But it was still possible for slave owners in the South to try to reclaim their errant 'property' in the north, and the Crafts were forced to make another escape, this time for England.

And this is where we find them, on 30 March 1851, at the house of Wilson and Mary Armistead in Springfield Place, Leeds. The census record from that year states that an enumerator found eleven people at the house that night: the Armistead family, including their three children, one mother-in-law, three household servants and their two visitors, William and Ellen Craft. The occupation for both Crafts is recorded as 'fugitive slave'.

The fugitives had sought out Wilson Armistead as he was a renowned abolitionist, and through his Quaker network the Crafts were helped in establishing themselves in Britain. The story of their perilous escape was picked up by the press – and William went on to set it out in a book, *Running a Thousand Miles for Freedom* – and they became figures on the anti-slavery public speaking circuit, along with popular fellow Americans Frederick Douglass and Henry 'Box' Brown – who had made a similarly high-stakes escape from slavery by posting himself to the US free states in a box. In the 1861 census we find Ellen Craft again, this time settled in Hammersmith in London, with her three children aged three to eight years old. William is not recorded, likely because he was away at the time in Dahomey (modern-day Benin), where he worked to discourage the slave trade at its origin. The Hammersmith house now bears a commemorative blue plaque: 'ELLEN CRAFT c.1826–c.1891 WILLIAM CRAFT c.1824–1900 Refugees from slavery and campaigners for its abolition lived here'.

If Britain was a safe haven for runaway slaves in the 1850s and in the vanguard of the abolition movement, it was on the tail of three hundred years of it having been a prolific participant in the trade which had enslaved them. It is estimated that Britain transported 3.1 million Africans (2.7 million of whom survived the journey) to its American colonies between 1640 and 1807, where British people enslaved them on plantations.[2] Around 767,000 slaves were transported in the thirty years that it took Parliament to debate and ultimately agree to end the trade via the Abolition of the Slave Trade Act 1807.[3] It was not until 1833 that the act of enslavement itself was made illegal in British colonies, with most former slaves then forced into a new apprenticeship scheme which did not end until 1838.

The UK economy was also bound up with overseas slavery until long after we had formally ended it in our colonial lands. All that cotton – which had turned Lancashire into a global hub of textile production and Manchester into the emerald city of Cottonopolis – wasn't picking itself. Of the raw cotton coming into Britain between 1840 and 1858, the key years of Manchester's expansion, three quarters came from the United States, where slavery was very much still in operation.[4] British cotton factory workers lived a precarious existence, with few opportunities other than to take gruelling, low-paid jobs in which they had no power to negotiate over conditions. And when the American Civil War interrupted the cotton supply, it caused a cotton famine which ricocheted through the textile-producing towns and cities of England. Imports halved, and in Lancashire over three hundred thousand people – or 70 per cent of the workforce – were temporarily laid off and had to depend on poor relief.[5]

The 1851 census recorded around one thousand US citizens living in Great Britain besides William and Ellen Craft. It was the second census to record whether individuals were born in 'foreign parts' but the first to record whether they were British subjects or foreign nationals. Beyond this we don't have much detail as to where these individuals came from or how many of them might also have been Black and mixed-race refugees.

In addition to the Crafts, we find a thirty-five-year-old woman named only as Emma living with a couple in Hackney, who is listed with the note 'had served late a slave'. Her place of birth is given as Africa. In Peebles, in the south of Scotland, we find George Lesslie, lodger to a family of Irish descent and described as 'pauper escaped slave', with place of birth unknown. Twenty-year-old Mary, again with no surname, is listed as a 'domestic serv[ant] emancipated slave' born in Africa, now servant to the curate of a church near Liverpool and his family.[6] What can it possibly have been like to have been abducted and transported across the Atlantic at such a young age, and to then cross it again, still without coming home? To witness every form of cruelty and then find chilly sanctuary in a God-fearing English home, stoking morning coal fires while listening to the sound of unfamiliar birds. In Liverpool we also still find a man listed whose occupation is given as a 'stock and slave broker'.[7]

The census had first tried to measure the size of the population from 'foreign parts' in 1841, before which time the data on migrants was fairly piecemeal. An Act of Parliament in 1836 had required all foreign arrivals to be registered at their port of entry but over time this had stopped being enforced. Ships' passenger lists sometimes gave information beyond mere numbers, like names, nationalities and places of origin, but such records were inconsistent and certainly not collected anywhere centrally. As was the case for people in general prior to the nineteenth century, the place we can find anything resembling detailed lists of the foreign population is in the assessment records for people who were being taxed.

Monarchs in the fifteenth and sixteen centuries were big on levying taxes on 'aliens', who were the target of periodic flares of envy and resentment from the public and the ruling classes. A tax assessment from 1440 is a particularly useful specimen in terms of numbers, recording around 16,800 foreigners across England (although this was likely far short of the true number). It also gives us a useful broad overview of their origins – mainly Norman French, Dutch, Flemish and Italian – but is slightly less useful as a genealogical record, since hundreds of names seem to have been somewhat lazily transcribed as variations of 'John Frenchman' and 'Jan Dutchman'.[8] But we do get some detail: Italian merchants in Poole, Irish labourers in Cornwall and Bristol, visitors to York from the rising medieval trade hub of Middelburg in Flanders. When Henry VIII introduced a graduated poll tax in the sixteenth century, 'aliens' were ordered to pay double the normal amount. Records of these taxpayers show remarkable numbers of foreign Protestants who had sought refuge from persecution. In 1540, one third of poll-taxpayers in London were listed as foreigners. In one ward, there were only six English to 207 foreign taxpayers.[9] This probably tells us more about who was comparatively wealthy and who felt they couldn't risk displeasing the state than it does about the proportion of the population that was foreign. Over time the scapegoating of foreigners became rarer, and the impulse to tally them waned.

The 1841 census introduced a question on country of birth and nationality but because it had quite a low response rate, it was not until 1851 that we really got an accurate picture of where migrants in the UK were from. Around seventy thousand inhabitants had been born in 'foreign parts' and a further forty-one thousand had been born in British colonies. At less than 1 per cent of the population, migrants were hardly altering the demography of the country in a significant way. There were also clearly more British-born people living outside the United Kingdom, particularly if you counted the Irish, who numbered close to a million in the United States alone.[10]

In certain areas, though, migration clearly was having quite an impact. In London, around one in a hundred people were foreigners from foreign parts, but around one in fifty-eight had been born abroad, whether foreigner or British. If counting the Irish as born abroad (which technically they were not, although they were very often treated as foreigners), one in seventeen Londoners fell into this category.[11] We also got a good grasp for the first time of the number of people of specific nationalities living in London. The most plentiful were Germans, with nearly ten thousand of them, followed by French, West Indian, Dutch and Canadian.[12] The 'country of birth and nationality' field on the census return for Prince Albert, who made a point of declaring himself German until the bitter end, is diplomatically left blank.

As time went by, we got even more detail from censuses, so that in addition to virtually all nationalities settling in their largest numbers in London, we could see pockets of Norwegians settling in the northern counties, Germans and Americans settling in the north-west, and people born in the colonies and India settling in Hampshire.[13] Migrants coming from 'foreign parts' were overwhelmingly male, while migration within the UK was a slightly more female phenomenon, which was put down to young women moving away from their birthplace for domestic service.[14]

We see a complicated wrangle over identities play out in these figures around the question of who should be considered 'foreign'. Initially the census simply tried to find out whether people had moved from their place of birth, whether that was to Manchester from Cheshire or from India. Later a clear distinction emerged between people based on their country of birth and nationality. People born in the UK colonies were one group, British nationals born in other countries were another, and 'the strictly foreign element in the population' consisted of people born outside the British Empire who also had the nerve not to be British.[15] Of these 'strictly foreign' individuals, we first obtained an accurate numbering of their population in 1891, when around 233,000 were recorded in England and Wales and 287,000 in the UK as a whole.[16] Around this time we also start to find the word 'natives' feature in the statistics, as a description of people originating from the British Isles.

The statistics reveal a gradual diversifying of the population and show quite clearly who the main groups of migrants were. By 1901, the 'strictly foreign' population numbered around 290,000 in England and Wales, with the increase mainly people from Russia, Italy and the Balkans. Italians had been migrating to the UK for quite some time and were a familiar sight on the streets of London as performers, singers and acrobats, and sellers of ice cream, coffee and fish and chips. By 1901 there were six hundred Italian professional cooks and the same number of bakers, along with thousands of Italians working in the restaurant trade, as street-sellers and as artists and musicians.[17] One occupation of Italians was to wheel a barrel-organ through the streets blasting out popular hits on request. This so irritated Charles Babbage, inventor extraordinaire, that he sued barrel-organists for damages on the basis that he was losing a quarter of his time to being distracted by their gleeful racket. They did not stop, and gradually the music became a sideshow for another event – the jingle that plays to announce the arrival of an ice cream van.[18]

Although not foreigners in any official sense, Irish people migrating to Great Britain were certainly treated as outsiders and often as unwelcome guests. They also experienced some of the greatest hardship of anybody in nineteenth-century Britain, and we find many suffering young Irish men and boys in Henry Mayhew's account of a London homeless refuge. Between 1841 and 1851 the Irish population in Great Britain rose from around 290,000 to 520,000 people and then peaked in 1851 at over 600,000. A Royal Commission on the

Poor Laws, reporting in 1836 when the Irish had been fully-fledged citizens of the United Kingdom for over thirty years, did not hold back in detailing 'filth, neglect, discomfort and insalubrity' in the ways of Irish migrant communities.[19] And this was before the largest and most suffering wave of Irish migrants came mid-century to escape famine and disease.

In London at the end of the nineteenth century, 5 per cent of the population was from Ireland but they made up between an eighth and a quarter of the population of northern cities from Bradford to Liverpool and around a fifth of the population of some Scottish cities. The Scots were not happy at the volume of arrivals from Ireland, with the census in 1871 reporting that 'this invasion of Irish is likely to produce far more serious effects on the population of Scotland than even the invasions of the warlike hordes of Saxons, Danes, or Norsemen'. And they didn't just mean in terms of numbers. 'As yet the great body of these Irish do not seem to have been improved by their residence among us,' the Scots lamented, rather that 'the native Scot who has associated with them has most certainly deteriorated'.[20] The Irish were cruelly stereotyped as being unintelligent, lazy and drunken, and were even regarded as racially inferior in the context of later ideas which we shall come on to. But data collected on occupations showed that very few adult Irish men were unemployed and that nearly half worked on the docks – work that could certainly be irregular but was no walk in the park when you did get it. Meanwhile, a far larger portion of the Irish population had travelled away from the United Kingdom for good: by 1881, the number of Irish people living in the United States stood at 1.9 million.[21]

Tens of thousands of Russians, Poles and Germans migrated to the UK in the second half of the nineteenth century, a large proportion of whom were Jewish. Throughout the nineteenth century, and before, Jews in Eastern Europe had been subject to pogroms, ghettoisation and expulsion. In 1866, a cholera epidemic in Russian Poland and famine in Lithuania, as well as targeted attacks on Jewish populations in Russia, encouraged a steady trickle of westward migration. The numbers increased in the 1880s, when the German chancellor Bismarck expelled 'alien Poles' (meaning Jews) from the north of Poland, in what was then Prussia, and Moscow and Kiev expelled their entire Jewish populations. The United States was the first choice of destination, but for those who couldn't afford the long passage by steamboat, Britain made a fine alternative.

From the census we get a snapshot of which countries people came from and we can deduce that arrivals from Russia and Poland were mainly Jews. But there was no official data on the number of people practising different religions. It seems like a pity that the census didn't ask about religion, especially considering the fact that the 1901 census-takers were at pains to enumerate London's Jewish population, including translating the census paper into Yiddish and having both the Chief Rabbi and the Jewish Board of Deputies send out circulars encouraging people to comply.[22] But they had their reasons, as we shall see in a later chapter.

In 1851, a one-off census of religious congregations estimated that there were around 8,500 Jews living in England and Wales.[23] By the 1890s, it was estimated that there were around sixty to seventy thousand living in London alone, nine-tenths of whom were living in the East End.[24] Without hard data, these estimates were made based on a variety of sometimes dubious methods. One attempt to measure the inflow of Jewish migration was to take passenger lists from London and Hull and to divide up the names so that 'Moses and Abraham are on one side of the line, and Smith and

Robinson on the other' – the only problem being a large and 'doubtful fringe' of names in between.[25]

It's now estimated that between 1881 and 1914, 150,000 Jews came to the UK and settled for good, a great many of them in London. They were for the most part very poor, often destitute, and completely reliant on the kindness of strangers. But if this put a strain on the resources of poor relief, it was typically only for a short while. Jews arriving at Tilbury Docks in Essex would quickly find their way into London's East End, where their inexperience was frequently exploited and they would find themselves trapped in the very poorly remunerated and borderline slave labour of the sweatshop. In 1901, over half of working people from Russia and Poland living in the UK were employed in clothing manufacture – and for women within this group the figure was two thirds.[26]

Poverty was the norm, and yet the fact that Jewish migrants were often to be found in the new 'model dwellings' being erected by the likes of George Peabody and Octavia Hill suggests they were doing better than some. Over time, these new arrivals or 'greeners' would become acclimatised to the pace and rules of this harsh existence and start working on another plan of escape. Gradually, the London Jewish community would collectively save enough money to quite literally move up in the world to the cleaner and more pleasant surroundings of Stamford Hill and Tottenham. Some of them would really make the big time in the retail industry and provide Britain with some of its most iconic brands. Michael Marks, who migrated from Polish Russia in the 1880s, started out with a market stall in Leeds and ended up with a national chain of shops called Marks and Spencer. A descendent of this generation, Jack Cohen, would many decades later turn a business hawking surplus post-war supplies in Hackney into one of

Britain's largest and most popular supermarkets, Tesco (the 'co' being a reference to his surname).

At the same time that the diversity of the UK population, in terms of country of origin, nationality and, to some extent, race, was being revealed through statistics, new forms of hostility based on these characteristics were starting to appear. British science and social research had begun to flirt openly with the idea that race was a determinant of a person's intelligence level and behavioural tendencies. Some even went as far as to theorise that people of different races were members of different evolutionary branches, even different species. These theories took as their starting point Darwin's *Origin of Species*, then used the evidence of Black, Asian and Indigenous peoples' subjugation at the hands of colonial powers to conclude that Europeans had won the battle of natural selection.

Some scientists leaned in to stereotypes about race and nationality and used them to construct quasi-scientific theories about a hierarchy of races. The French anthropologist Gustave Le Bon devised an evolutionary pyramid with white Europeans at the top.[27] In Britain, Francis Galton extended these ideas by introducing the added element of social class. His theory was that some genetic strains of humanity were inherently better than others, and so the propensity to be poor, unhealthy or in other ways unproductive would be passed on until the faulty genes were bred out. He believed that social inequality was evidence that some people were born to serve and others to lead; that a 'degenerate stock' of people existed whose numbers should be reduced for the good of democracy.[28] This was a school of thought which came to be known as eugenics. And although these ideas were extreme, they were fairly influential in the late nineteenth century. Even if eugenics itself wasn't mainstream, the British people couldn't escape an overall environment in which the idea that Europeans – and specifically the white British – were superior was being constantly drip-fed via education, the media, the government, literature and the arts.

The fact that social research, as well as the trend of realism in literature and art, were bringing the lives of society's poorest out of the shadows became a mixed blessing. On the one hand, statistics showing that a disproportionate number of new foreign arrivals lived in some of the worst conditions imaginable generated compassion and sympathy. On the other, the unflattering image of lives lived in filth and poverty was now out there for the world to see, and for some people it only confirmed the idea of something 'degenerate' about the people themselves. In his study of London poverty, Charles Booth had diligently recorded the unavoidably foul living and working conditions of Jews in the East End but also noted their polite manners, work ethic and sobriety. But his positive observations didn't seem to have as much of an impact as the images of squalor that fell in harmony with antisemitic, anti-foreign and racist tropes of the time.

A feeling grew among the wider population that there were too many immigrants of the 'undesirable' sort. In 1903, a royal commission which had been convened to look into 'alien immigration' reported its findings after holding an admirable forty-nine evidence sessions in just under a year. Much of this evidence was of the anecdotal kind and the commission concluded that it remained 'impossible to state with accuracy the number of aliens in the UK'. Undeterred by this evidential thinness, the commission nonetheless reported that a great many 'aliens' were impoverished and destitute, and that 'among them [were] criminals, anarchists, prostitutes and persons of bad character in number beyond the percentage of the native population'.[29] A failure of integration meant the Jewish community in the East End formed a 'solid and distinct colony' but equally, when migrant labourers strayed outside majority-immigrant job sectors like tailoring, 'ill-feeling and friction' was wont to result.

What the commission seemed to miss, wilfully or otherwise, was that the evidence actually showed a remarkable degree of self-sufficiency in these migrant communities. Including medical relief, 2.4 per cent of London poor relief was going to 'aliens', while their share of the population was 5.5 per cent.[30] They were under-claiming poor relief, which was especially surprising given the mountain of other evidence pointing to their poverty. Facts such as these were, however, no match for the distaste towards people seen as 'generally dirty and uncleanly in their habits' that was building by the day, along with resentment towards communities that seemed to be isolating themselves from the mainstream.[31] It seems to have not been considered that separation could have been a form of self-protection or that ghettos were all some of these new arrivals had ever known.

The Aliens Act, passed in August 1905, was the first immigration law in seventy years and the first ever to introduce systematic control of immigration at the border. Until this point, there had been no controls on immigration to speak of, with the exception that foreign nationals were supposed to sign a register on arrival at port, but the system had 'fallen into disuse' (notwithstanding some registration lists that were evidently still being made in order to sort Abrahams from Smiths for statistical purposes).

UK politicians admired the American system, whereby shipping companies had a responsibility for only delivering passengers who were in a healthy condition; the sick were effectively weeded out before they could even embark. The British alternative was to give customs officers the power to turn people away at their port of arrival if they didn't seem able to support themselves or were otherwise 'undesirable'. They were expected to hop back onto the next returning boat. Whole ships could be turned away if they were not considered to be of the right sort. But since the rules only applied to ships with twenty or more passengers, people started travelling in smaller boats to cruise in under the radar. And since the decision-making was so subjective, it was also hard to enforce. In 1906, of the 935 people initially denied entry, around four hundred were ultimately allowed in after making an appeal.[32] Parliament also had to introduce amendments on people fleeing persecution, which exempted a lot of the most desperate people who had been deemed 'undesirable' in the Alien Act's original spirit.

What was curious was that while politicians were working themselves up into a vein-popping frenzy over the 290,000 'aliens' in the UK – less than 1 per cent of the population – there had been no real suggestion of ending the open-door policy towards subjects of the British Empire, who at that time numbered around four hundred million and made up a quarter of people on earth.[33] The Aliens Act applied only to the 'strictly foreign', such as Germans, and in theory any number of people could have come from India or British Sudan. Of course, there was no prospect of the vast majority of British subjects making use of this opportunity. It was an empty promise, and Britain knew it. Traffic was one-way, from the motherland to the colonies – and sometimes by force, as in the case of around 160,000 criminals who had been transported to Australia in the eighteenth and nineteenth centuries for offences as minor as shoplifting.

The 1905 Alien Act was nothing new in terms of its aims. In addition to punitive taxes on foreigners over the preceding centuries, there had been various attempts to try to discourage immigration entirely.[34] And like many of those other efforts, the Aliens Act did little to nothing to halt immigration, as we can see from the steadily growing number of people from 'foreign parts' in the censuses that came after. The diversifying of the population was unstoppable – inevitable, given the colossal volume of traffic to and from the UK during the time of its empire.

One place where the diversity of nineteenth century Britain is preserved in amber is in the census returns for the east London neighbourhood of Limehouse. Nowadays, Limehouse doesn't feel like much of a defined place at all. Aside from a few pretty streets and a desirable marina featuring luxury flats, it mainly consists of a restless thoroughfare between the City and the Isle of Dogs, where a busy A-road pounds past a collection of helpless-looking council blocks. But in the nineteenth century it was a dockside community interwoven with warehouses; a riverside location for well-off merchants while also a refuge for weary sailors seeking comfort in drink or even in one of several Chinese-run opium dens.[35]

It is here in 1861 that we find a house with twenty-nine inhabitants, one of whom was listed as thirty-six-year-old John Johnson who, like Ellen and William Craft who we met at the start of this chapter, is described as an 'escaped slave'.[36] The house was known as the Strangers' Home for Asiatics, Africans and South Sea Islanders. It was a purpose-built three-storey brick building which the community had funded to provide shelter to destitute sailors. The residents that night were a married couple and their four young children, four servants and nineteen lodgers: Johnson, as well as one student, who appears to have been a Russian Jew, one Indian cook and sixteen others described as 'lascars'. This term referred originally to very low-paid sailors recruited in India to work on British fleets, although several of the lascars in Limehouse were Chinese. Their names suggest a variety of origins and the majority seem to have been Muslim. When the Strangers' Home appears again in 1881, its lodgers are largely sailors and soldiers from China, Arabia, India, Ceylon and the Kru Coast (likely modern-day Liberia or Ivory Coast). By 1901, its residents were from India, Mauritius and Japan, and by 1911 over half of its forty-five boarders were from China or Hong Kong. Some were listed in the census with specific cities of origin, such as Manila, Cape Town and Rangoon.

Censuses provide us with these snapshots of human driftwood, left high and dry by the tide of imperial expansion. Their origins hint at the incredibly wide reach of British rule, which had touched virtually every corner of the globe, while they themselves were the remarkably scanty residue of people who had travelled against the flow and found a cold welcome or perhaps even open hostility in the motherland.

As the empire approached its peak in the early twentieth century, British superiority was already starting to fray. So too was the confidence of the British establishment in the nineteenth-century way of doing things, which had involved exploiting people first and worrying about the consequences much later on. The data collected through censuses and social research had played a part in enabling and encouraging this new self-reflection. Many people – be they working class, poor, sick and destitute, or foreigners working in thankless and barely paid jobs – had not necessarily been seen before as individuals but rather as a pliable mass which would adapt to any conditions.

But the long Victorian age was ending. New ideas about democracy were in the wind, and it was time for another reckoning. It didn't take a statistician to work this one out: half the population was getting a raw deal.

8

The Second Sex

On Friday 24 March 1911, a letter appeared in London's *Evening Standard* newspaper. 'I venture to appeal to all suffragists to reconsider their intention,' wrote the correspondent. 'The method chosen for the intended protest is anti-social [and] considerable trouble and pecuniary loss will be inflicted.'[1] The writer was a registrar for one of London's districts, and the protest a boycott of the 1911 census by women demanding equal voting rights with men.

Suffragists – as those campaigning for women to get the vote were known – had come up with the plan of using the new census to make a symbolic statement. If women weren't counted by the state as full citizens, they would refuse to be physically counted in official statistics. The instructions for those wanting to participate were to leave their census entry partly or entirely blank, or to fill it with slogans about women's rights.

'The Census is a numbering of the people,' explained the leader of the Women's Social and Political Union (WSPU), Emmeline Pankhurst. 'Until women count as people for the purposes of representation in the councils of the nations as well as for purposes of taxation and obedience to the laws, we advise women to refuse to be numbered.'[2] In terms of specific demands, the WSPU was asking for assurance from the government that it would not veto a Women's Suffrage Bill which was scheduled for its second reading in the House of Commons on 6 May, but allow time for debate. More generally, though, it was an opportunity to register the presence of the women's suffrage movement in an official public record, through absence.

The overall argument for suffrage was that if Parliament was empowered to make laws affecting women – and even laws which exclusively affected them – they should have an equal say in who got elected to that Parliament. 'Women, being voteless, are powerless,' was Pankhurst's argument. And being subject to decisions made by people whom one had no power to un-elect was akin to 'being governed without consent'.

Some opponents dismissed the protest as a tantrum or a sign of women's stupidity. A Professor Sadler, in a letter to *The Times*, said it was 'a crime against science' and warned that 'to sulk against the Census would not be a stroke of statesmanship but a nursery fit of bad temper'.[3] A later piece in *The Times* called the planned protest a 'childish threat' and crowed that the only way in which the government would be 'impressed' would be 'by the moral obliquity and mental deficiency of those who have invented the plan'.[4] Critics of suffragists' methods often used this tone of telling off a naughty child combined with intellectual point-scoring. The *Spectator* simply dismissed the protest 'a piece of criminal folly'.[5]

What is interesting for our purposes is just how much the census itself was centre-stage in these arguments. It hadn't been so vigorously defended since first coming into being over one hundred years earlier, but suddenly there was a choir of voices on both sides loudly singing its praises. The census was defended as 'a work of high social utility', producing statistics by which we could measure health and happiness, and confront poverty and disease.[6] If the census were wrong, then 'serious mistakes would be made affecting every field of national activity' and some went as far as to call census vandalism a 'grave public injury'.[7] The census was characterised as an innocent victim, the line being that it was 'entirely non-political'. But if disrupting the census was antisocial, the suffragist response was that 'the legislation which will be based upon this Census will be *anti-social* so long as women are excluded from any direct voice in it'.[8] This comeback was delivered by suffragette activist Emily Wilding Davison, who had a particularly audacious census protest up her sleeve, and about whom we will hear more later on.

Censuses are non-political in the sense that they are not supposed to be swayed by party politics. The questions on the form should not be placed there according to party interests but by consensus as to what vital statistics the nation needs for the business of governing. But the reality is that statistics are always political – with a small p, you might say – because they are shaped by the norms, attitudes and judgements of society at a given time. Censuses, like any form of population statistics, reflect back at us what we choose to measure, what we *don't* measure, and who or what we give importance to. To treat numbers as inherently objective and neutral – as if they appear written on the wall by the hand of God – is to miss one of the most fundamental features of statistics: they are man-made.

Perhaps the most extreme illustration of this comes from the first US census, for which it was decided that slaves would each count as three fifths of a person. This was a compromise between the northern states arguing that slaves should not be counted at all since they were denied any right to public participation (an unintentional suffragist-style argument) and the southern states wanting to boost their numbers for the sake of greater representation in Congress. It was never suggested that counting slaves equally with free people should come with an equalisation of civil rights. This was also a debate about whether slaves were to count as people or property. There were around 700,000 people in slavery in the United States at that point, or, if applying the three fifths arithmetic, 420,000.[9] There is obviously something political going on when some living and breathing residents of a country aren't considered full people.

Even when it isn't designed to send a message about 'who counts', exclusion from statistics can powerfully demonstrate the lack of worth that society and the government places on a category of people or some aspect of their experience. Until sixty or seventy years before the suffragists planned their 1911 census boycott, there were barely any individual-level statistics on women in the UK. At that point, it had only been just over a hundred years since the first definitive statistics on how many women there were in aggregate, thanks to the 1801 census. You could say the same of men, but the data gap was a lot smaller: they appeared on lists for taxation purposes and a great many, regardless of social class, had been enumerated on military rolls.

The Domesday Book contains more records of pigs than of women.[10] This was because it was ultimately a census of the country's production capabilities; women were recorded mostly as the wives, widows or daughters of men with some quantity of assets or land. A solitary widow would tend not to appear, and nor would the whole of a poor family employed in a cottage industry and living off a small vegetable garden. A few women were listed in their own right because they were some of the country's biggest landowners, most notably a Countess Judith who was associated with 193 tracts of land from London to Lincolnshire. In another case we find the widow Leofgeat, who held a large but badly diminished portfolio of land after her husband had been killed by the invading Normans. A few quirky details also survive in Domesday, without apparent reason. Leofgeat did 'gold embroidery for the King and Queen', and there is a record of a female jester called Adelina working for an Earl Roger in Hampshire, which does seem unusual.[11] In the centuries that followed, women continued to appear in lists wherever they had something to tax.

The nineteenth century was the first time we had individual-level statistics containing detail on the lives of all women. (The same can be said of a great many working-class men, and of children.) The 1841 census recorded the names of every person living in a household, along with sex, age and some information about occupations, although this was mainly aimed at men over twenty years of age. The census in 1851 was much more comprehensive, collecting information about the occupations of all persons in the household, which is why it is thought of as a pivotal moment and a 'catalyst for British feminism'.[12]

But before we get carried away with how great this egalitarian new approach was, we need to pause and look at an oddity in the 1851 census. As we saw in Chapter 6, occupations were grouped and ranked into what was effectively a hierarchy of social class. In 1851, a new category was introduced for the occupation of 'wife'. 'The fifth class ["wife"] comprises a large number of the population that have hitherto been held to have no occupation,' announced the census report. 'But it requires no argument to prove that the wife, the mother, the mistress of an English Family fills offices and discharges duties of no ordinary importance.'[13] This notion could be described as quite radically feminist. The idea of recognising women's unremunerated labour in the household as *work* would seem to only be a small step away from the idea that she should be compensated for it, at the very least in terms of individual rights. But this was a time when women were banned from owning property or assets if they were married, when there were no widows' pensions (or any pensions to speak of) and slim prospects for women of obtaining a settlement after divorce.

It was not, in fact, a feminist statement, at least by our standards today. Rather, creating a specific and highly ranked class for wives was done to make the point that 'the duties of a wife, a mother, and a mistress of a family can only be efficiently performed by unremitting attention'.[14] The aim was to promote marriage and, more specifically, to promote women giving up their jobs when they did marry. Around one in four wives in England and Wales also had some 'extraneous occupation' and the censors did not like it.

The wider context was also that every single census taken since 1801 had shown a 'surplus' number of women, and this number was rising. In England and Wales in 1851, there were 350,000 more women than men (notwithstanding the fact that a substantial number of men were away at sea). In 1861, the excess was over half a million – a number which, as the *Manchester Guardian* put it, 'would have filled the Crystal Palace four times over'.[15] Looking more closely at the statistics, it was apparent that a large proportion of this surplus consisted of unmarried women. This was a particular cause for alarm as it was interpreted as women holding out against their duty of marriage. Fundamentally, women were seen as unproductive if they did not marry, no matter how many hours they toiled in the cotton factory. They were also seen as taking men's jobs, which was another driver of the cultural propaganda campaign to get women to see wifedom as full-time work.

A solution put forward by both male and female commentators in the 1850s and 60s was that single women should be encouraged to emigrate. Some of the colonies – Australia, New Zealand, South Africa and Canada – were known to have a surplus of men, so exporting women there seemed like a natural act of rebalancing.[16] Between 1860 and 1890, one hundred thousand British women and girls migrated to Australia under a scheme for single women, with their passage paid by the government of their new homeland.[17] Naturally, these women were not portrayed in a flattering light but rather as 'unmarketable womanhood' whom the UK had dumped on her colonies in the manner of an 'outfall sewer' (at least this was the take of one popular British newspaper).[18] The push for emigration stalled and instead commentators started to point out, using the very same census statistics, that unmarried women were likely to be working and therefore not 'unproductive' at all.

The final decades of the nineteenth century saw an increasing tension between moral expectations for women and a reality of modern life which made it all but impossible for them to be met. A great many married women simply had to work in paid employment because the wages of one earner were not enough. The movement to cities meant smaller houses and fewer relatives around to help with child-rearing, and so women were less able to fulfil their wifely duty of supplying a vast brood of offspring. There had also been milestones in women's rights, including women and men being able to apply to the civil courts for divorce and, in 1870, the ending of the centuries-old practice of married women being barred from owning property.[19] And at the start of the twentieth century a generation was growing up where boys and girls had both for the most part attended school, without there having been any noticeable difference in intellectual capability. Yet the attitudes of some men towards women were barely distinguishable from those of a hundred years earlier. There was still a heavy, even a growing, emphasis on women's duty to be a wife and mother, at least in the conversations taking place in the corridors of power.

In this pressured situation, opposition to sexual and social double standards became increasingly vocal. In 1887, the headlines were grabbed by an episode in which a woman had been arrested one night while strolling on Regent Street, an upper-class shopping street in central London, on the grounds that she was soliciting for prostitution. Elizabeth Cass, who had moved to London only a few days prior and was by all credible accounts of impeccable character, denied the charges and kicked up something of a fuss. The judge at her hearing opted to caution her, on the basis that she may or may not have been guilty of the crime, but being out on the street at such an hour was enough to suggest something nefarious. 'Just take my advice,' he said. 'If you are a respectable girl, as you say you are, do not walk Regent Street and stop gentlemen at 10 o'clock at night. If you do, you will either be fined or sent to prison.'[20] This judgment effectively placed a curfew on women in central London, which generated considerable outrage.[21] An official inquiry followed, and it was rumoured that Queen Victoria herself was closely following the case and a supporter of Miss Cass.[22]

Eventually the police's case crumbled and Cass was vindicated, but the episode had touched a nerve that would not be easily soothed. The late 1880s had also seen the spate of horrific unsolved murders in Whitechapel attributed to serial killer Jack the Ripper, and the police had been criticised for a lacklustre response because the victims were said to have been engaged in prostitution. In 1864 an Act had been passed which allowed the police to detain women suspected of prostitution and subject them to an intrusive examination for venereal disease.[23] There was a public outcry about the hypocrisy of no such inspections being required of men, given that the Act's ultimate purpose was aimed at reducing venereal disease in the entirely male armed forces. It was within this atmosphere that the women's suffrage movement developed.

The movement is sometimes seen as a campaign by primarily upper- and middle-class women. There is some truth to this, given that they were the women who could generally afford to engage in activism, both in terms of the time commitment and the risk to reputation. In addition, a Reform Act in 1884 had extended male voting rights without including all men – and particularly those who were neither owners nor occupiers of property – so it's plausible that some working-class women didn't see the point of campaigning for 'equal' rights which wouldn't affect them anyway. But there were efforts to draw in working-class women, including a petition that circulated in the 1890s – 'An Appeal from Women of All Parties and All Classes' – which amassed nearly a quarter of a million signatures.[24] In 1896, the National Union of Women's Suffrage Societies (NUWSS) was established to coordinate the activities of groups around the country. When the WSPU was formed in Manchester in 1903, its co-founder Christabel Pankhurst stated that their 'main concern was not with the numbers of women to be enfranchised but with the removal of a stigma upon womanhood as such'.[25] In other words, the first goal was to have it acknowledged that men and women were equal *within* their social class. Some went further and argued that step two should be universal suffrage, as well as the remedying of broader social inequality.

Over time the suffragists' tactics became more militant and the women who engaged in them came to be known as 'suffragettes'. From disrupting public meetings and an unprecedented women's march (dubbed the 'Mud March') through the filthy streets of London, their activities escalated to bombings, arson and vandalism. Following an attempt to force their way into Parliament, a group of women was beaten, 'flung hither and thither', and 'handled with gross indecency' by the police, who apparently had been primed not only to hold back the protesters but to 'terrorise' them.[26] Often the aim of these tactics was to be imprisoned, as this drew greater attention to the cause. In 1910, 116 suffragettes were imprisoned for criminal offences, 188 in 1911, and 240 in 1912.[27] In prison, some women (and occasional men) went on hunger strikes and were force-fed, in scenes which attracted public horror. To overcome extreme resistance, subjects were restrained by physical force before a tube was inserted into the nose or mouth. Women reported bruising, lung problems, throat lacerations and damage to the eyes and ears. After ten weeks of brutal force-feeding, Mary Richardson recalled being 'little better than a breathing corpse'.[28]

Emily Wilding Davison went on hunger strike on seven occasions, after being imprisoned for setting fire to post boxes, vandalism and assaulting the police. She is one of the best-known suffragettes and the only one to die as a direct result of her activism, in a high-profile, separate incident in 1913. Back in 1911, Davison had heard the call to disrupt the census count and, in typical fashion, decided to take it one step further.

She was fairly familiar with the Houses of Parliament, it having been the stage for many of her previous protests, and from which she had been ejected on no less than five previous occasions.[29] On the afternoon of Saturday 1 April 1911 she entered the Palace of Westminster and spent some time tacking herself on to various groups of tourists wandering through the building. Some time after 4 p.m. she joined a large group of visitors being shown around by an MP, which gave them privileged access to the Chapel of St Mary Undercroft, the crypt underneath Westminster Hall. Situated at the bottom of a narrow and dingy stone staircase, entering the underground chapel is like discovering a cave of dragon's treasure – a dazzling, glittering pile of gold ornamentation beneath jewel-coloured Gothic arches. As the tour made its way back out of the crypt, Davison peeled off from the group and slipped into a broom cupboard at the back of the chapel. As her eyes became accustomed to the gloom, she noticed with astonishment words written on the wall declaring 'Guy Fawkes was killed here'. (Dear reader, he was not.) Davison settled into the cupboard for a spooky night.

She was down there for nearly two full days, taking occasional walks in the crypt to stretch her legs and snacking on some provisions she had brought. At one point an MP threw open the cupboard door to triumphantly show a couple of guests the Guy Fawkes inscription, with none of them seeming to notice a suffragette crouching behind some boxes.[30] On Monday, satisfied that she had avoided census day entirely, Davison let herself be discovered by a workman who had come to the cupboard for supplies.[31] She was escorted to a nearby police station where, perhaps to her disappointment, no charges were made and the only action recommended was that she be duly enumerated in the census.

This episode might have become just an amusing footnote in suffragette history, had it not been for the fact that two years later Emily Davison was killed in dramatic scenes at Epsom racecourse after running out onto the track into the path of the thundering horses. In footage which survives from the incident, she appears suddenly among them like a dark apparition. She seems to reach out for one as it careens towards her and they collide head-on, sending her tumbling under horse and rider, who are thrown jaggedly to the ground. Under her coat she was wearing a sash in the suffragette colours, and she had two WSPU flags with her, which some have speculated she was trying to pin to the bridle of the King's horse. In her bag was the stub of a return train ticket. Newspapers at the time fumed at her 'misguided zealotry' and 'militant lunacy' but she was also held up as a martyr to the suffragette cause.

When the 1911 census returns were examined in light of Davison's later celebrity, a record was indeed located of a 'Miss E Davidson' who was 'found hiding in the crypt of Westminster Hall'. Her name is misspelled and her occupation out of date – she had not been a schoolteacher for some years but rather a full-time political activist – perhaps because she refused to supply the details herself. The chapel broom cupboard is still sought out by many a visitor to the Palace of Westminster, but no longer for its Guy Fawkes fame. In 1991, Labour MPs Tony Benn and Jeremy Corbyn secretly installed a plaque there, 'In loving memory of Emily Wilding Davison ... [who] hid herself, illegally, during the night of the 1911 census'.[32] As it turned out, Davison's landlady had recorded her at home on Coram Street in London on census night. Ironically, rather than being absent from the census, Davison appears in it twice.

CENSUS OF ENGLAND AND WALES, 1911.

SCHEDULE.

Prepared pursuant to the Census (Great Britain) Act, 1910.

This space to be filled up by the Enumerator.

Number of Registration District.......5
Number of Registration Sub-District...3
Number of Enumeration District......24

Name of Head of Family or Separate Occupier. } Miss E. W. Davidson

Postal Address... Found hiding in crypt of Westminster Hall
WESTMINSTER

NOTICE.

This Schedule must be filled up and signed by, or on behalf of, the Head of the Family or other person in occupation, or in charge, of the dwelling (house, tenement or apartment).

Other suffragettes were more successful in evading the censors. Kitty Marshall, a bodyguard to Emmeline Pankhurst, organised three caravans in which she and some friends planned to hide out, deep on Putney Heath in south-west

London, on census night. The police did track them down, but the census record simply lists 'Mrs Marshall' and '9 other females' who refused to even give their names.[33] Others tried to avoid being counted in their true place of residence by gathering en masse in public places or at parties which went on late into the night. The police already had intelligence on parties of up to a hundred people planned at various locations in central London and went around trying to uncover the clandestine census-dodgers. A census listing for Aldwych Skating Rink records '500 women [and] 70 men', without any names or other details.[34] This seems to have been a particularly successful mass evasion, apparently thanks to the sporty suffragettes circulating constantly back and forth between the roller-skating rink and restaurant to the bafflement of enumerators.[35] In Edinburgh, a 'large gathering' hid out in the Café Vegetaria all weekend, returning a census form on the Monday which was blank except for words to the effect of 'No Vote' and signed by Lucy Burns, a prominent WSPU activist.[36]

Some filled in the form but defaced certain parts of it to put their point across. Mary Howey of Cradley, Hertfordshire, did complete details for herself and a servant in the household but garnished it by writing 'VOTES FOR WOMEN' in large letters across the remainder of the form and, in the column used to record any infirmities, wrote 'no enfranchisement'. One form was returned blank but for a 'No Votes for Women, No Census' poster pasted across half of it and 'No persons here, only women' written across the remainder. Not wanting to ruffle so many feathers, two headteachers in Walsall, Staffordshire, diligently filled out all their information before adding a stealthy 'no vote' in the infirmity column.[37]

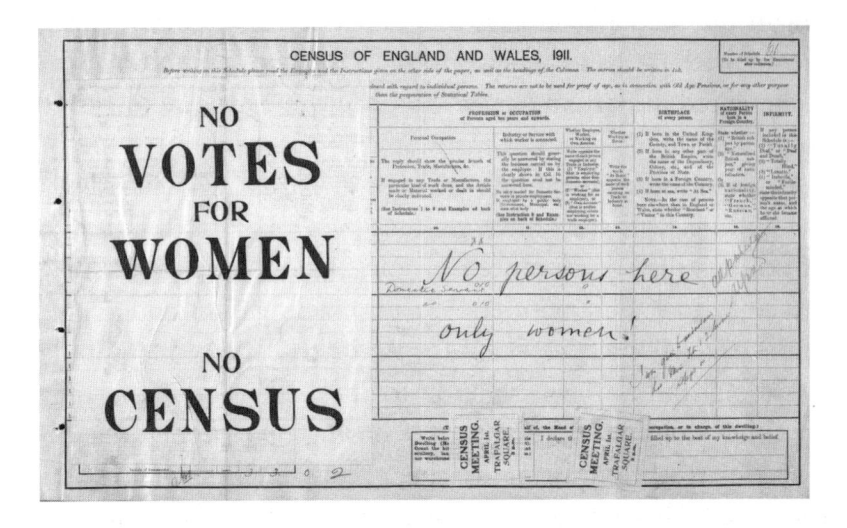

Some took it further and used the occupation column to send a message. Gertrude Pidoux in Buckinghamshire recorded herself as a 'Militant Suffragette'; in London, Ethel Burrow of Hampstead was a 'Suffragette', while Dorothea Hope of Hammersmith wrote under occupation, 'I demand the right to a political vote'.[38] One curious entry by Laura Bell in Letchworth, Hertfordshire, describes her occupation as 'husband's chattel', infirmity as 'no vote' and around the edge of the page are written disconnected witticisms and political commentaries: 'the law's an ass', 'if women are classed with lunatics why ask them to give information that will be used as a basis for legislation?'[39]

It's evident that a lot of the women defacing their forms were 'of independent means', with an affluent husband and servants, and nothing much to fear from committing an act of light vandalism and a possible punishment of a £5 fine for refusing to provide true information. Some even made it clear on the census form where their own interests lay. 'Being a woman householder but having no vote I decline to fill up this paper,' wrote Edith Schweder, living on private means in Kent, and 'no work and no vote, taxed but not represented in Parliament' wrote Annie Packer of Lambeth, south London.[40]

Understandably, it seems few working-class women risked the £5 fine, which would have been equivalent to hundreds of pounds in today's money and weeks of earnings for the lowest-paid female workers at the time.[42] We do find a few brave exceptions. The entry for Emily Smith, twenty-seven years old and a domestic cook to the Jenkin family in the wealthy London borough of Kensington, simply reads, 'Refuses to give information because women have not got the vote.' This would have been written by her employer, who filled out the household form, so it demonstrates that Smith had some serious guts.[43] On the other side of London, sixty-nine-year-old Canadian Jane Sbarbaro, has 'suffragette' recorded under her occupation and the form is graffitied with '6 weeks in Holloway for wanting the vote'. Someone, possibly Jane herself, seems to have got cold feet later and added another occupation: 'office cleaner'.[44]

Some of the 1911 census returns also provide an intimate glimpse into the dynamics of families clashing over the issues of women's voting rights. Henry Twells of Lincolnshire comes across as slightly fatigued in his description of his wife's present occupation: 'At present agitating for votes for women.'[45] On a form filled out by Edward Maund in Hammersmith, his wife Eleanora's entry is crossed out with a thick black line. Maund has replaced the crossed-out entry in livid red pen, adding, 'My wife unfortunately being a Suffragette put her pen through her name, but it must stand as correct. It being an equivocation to say she is away. She being always resident here and has only attempted by a silly subterfuge to defeat the object of the census to which as "Head" of the family I object.'[46]

Although we find more examples in this census than in any previous one of 'spoiled' forms for a political cause, it certainly wasn't the first time that people used the census for protest. In 1881, there are several instances of women describing themselves as 'slaves', seemingly to make a point about their under-appreciated work. Elizabeth Blanch, wife to a carpenter in Westminster, is a 'Brittish slave'; Ellen Harford of Euston, mother to three children, is a 'slave of the family'; and Charlotte Niblett in Gloucestershire is listed as 'Maid of All Work and Slave', with her infirmity being 'scarcity of money'. As early as 1851, we find an entry for thirty-eight-year-old Mary Round, recorded in Staffordshire with her husband and four children as a 'work slave'.[47] There were also cases of men using the census to make a similar point: in 1851, Thomas Allen in Paddington declared his occupation as 'Bricklayer white slave', while Abraham Stoker, a milk deliverer and self-declared 'slave' in Staffordshire, used the empty part of his family's form to write 'Hail to the Social Revolution' in large letters.[48]

Most of these were well before the days in which people filled out their own census forms. Information would only make it onto the census paper if someone said it out loud to an enumerator and they wrote it down. Perhaps awkwardness or apathy stopped enumerators from asking any follow-up questions to these theatrical declarations of enslavement. Or perhaps, given that by the 1880s a substantial proportion of enumerators were women, they were willing partners in these small acts of subversion.

Overall, not enough people participated in the 1911 census 'boycott' for it to have any impact on the statistics. The census was not ruined; the statisticians at the GRO breathed a sigh of relief and the whole affair was more or less forgotten (the protest doesn't even get a mention in fourteen volumes of census report). But the impact in terms of publicity for the suffragist cause was huge. They had managed to irk some very powerful people who had come out to defend the census almost as if it were a sacred document being vandalised. The suffragists had made a powerful point too: we won't let you count us until we really count. The campaign continued up to and to some extent throughout the war which broke out in 1914 and changed life beyond recognition for many people. In 1918, the Representation of the People Act extended the vote to women over the age of thirty who either owned or occupied property, or whose husband did. This represented around 8.5 million women, and at the same time the Act likely enfranchised another three to four million men through the removal of the property rule for them.[49] The ultimate sacrifice made by so many young working-class men had given weight to the argument that life-and-death decisions shouldn't be made about people who had no power to decide who they wanted as decision-makers. In 1928 the vote was extended to all women over twenty-one, putting them on equal terms with men, and in 1969 the voting age for everyone was lowered to eighteen.

For the census, the episode was an absolute gift in terms of public relations. Critics and proponents of the protest emphasised – perhaps even over-hyped – the importance of population statistics for policymaking and acknowledged the census as a cherished public document. The data was presented as the backbone of public policy, which could not function if one or more of its vertebrae were missing. Whether the census really was that important is up for debate. We had, however, well and truly accepted the role of numbers within policymaking. Data was now seen as a vital and immensely powerful public resource and the glue between government and the governed.

The story that we've heard so far in these pages has been about how counting people makes them visible to others and gives them a social identity, which tends to lead to recognition of an injustice. For the most part, this seems to happen as quite a passive process because people who are uncounted generally also lack political influence. What we have here is an unusual case in which a group *actively* refuses to be counted unless more power is granted to them in exchange. Effectively, it was a data hostage situation.

When people are given the opportunity to enumerate themselves in a public list for the first time, many – if not the large majority of people – will jump at the chance to finally make their official mark: 'I exist'. But it arguably hadn't happened like that for women because in a large proportion of cases it was still the male householder filling out the form, and for a long time they were not allowed to record their true occupations, instead being told that they were just 'wives' or 'the residue'. Census boycotts are often a protest about a perceived breakdown of the consensual relationship between citizen and government. Withholding data was a way of disrupting a relationship that seemed to be all take and no give: 'I exist, but you treat me as if I don't. Is this what you want?'

The suffragette census protest and the outbreak of war shortly afterwards overshadowed the results of the 1911 census. They also somewhat obscured the fact that some of the data collected was unusually intrusive and unconventional.

For the first time, the householder had been instructed to state 'for each married woman entered on this schedule' the number of years her present marriage had lasted and how many children it had produced. The householder filling out the form was to declare how many of those children were still living, and how many had died. The report on this fertility data, which was not completed until 1923, includes some amazingly detailed information about people's marriages, including age at marriage and the age difference between partners. There was no attempt at suppressing small numbers, which is what statisticians do now to avoid singling people out in categories. We can clearly see that there were four men and two women in England and Wales who were more than sixty years older than their respective spouses.[50] Because there is also a breakdown by occupation, we can see that there was one railway worker aged over forty-five with a wife aged between fifteen and nineteen. We're not here to judge – just to marvel at how sordid it feels to have so much detail on people's personal relationships. But terms like 'ante-nuptial conception' and 'sterile unions' give the report a Victorian feel, as if scientific abstractness can disguise the fact that this was a huge national effort to satisfy official curiosity about people's sex lives.

And what precisely was the point of it? Historians are in different camps as to why these questions got the go-ahead, given the hassle and expense of such a large expansion of the census form, but the overall argument was that it was 'for the study of certain social problems, such as comparative fertility in classes of different social positions, ... occupations, [and] age and upon certain questions relating to infant and child mortality'.[51] In other words, it was to figure out which social classes were breeding most intensively. From the census report we do gain insights such as 'Class VI, the textile workers, [show] a total fertility about the same as that of Class II [middle class "skilled" workers], but as its child mortality is much heavier its effective fertility is decidedly less'.[52] Families were arranged in eight classes by social 'status' and, overall, marriages further 'down the social scale' tended to produce more children.[53]

The fertility rate in England and Wales was declining – it had peaked in 1876 – and that was another reason why some had adopted it as such a fixation. The census report itself ruefully mentions mysterious 'influences, whatever their nature, which commenced so definitely at that date to lessen reproduction'.[54] Some historians have argued that statisticians at the GRO had pushed for an investigation into social class, fertility and child mortality either because they wanted to deflate arguments in favour of eugenics or because they were attracted by the ideas of eugenics themselves.[55] An official argument for the fertility questions was that we could use the data to discover why children were dying and do something to prevent it. Given that they were mainly testing the effect of women's marriage age and social class on child mortality, what exactly were the solutions going to be if either of these factors proved influential? Put a stop to marrying at certain ages for people of certain classes? It also seems rather unnecessary, given that child mortality was already going down.

Women's participation in the labour force ended up increasing during the First World War, before a backlash in the 1920s. Women were then partly excluded from the new unemployment insurance, forced to give up their jobs in certain industries when they got married, and even banned from playing competitive football despite their games having drawn larger crowds than men's matches.[56] Whatever the impetus for the fertility census, the analysis which it produced in the 1920s fed into an atmosphere of hand-wringing about women's 'proper' role. Some argue that the fertility analysis may have also been an excuse to try out the new Hollerith tabulation machines which had been acquired to mechanically sort the census data with speed and sophistication that far surpassed the power of human hands.[57] But as the suffragettes may well have asked, where was the consent for this line of questioning in the first place?

9

A Downward Slope

In 1919, Britain was still picking itself back up after four years of brutal combat in Europe when it started making plans for its next census. Victory was ours, though it had come at a terribly high price. The khaki-clad soldiers returning from the front were received as heroes but drifted home like ghosts. The horrors of the trenches would leave many of them psychologically scarred for life, while the physical toll taken by being cold and soaked for weeks at a time and without enough food would have a lasting impact on their health. The economy had taken a hit and national debt was at 140 per cent of GDP, the highest for three quarters of a century and five times what it had been in 1913.[1]

But more costly and more keenly felt was the cost in human lives. Over seven hundred thousand British men had died and 1.7 million had been wounded, meaning around one in five working-age men had either returned from the war injured or not come back at all.[2] When the 1921 census was completed, the deaths of so many young men in war loomed from the page in the form of a large chunk missing from the population aged twenty to forty. The war had a second bite of the cherry in the age category 0–5 years old, for both sexes: during wartime, for obvious reasons, far fewer babies than usual had been born.[3]

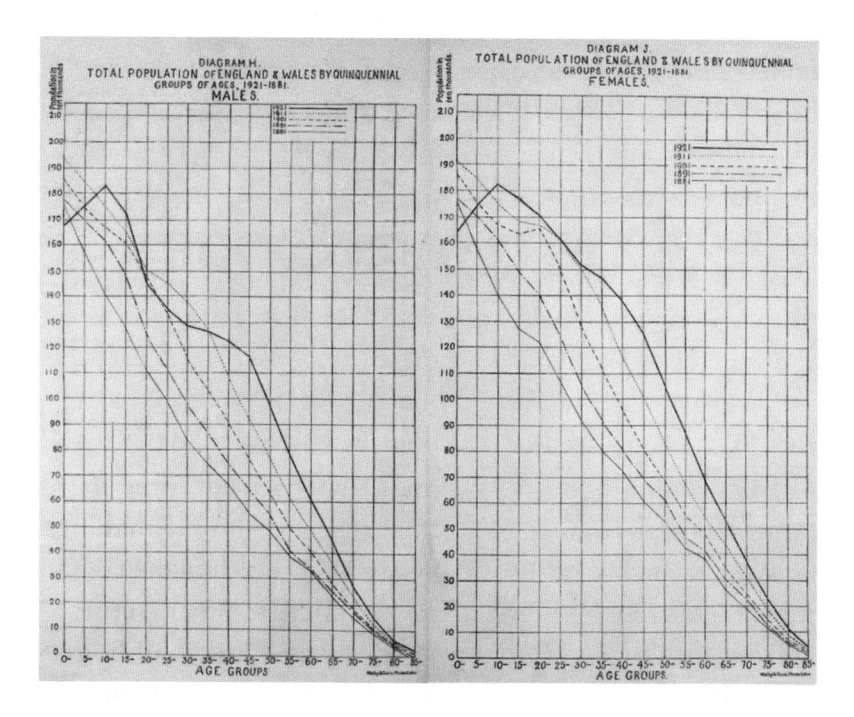

DIAGRAM H.
TOTAL POPULATION OF ENGLAND & WALES BY QUINQUENNIAL GROUPS OF AGES, 1921-1881.
MALES.

DIAGRAM J.
TOTAL POPULATION OF ENGLAND & WALES BY QUINQUENNIAL GROUPS OF AGES, 1921-1881.
FEMALES.

There would be no census in Ireland in 1921. In fact, there would never be another single census for Ireland as a whole because in May 1921 the country was formally divided into two self-governing territories. (In 1922, Southern Ireland would split off as the Irish Free State, later becoming the Republic of Ireland, while Northern Ireland remained part of the United Kingdom.) The last time politicians in Westminster talked about holding an all-Ireland census, in 1920, many had voiced extreme doubts about the wisdom of even trying. It was asked why the Treasury was planning to spend the equivalent of several million in today's money printing census forms which would inevitably end up as bonfires on the streets.[4] By then, there was a considerable separatist movement, which had only grown since the 1916 Easter Rising. Ireland was effectively in a state of war and had certainly reached the point of being ungovernable, despite the efforts of the British army and the police. 'How many tanks will be required for the collection of the census forms?' the Attorney General for Ireland was asked in Parliament, even as he insisted right down to the wire that the 1921 count would go ahead.[5]

But it would not be until 1926 that the next – and indeed the first – census would be held in Northern Ireland. The six counties of the north had gone through a period of stress and violent upheaval, and a heavy military and police presence had been installed in the urban areas of Belfast and Londonderry. Despite some people's understandable mistrust of the authorities, it was decided that, as was usual in Ireland, police constables would be the ones to go house to house, filling in the census forms.

A piece in the *Derry Journal* reported a conversation between two women, overheard in the golden evening light on the banks of the River Foyle. 'When I seen him up the street with papers I thought to fly out the back door,' said one, recalling the constable's approach with census forms in hand. When asked to provide some particulars on the family, she had responded, 'Well, their names you might get, but I'll tell me age to no man.' The question on religion provoked greater suspicion still, with the other woman cautioning, 'I know the form says to put down the sort of Protestant you are ... but the safe thing to do is to put down "Orange" and be done with it.' The question on occupation had given them much amusement. 'When I told me husband the police want to know what work he was at he went flaming mad, for he hasn't done a stroke these five years,' commented one of the women. 'I'm putting him down as "Gentleman, retired".' 'That won't do,' replied her friend. 'Mine is going down as "Brass Finisher". He finished all ours.'[6]

When the first Northern Ireland census results were released, they showed a population that seemed to be at a standstill. But the headline figures disguised a great churn below the surface. Like the rest of Ireland, the north had seen its population shrink over the preceding decades as a result of famine, disease and mass emigration. The population of the island of Ireland had nearly halved from 8.2 million in 1841 to 4.4 million in 1911.[7] In Northern Ireland, even though births had exceeded deaths between 1871 and 1926 by around 440,000, the number of people who had emigrated during that time was higher still, at 530,000.[8] The population started to recover, partly thanks to an influx of around twenty thousand people at the time of Ireland's division.[9] Unfortunately, who exactly these 'immigrants' were – likely Protestants from the south – will in some cases never be known. Nearly a century later, it came to light that the 1926 Northern Ireland census returns had been pulped during the Second World War under a directive to dispose of 'waste paper' in buildings for the sake of reducing fire hazards.[10]

Great Britain in the early twentieth century was also experiencing high levels of emigration, to the extent that the population lost to emigration in the ten years before the First World War was double the number of men lost in the war itself. The scale of this emigration – although not as traumatic to the remaining family members as a loss from war – is really quite staggering. It has been estimated that almost every family in the country would have seen at least one member emigrate in the decades preceding the war.[11] Between 1911 and 1913, close to half a million British citizens were emigrating each year – a considerable number and around four times higher than we see nowadays, in this era of global mobility.[12] After 1918, the pace abated slightly, but in Scotland the net number of people leaving every year remained higher than the number of babies being born.[13]

Why were so many people leaving the UK around the turn of the twentieth century, when the country was the envy of the world in many respects? For the most part, emigration seems to have been driven by the prospect that there were higher wages to be had in the main destinations – the USA, Canada, Australia and New Zealand – along with lower living costs, less overcrowding and an all-round better quality of life.[14] A Scottish crofter could trade in a barren patch of highland for acres of lush Canadian estate and also feel part of something new and vigorous, as opposed to forgotten by a country hellbent on industrialisation. The UK was also nearing its peak of colonial expansion, and British settlers were needed as part of the strategy to maintain influence and control over such an enormous empire.

For some, it was not the prospect of higher wages but of finding employment at all that led them to look abroad. Towards the end of the nineteenth century, it turned out industry didn't necessarily need as many workers as it had, and the 'surplus' were encouraged to look for work elsewhere. People were, for the most part, moving voluntarily, but this was less the case for some poor families who were given assistance from charities to emigrate, with much less generous help offered if they refused. Much like encouraging 'surplus' single women to emigrate, this was a way of offloading people seen as unwanted and a burden.[15] Often when people emigrated, it was on a one-way ticket to destinations which took weeks to reach by boat. They left with next to nothing and with no guarantee that they would ever be able to afford a return journey.

But if politicians and charities had thought there was too much surplus labour – not to mention humankind in general – in the late nineteenth century, it was nothing compared to what was coming down the pipe. Once the dust had begun to settle from the First World War, one thing became clear at home: the major industries – shipbuilding, coal mining, steel and cotton manufacture – had gone into terminal decline. Shipbuilding and repair had always fluctuated wildly with demand, and after 1920 there were just not enough people commissioning big ships for the industry to survive at the same scale. It was the same story with steel and iron production: the demand was just not there for Britain's furnaces to continue blasting at the same pace as before the war. Coal production fell by a quarter during the interwar period and, with 80 million tonnes less of it being mined each year, there was no need for the same quantity of manpower. It didn't help the more than half a million people who were trained to hew coal by hand that, by 1939, 60 per cent of coal was being cut by machines.[16]

Cotton was another 'ailing giant' and one which saw the most drastic fall. The industry had bounced after the 'cotton famine' caused by the American Civil War in the 1860s and, by the time of the First World War, 80 per cent of British cotton was being exported and accounted for two thirds of the global trade.[17] By the mid-1930s, production had halved and exports had fallen by three quarters. The problem for Britain was that other countries had caught up. We had been ahead of the game in manufacturing during the nineteenth century and had also benefited from selling cotton goods to British colonies, which were behind in terms of industrialisation. India had previously bought 2,700 million square yards of British cotton fabric each year; by 1938 it was importing less than a tenth of that amount, having industrialised to the point that it was becoming a global producer itself. In 1870 the UK was responsible for nearly a third of total world manufacturing production in general, before the USA and Russia came along and reduced this to a tenth by the 1930s.[18]

As it became clear that these industries were never going to return to their former size and importance, Britain discovered the new problem of mass unemployment. In 1911, when industry was still thriving, the UK had introduced its first compulsory unemployment insurance scheme, which meant around 2.5 million workers had to contribute part of their salary to a rainy-day fund in case of job loss. By 1920, though, it was obvious that the potential for mass unemployment was far bigger than that, and the scheme was extended to around twelve million workers.[19] The other issue was that the unemployment benefit was only supposed to cover six months of being out of work, but by 1927 there were so many claimants who had gone beyond this time limit that it had to be extended.[20] This all made the scheme phenomenally expensive. By 1928 it was £25 million in debt; by 1931, £75 million.

The Wall Street Crash of 1929 delivered a knockout blow to Britain's flagging industries. The unprecedentedly large financial crash saw the United States stock market lose nearly 90 per cent of its value, triggering the Great Depression in the USA and having knock-on effects for economies all around the world. Britain, a close economic neighbour of the US, was hit full-on by the ripple effects and even more people found themselves out of work.

Mass unemployment meant that living conditions in certain parts of the UK began to stagnate or even became considerably worse. Throughout the 1920s, in some parts of the north-east of England, as well as Wales and Scotland, living standards were the same or worse than they had been twenty-five years previously. There were still tens of thousands of people living in unsafe and overcrowded slum housing in Liverpool, Manchester, Birmingham and London's East End.

In Scotland in 1931, over 330,000 people were still living in one-room dwellings (although no houses without windows had been recorded since 1911). Around forty thousand of these one-room 'houses' had more than three people living in them, and in one part of Ayrshire a quarter of the population was living in such conditions.[21]

Inequality began to grimly manifest itself through widening differences in child mortality. In Great Britain overall, the child mortality rate had fallen dramatically from 142 deaths per 1,000 live births in 1901 to 68 per 1,000 in 1931.[22] But while in the south-east the child mortality rate was 47 in the early 1930s, it was 63 in Wales, 68 in the north of England and 77 in Scotland.

There were also places where the rate started to rise. Wigan, in the north-west, went from a rate of 93 infant deaths per 1,000 in 1928 to 110 in 1933. In St Helens, Merseyside, the rate had risen to 116 per 1,000 by 1933. At the same time, the infant mortality rate in affluent Oxford had shrunk to around 32 per 1,000 births and was still on the decline. These differences are remarkable: one in nine babies born in St Helens would die in 1933 – one in nine! – compared with one in thirty-one in Oxford.[23] Various social investigations at the time found high levels of ill health and malnutrition among children in places such as Newcastle upon Tyne. The time when life could be relied on to continuously improve had slipped away like a dream.

Wanting to get a handle on this situation, Parliament decided that the 1931 census should collect official, comprehensive statistics on people who were 'out of work'. In England and Wales, it was found that 12.7 per cent of males and 8.6 per cent of females over the age of fourteen were out of work, although there was huge variation across different areas and industries. Overall, one in five miners, one in three cotton weavers and two in five shipbuilders was unemployed.[24] The situation was worst for people over the age of sixty who still intended to work, and far more of them were out of work than in it, in certain industries. The census report did, however, take the trouble to point out that some industries continued to show a healthy demand for labour: Catholic priests and nuns, for example, were almost never out of work – not that nuns were really 'employed' as such.

But unemployment was at staggering levels in some specific places. Over a third of men in the mining and shipbuilding districts of South Shields, Sunderland and Merthyr Tydfil were out of work, as were over 40 per cent of female workers in the cotton-weaving town of Blackburn. These places came to be described as 'depressed areas', later rebranded as 'special areas' in the mid-1930s so as to make it seem like they were getting more attention than others, rather than less.

On 30 October 1936, a column of around two hundred men draped in waterproof groundsheets made a forlorn spectacle as they walked through the pouring rain into north London. They entered the capital on blistered feet to a marching tune played on harmonicas and a smattering of applause from the curious suburban onlookers. They had just completed a march of 291 miles from Jarrow, in the north-east of England, which was intended to grab the attention of Parliament and pressure them into doing something to save their town.

The closure of Jarrow's shipbuilding industry had removed the only realistic source of employment for a large number of men. Fifteen years after the shipping industry tanked, Jarrow's shipyards were still silent – growing over with rust and seagull droppings – and its men restless. Unemployment in September 1935 was at 73 per cent. Infant mortality in Jarrow was 114 per 1,000 at the same time that it was 47 in the south-east of

England.[25] No new business had swooped in to save the town and unemployment had not abated on its own.

After a proposal to establish a steelworks fell through and Jarrow was told it 'must work out its own salvation', anger galvanised the unemployed workers.[26] The local MP, Ellen Wilkinson, got involved and Jarrow Council voted to approve a march to London, not only to petition Parliament but to '[rouse] public opinion in England to the plight of Jarrow, and the forgotten areas like it'.[27] Two hundred men were vetted and approved to go, each supplied with a groundsheet, leather and nails for mending their boots, and some rudimentary camping supplies. Ellen Wilkinson marched with them whenever a break from her Parliamentary duties allowed. One sixty-year-old man who didn't make the cut had begged to be part of it, saying, 'I have suffered all that a man may suffer. Nothing that can happen on the road between here and London will be worse than that.' He died before the group returned home.[28]

As the men set off on 4 October 1936, townsfolk waved their handkerchiefs and one woman was heard calling out, 'Good luck to ye, Geordie, and bring yersel back a job!'[29] Almost immediately they picked up a stray dog, which was given the name Paddy and adopted as a march mascot when it became clear he intended to follow the group the whole way. At Chester-le-Street, just one day in, the marchers were informed by the Unemployment Assistance Board that their benefits had been stopped for the duration that they were on the road.[30] Two weeks later, the government issued a statement deeming such marches 'altogether undesirable' and announcing that Cabinet ministers would be banned from meeting with the men in London.[31] The press, on the other hand, largely sided with the marchers. Even newspapers which disapproved of the protest tactic acknowledged that

Jarrow had 'been treated shabbily, even shamefully'.[32] In the wealthy, Conservative-leaning town of Harrogate, they were welcomed and given shelter for the night in an army barracks.

The marchers were met with many such acts of generosity and kindness. A group of medical students who volunteered to travel with them ended up diagnosing a great many ailments that had been troubling the under-nourished men for years. They managed to secure pro bono dental treatment and even a tonsillectomy for one of the marchers en route. Some of the 'Jarrow Crusaders' were, if anything, suffering from 'over feeding', chortled local north-east newspaper the *Shields Daily Gazette*. It was true though that the medics were reporting large numbers of the men presenting themselves after meals to ask for indigestion remedies, their stomachs not being accustomed to anything but meagre quantities of plain food.[33] After staying the night in Leicester drill hall they were sent on their way with a breakfast of beef and tea, and each given a large packet of cigarettes. The makers of the nourishing meat-based drink Bovril at one point seemed to unofficially sponsor them as an advertising opportunity. No wonder some of them were feeling a bit queasy.

In Leicester, shoe-makers from the local cooperative society sat up all night repairing marchers' boots for free, while an autumn storm rattled the windows.[34] In Leeds, a newspaper proprietor had treated the men to a free meal, with beer, and in Barnsley the mayor arranged for the municipal baths to be heated so that they might soothe their aching muscles (Ellen Wilkinson reported having exclusive use of the 'ladies' foam bath'). One marcher was amused to receive a letter at Loughborough, saying that people had been turning up at his house back in Jarrow to pay respects after a rumour had circulated that he had died. He was very much alive and confirmed this to the press for the avoidance of doubt.[35]

Other stretches of the journey were comfortless and bleak, like the twenty miles between Bedford and Luton in a relentless downpour where the wind blasted so hard that it drove rain between their teeth. Despite the help from the cobblers of Leicester, boots were wearing thin, and the blisters were so bad that people's socks had to be cut off. But they arrived in London on schedule, to the flashing of press cameras and the approving comments of journalists that they looked 'the picture of a walking "distressed area"'.[36]

They presented their petition to Parliament along with postcards and letters from Jarrow, the Commons galleries creaking with rows of the weary marchers. The petition was received, a couple of MPs asked questions, and within minutes the House had moved on to other things. Nothing was done by the government, and although some business owners suggested they might step in and help, nothing significant came in the way of new jobs. Disappointed, the marchers slowly returned to Jarrow, slightly better fed but still with empty hands. Ironically, it would not be a peaceful march but the outbreak of the Second World War which would revive Jarrow's steel and shipbuilding industries, albeit temporarily and at the cost of attracting bombardment from the Luftwaffe.

It was not the only, or even the first, 'hunger march' to take place during this period, although the Jarrow march is the best known. The first hunger march was organised by the National Unemployed Workers' Movement (NUWM) in 1922 and involved around two thousand people marching from various starting points into London to draw attention to their desperate state. In 1931 it organised a march of mineworkers from South Wales to Bristol to demonstrate at a convention of the General Council of the Trades Union Congress (TUC), where they were met by a cordon of police.[37] In 1932, a Great National Hunger March was organised and the Metropolitan Police put two thousand officers on standby in anticipation of their arrival in London. Some said that a subsequent rally in Hyde Park had attracted ten thousand attendees; others said a hundred thousand.[38] Rallies of twenty-five to thirty thousand people in Hyde Park and Trafalgar Square started to become a regular occurrence.

It was the first time individuals had physically assembled in such large numbers, or been aware of a purposeful connection with so many others. Mass demonstrations had, of course, occurred in the past. The Chartist movement, which began in the 1830s and campaigned for democratising reforms including universal male suffrage, had managed to successfully assemble and coordinate people in their thousands. A petition presented to Parliament in 1839 contained the signatures of 1.3 million men, which would have had to be gathered literally by hand from all around the country. Trade unions had also pulled off mass acts of industrial and civil disobedience, and the women's suffrage movement had managed to successfully coordinate the activity of many cells all around the country.

Mass protest reached its zenith in May 1926, when workers from all industries – but largely those in manual labour and transport – went on strike for nine days. This General Strike was unprecedented in scale, involving around 1.7 million workers and leading to the estimated loss of 162 million working days.[39] The dispute was over proposals by coal mining companies to decrease the hourly pay of their workers, in response to the reduced profitability of British coal exports, and the TUC had mobilised workers in other industries to strike in solidarity. It came to nothing. The miners were not able to hold off pay cuts in the end, and the government responded to the episode by introducing a law, the Trade Disputes and Trade Unions Act 1927, banning sympathy strikes.

If little was done to alleviate unemployment, it was not for a want of evidence on the nature of the problem. The interwar period saw a new boom in social research, which was focused like a microscope on conditions in the 'special' – meaning depressed – areas.[40] Parliament and the government commissioned numerous official investigations and inquiries into social and industrial conditions.

Seebohm Rowntree, the pioneering social researcher, did another round of his poverty survey of York in 1936. When comparing people's income and situation against the poverty line he had set in 1899, just below 7 per cent of the city's population were in primary poverty in 1935, about half of what he had found the first time around. But after updating his poverty line to reflect higher costs of living in the 1930s, this figure rose to 9 per cent. And looking specifically at the working classes, Rowntree calculated that around a third of them were in primary poverty in the 1930s – a thoroughly joyless state in which there was essentially no spare income after the basics of survival were accounted for. A lot of the observations he made on individual households show the uptake of various new forms of assistance – school milk, unemployment benefit, National Health Insurance benefit, money from the Public Assistance Committee.* But these schemes were generally contributory; in other words, you had to pay in to get something back. Rowntree's evidence clearly showed that this was not really working for the poorest. The assistance that was available was enough to keep them alive but not to alter their situation in any permanent way.[41]

It is perhaps because there was so much evidence produced on the 'depressed' areas that the actions of the government were regarded as so inadequate in response. It did take some steps to try to create jobs, but this barely made a dent in the number of the unemployed and there seemed to be no appetite for big or radical ideas.[42] Yet no one could deny that millions of people were out of work: the statistics said so, plain as day. We even knew who was worst affected, since our cherished census was recording hundreds of thousands of people 'out of work' in specific industries. But there were no comparisons being made to Crystal Palaces full of the unemployed. If there had been, at the peak of unemployment in 1932, it would have revealed that it would have taken twenty-five days for Britain's unemployed to file through the structure at full capacity.†

Another issue might have been that even though these numbers were large, the people affected were still a minority within the country as a whole. For most people in the UK,

---

* The replacement established in 1930 for the Boards of Guardians who used to oversee the distribution of poor relief.
† Incidentally, the Crystal Palace, which was at that time being relocated to Sydenham, south London, was destroyed by fire in 1936. Winston Churchill remarked that it was 'the end of an age', and it really was a fitting symbol for the demise of Britain's empire.

life was getting *better*. For those who were in work, labour conditions were the best they had ever been, and a lot of people had noticeably more spending money and free time. Average working hours had gone down by a third since 1870, meaning that instead of a typical worker devoting sixty hours per week to work, he or she was now working around forty-six – equivalent to getting at least one, if not two, full days of time back in the week.[43]

The marvel of electricity also revolutionised life for many people. Across the country, homes were being connected to the grid at a considerable pace: in 1920 just one in seventeen houses had electricity; by 1930 it was one in three, and by 1939 it was two in three.[44] Europe's largest power station had been constructed in Chelsea in 1905, and other huge ones were built in Stourport, Greenwich, Battersea and numerous other places during the 1920s and 30s. All this coal-, oil- and gas-fired power meant that ordinary people could have devices in their homes which, at the flick of a switch, would animate themselves and start doing the washing, cooking and cleaning. Cookers, electric irons, radios, gramophones and even vacuum cleaners became ubiquitous in middle-class households.

This was accompanied by massive improvements in housing. After the First World War, substantial sums were invested in housebuilding to provide 'homes for heroes' and to address the damp and dingy state of much of Britain's housing. In the 1920s, three million new homes were built, and one million more in the decade after. One popular development style was to plop thousands of units of pleasant but rather plain, identical houses with gardens front and back onto roads which had a slight wiggle in them to provide some semblance of 'nature'. Buildings were often mock Tudor in style, with details in pebbledash, timber and brick. The suburbs, as we still know them now, were born, in areas such as Becontree in east London, and Solihull, near Birmingham. A large portion of the new housing was in the south-east, creating the leafy cul-de-sacs and semi-detached dwellings that typify parts of Surrey, Essex and Hampshire. This abundance of relatively affordable new homes provoked a population boom in these areas and 60 per cent of the total population increase in the UK during the interwar years was around London.

Life on a steady income for people living in the south-east or the Midlands was pretty sweet. Although wages had not really risen, the cost of living had become considerably cheaper by the 1930s, and so people felt their money stretch a lot further.[45] The availability of new contraceptive products meant couples could put off having children until later, and with the holy trinity of vacuum cleaner, cooker and iron doing the bulk of housework, there was ample time for going out to socialise and dance, and driving out of town at the weekend for a hike or a minibreak to Clacton-on-Sea. In 1901, around one and a half million workers had paid annual leave but by the 1930s fifteen million people were taking holidays each year, chiefly to the seaside.[46] The small town of Skegness hit the big time in 1937 when Billy Butlin chose it as the site for his first all-inclusive holiday camp. By the 1930s, it was also increasingly common for middle-class families to have a car; those that didn't had the option of tram, bus or train. One of the first electric cinemas opened in 1910 in Notting Hill – and is still running over 110 years later – and by 1939 there were no fewer than five thousand cinemas operating across the UK.[47] The well-off in 1930s Britain were already living the life of the 1950s or 60s.

But this was an era of contrasts. There were parallel lives: one blasting off towards a modern future and another left stranded at the launchpad, abandoned by both the old world and the new. There was a feeling of greater connectedness, while at the same time new political divisions were emerging.

One development which might have done more than anything else to connect people and to establish mass consciousness of social issues was the creation of the BBC in 1922. Very quickly, everyone became connected by the radio and on the same cultural wavelength at the national level. Thanks to this wider-than-ever proliferation of different viewpoints (and everybody now being aware of the news), society started to cleave on a bigger scale than ever around a range of new '-isms' and their associated symbols: socialism, communism, fascism, liberalism, internationalism. The black flag and the red. The phenomenon of identity politics, which we will see emerge later on in our story, in many ways starts here. But mass culture also provided a window into completely different lives and made people realise that their own life might be interesting to others.

The idea that ordinary people could have a public voice quickly morphed into acceptance that their opinions were also deserving of airtime. In 1937, an American called George Gallup introduced opinion polling to the UK, having already made a success of the technique in the United States. The polls involved taking a random sample of the British public each month and asking them to give their honest and anonymised answers to questions on subjects of current and national debate. The very first poll in 1937 asked people whether they thought the grounds for divorce should be made easier, to which the majority (58 per cent) said 'yes'.[48] Over the years, the range of questions expanded to cover all aspects of the trivial and deadly serious. Some were straightforward market research ('Did you buy a hat during the past twelve months?', 'Do you read magazines regularly? If so, which is your favourite?'), many were focused on voting intentions and politicians

('On the whole, do you approve or disapprove of Mr Attlee as prime minister?') and others were gauging where public opinion lay on important policy issues ('Do you think we should or should not make the H-bomb?')[49] Some questions seem to have been asked out of pure curiosity, such as 'What is your normal time for going to bed?' and 'As a child were you afraid of the dark, of burglars, both, or neither?'[50]

But while some of the subjects of these polls might have been trivial, the practice of polling was a hugely significant development for the public at large. Until then, the only people who really had a 'public' opinion, in the sense that what they thought and felt was widely broadcast, were the powerful, the rich and the famous. Now, any individual in the population had a chance of being picked to air their views. It was framed by popular newspapers as a kind of revolution for democracy: that all individual voices were as audible as those of politicians, through the power of speaking together as one.[51] And if anyone – politician or business figure – offered a questionable take on what the opinion was of 'the masses', this could be swiftly debunked by means of a Gallup poll.

It was in a similar spirit that, in 1937, a project began, called Mass-Observation, which was an attempt to amass an 'anthropology of ourselves' through the unstructured observation of ordinary lives. One of its founders was a young anthropologist named Tom Harrisson, who had recently been studying cannibal tribes in the western Pacific and was now trying to observe working life in the north-east of England. Its other founders were Charles Madge, a poet and Cambridge dropout who had a gnawing hunger for authenticity, and film-maker Humphrey Jennings. All three were dissatisfied with the way politicians and journalists presumed to give opinions about 'what the country thinks' when there was no verifiable evidence, short of, in some circumstances, a Gallup poll.

What the man and woman in the street really thought was not on record anywhere, which meant not only that it didn't but *couldn't* really matter in the conversations of the powerful.

Madge, Harrisson and Jennings set out to change that by recruiting hundreds of people to record observations in the form of a diary and sent out observers to make a detailed record of what was going on in certain settings, like pubs and seafront promenades. One diligent observer went as far as to record the number of couples he observed 'embracing' on Blackpool dunes, listed according to the position they were in.[52] The whole idea was for observations to be organic, loose and subjective: to 'tell us not what society is like but what it looks like to them'.[53] Many of the observations capture the mundanities of life: lying in bed smoking a morning cigarette; eating eggs for breakfast and a pork chop for dinner; simply walking around in the evening for want of any other entertainment; airing opinions on party politics, the betting pools and horoscopes. They also capture a startling parade of kooks and oddballs, and many unfiltered accounts which seem totally at odds with the crisp, restrained style of official communications.[54]

Mass-Observation was an immediate success, and thousands of keen observers continued filling out diaries throughout the 1940s. Like Narcissus gazing into a pool, we became enraptured by the sight of our individual humanity reflected in a multitude of others. And before long, as the 1930s came to a cataclysmic end, we would be brothers and sisters in arms again.

10
All for One and One for All

Britain entered a state of war in 1939 for the second time in twenty-five years. It was early September and the public had become aware over the past months that war in Europe was all but unavoidable. In the spring a call had already gone out for people to sign up for the armed forces and for national service on the home front, and hundreds of thousands of people had registered. Public awareness campaigns had shown how to prepare your home against an air raid and how to plan for food shortages by starting a vegetable garden. Railings were being taken down to bolster the country's supply of metal for the making of armaments.

On Sunday 3 September, most people were likely pottering around their homes enjoying a day of rest when at 11.15 a.m. a radio broadcast interrupted the usual programming. Through the crackling airwaves came the voice of Prime Minister Neville Chamberlain, announcing that, as of eleven o'clock, having received no assurance that Hitler's army would cease its invasion of Poland, Britain was now at war with Germany. 'There is no chance of expecting that this man will ever give up his practice of using force to gain his will,' Chamberlain gravely informed the people. 'He can only be stopped by force.' Like the Great War that was still fresh in the minds of many, this would be another full national effort in which every person would be expected to play their part. The assembly bell had been rung once again, calling people together: 'you will report for duty in accordance with the instructions you have received'. Chamberlain's broadcast was followed by a series of instructions from the BBC about what would happen from this point forth, including what should be done in case of an air raid. Just eight minutes later the first air-raid sirens sounded in central London. Staff at the BBC, ignoring the instructions they had just given, threw on tin helmets and rushed to the roof of Broadcasting House to watch the bombs falling. It turned out to be a false alarm.[1]

Three years later, in 1942, it was doubtful that anyone would have been rushing to the rooftop at the sound of an air-raid siren. War had consumed every aspect of life. People had been uprooted and transplanted all across the country and beyond. Swathes of the capital and other towns and cities had been completely obliterated by enemy bombs, or transformed beyond recognition through the churning of the domestic war machine.

In a compound of warehouses in Hayes, west London, a nightwatchman was surprised by the unmistakable gleam of fire in one of the buildings. By the time the fire brigade arrived, flames had engulfed the entire warehouse, and it was all the firemen could do to stop it spreading across the whole estate. The blaze left nothing but the smouldering carcass of the building and a few charred pieces of paper lying in soggy piles outside in the mud. These were the original returns of the 1931 census of England and Wales. All the individual names, family records, details of who lived where and who did what – a priceless, irreplaceable historical record – had gone up in smoke. Not a single record could be salvaged.

It being the height of war, it was speculated as to whether

the warehouse had been the victim of an enemy attack. There had been six paid firewatchers on duty that night and the building itself – given that it was storing large quantities of paper – had been fitted with a special hydrant system. Despite this, reports concluded that 'the fire was not occasioned by enemy action' but was, most likely, the result of negligence.[2] A police investigation wasn't able to shed much more light on the cause and all it could offer was that the fire 'may have been due to a lighted cigarette thrown down by one of the firewatchers'.[3] Owing to the lack of concrete evidence, no one was ever held accountable. And in 2031, when the census records would have been unsealed after a hundred years and we would have been able to pore over the details of our relatives' personal lives, we will instead have nothing.* We won't have any records to look at in 2041 either, because there was no census that year due to the war.

The First World War had come as more of a surprise to people in the UK. War was declared on Germany on 4 August 1914 but, this being in the time before radio, there was no immediate announcement to the public. The following day, Prime Minister Asquith announced to the House of Commons that 'since eleven o'clock last night a state of war has existed between Germany and ourselves' and Parliament approved an immediate budget of £100 million for the war effort (the equivalent of around £10 billion in today's money).[4] There was hope that the war would be 'over by Christmas' – a short, sharp affair to bonk the Kaiser on the nose, send him back to his cage and reshuffle a few colonial possessions during

---

* As mentioned in Chapter 2, the hundred-year rule is not statutory so it would have been up to the government to agree to its release, although a hundred years is now the standard.

the general shake-up. In fact, the war would drag on for four years, cost thirty-two times as much as its original budget and result in the death or wounding of around two and a half million men and boys.

At the end of 1914 things still seemed to be going relatively to plan – although clearly the whole being home for Christmas thing had not worked out. The Allies had held off the German advance towards the Channel, which was a strategic necessity, but it had come at a great cost in human lives. There had been fifty-eight thousand British casualties in the first battle of Ypres alone.[5] Both sides had literally dug in to wait out the winter in freezing trenches. Britain's generals had started to talk about needing *a great many* more men. But the question was how to find them.

In June 1915, a Bill was introduced into Parliament for the for the compilation of a National Register (NR). This was to be a stock take of the country's manpower – like a census – but with a power provided to the government to use the information to organise labour towards the war effort. As the president of the Local Government Board Walter Long, MP innocently put it, while announcing the Bill, 'Before we decide what we are going to do with our resources in a time of great national crisis ... we must ascertain as carefully as we can what those resources are.'[6]

'What was the need for it?' some people asked, given that the British forces appeared to have an ample supply of voluntary recruits. 'Amateur help,' wrote a columnist in the *Nation*, 'has poured out from men and women in an abundance with which the authorities have not been able to cope' and it was true that hundreds of thousands of people had already put themselves forward (including eighty thousand women) by the middle of 1915.[7] Long himself even appeared to suggest that men and women were spontaneously amassing themselves into a defensive force, like a disturbed beehive which had spewed out 'a busy crowd of little insects determined to defend themselves, their lives, and their possessions'.[8] Many people were leaping to the country's defence, not least after the shores of Scarborough, Hartlepool and Whitby had been attacked in 1914 by the German fleet in the manner of a Viking raid, killing several hundred people.

But an initial flurry of indignant volunteers would not be enough for the total war situation which the government had to consider. And the government was clearly not proposing a stock take of the country's human 'resources' just for curiosity's sake. As sections of the press rightly speculated, it had to be, in effect, 'a preparatory scheme for bringing pressure to bear on the men and women of the working classes ... either to enlist or to change their occupations'.[9] In other words, it was laying the groundwork for conscription. Obvious as this possibility was, the government at first insisted that it saw no need to conscript. If people had not yet come forward, Long asserted, they were not slacking out of an absence of patriotism but out of a natural English shyness and a lack of clear instructions. The NR would make it easier to target certain groups and suggest that they volunteer. It all sounded very dignified, for now.[10]

Motives aside, the reason we couldn't just use the 1911 census was because it was already out of date. The ambition was for the NR to be a live database or population register.[11] Instead of being a snapshot of each individual in the population on one particular day, like a census, it would constantly be updated. Babies born are added to the register and people who die are removed. When people change their address or their name, or they marry or divorce, the register is updated.

Despite rumblings of concern – and after a complete exemption for Ireland – the National Registration Act was passed in August 1915. Two days later, instructions went out to local authorities to recruit twice as many enumerators as they would for a census (around sixty-five thousand in total) and for them to go from house to house, making a list of all persons there between the ages of fifteen and sixty-five.[12] By 30 September 1915, a population of around 21,631,000 had been registered and certificates were then sent out to each individual as proof of their registration.[13] Due to the season, nearly a million people had been enumerated away from home because they were on holiday.[14] The records were transferred to cards – one card for each individual – which contained a person's name, sex, age, address and occupation, with occupation having been condensed to forty-six categories for men and thirty for women, rather than the usual five hundred or so that would be listed in a census. The idea was that *if* it should be decided that more recruits were needed, the government could select, say, twenty thousand young men from 'some unimportant luxury trade' and contact them to encourage their enlistment.[15] Despite the government's insistence that voluntary recruits were coming thick and fast, it is notable that an immediate step taken was to duplicate all the cards for men aged eighteen to forty-one and send these to the local recruiting authority.

In October 1915, the Registrar General had provided the government with statistics from the completed NR, showing that, at a 'rough estimate', there were 4.4 million men of military age in England and Wales, around 1.4 million of whom could be deemed 'available' for service without disrupting the economy.[16] These figures were taken up by Lord Derby, the Director-General of Recruiting, who applied a less cautious approach. Largely ignoring the notion of essential workers – those in infrastructure and key services who could not be spared – Derby used the figures to claim that there were around 2.2 million military-age men in England and Wales who had so far failed to present themselves for service. The focus fell on the one million of these who were single men, and whom it was felt should put themselves forward first or, as Derby vaguely threatened, be encouraged 'by other means'. The press made much of these figures and of the 'Derbies' who were avoiding military service.

In January 1916, military conscription was introduced in Great Britain. But still, in some cases, men failed to appear following call-up and were unable to be found. '"Derby men" missing', ran one article about the discovery in Hartlepool that a number of men had seemingly given fake names and addresses, or had moved. Similar scenes unfolded in Birmingham, where around ten thousand people could not be located because they were not at the address listed on their form. But although this was portrayed as draft-dodging, it's likely that most of the failure to find people came down to problems with record-keeping. Even as Derby was compiling his figures on the 2.2 million missing men, the Registrar General was pointing out that the central enlistment records were not up to date: thirty out of sixty-four recruitment offices had not notified the GRO of a single enlistment as of November 1915, even though hundreds of thousands of people had signed up.[17] It was also clear that, although people were supposed to notify their local authority when they moved house, so that their record could be updated, in many cases this was not being done. The scheme was dealing with a hundred thousand changes of address every month and those were just the ones we knew about. In the general chaos, it was hardly surprising that in a city the size of Birmingham, ten thousand people would slip off the radar. It really wasn't guaranteed that the statistics showing 1.4 million, or even 2.2 million, un-enlisted, available men were accurate.

But it certainly wasn't a good look for the registration scheme. After being presented as a harmless stock take, it had almost immediately been used to 'expose' millions of apparent slackers (the finger being pointed in particular at unmarried men). Conscription eventually was introduced, in 1916, with the NR playing a key role in justifying this and in enabling the authorities to track people down.*

This mess frustrated Sylvanus Vivian, an official at the Ministry of Food who was overseeing food rationing. He was not surprised the register had become a mess, because it had lost public buy-in completely.[18] He had also developed a register to keep track of people receiving food rations and considered this to have gone much better. When people needed rations, they had to send in a form and then would be posted a ration paper and eight weeks' worth of food coupons.[19] The key feature of this system was that if an individual didn't keep the record of their current address up to date, they would not receive the coupons: in other words, accuracy was guaranteed by self-interest. Dealing with the deluge of address-changes was, however, an enormous amount of work, and by the time the rationing scheme was up and running there were six hundred 'girls' employed on the register, working around the clock to update and re-index all the cards.[20]

When the war ended in 1918, the NR and the food ration register were both swiftly dismantled. Vivian's work on rations had, however, impressed the higher-ups, and in 1921 he was promoted to Registrar General.

*

---

* The Military Service Act in January 1916 introduced conscription for all single men aged between eighteen and forty-one. In November 1917, responsibility for recruiting shifted to the Ministry for National Service. In 1918, an amendment was made to the National Registration Act so that boys who had missed the initial registration because they were under fifteen years of age at the time could now be brought on to the register. Although the age of army enlistment was eighteen, records suggest that more than a hundred thousand boys under the age of eighteen were recruited to the Royal Navy.

For hundreds of years, it was common practice in the UK – and in many other places – for small areas like parishes or villages to have a local population register. This was because parish clerks, who were typically linked to the church, were responsible for keeping track of births, deaths and marriages. They would also often compile naughty lists of non-churchgoers, to fill in the blanks for those people who were eschewing baptisms and funerals. It was not until the twentieth century that some European countries tried properly to construct versions of this on a national scale. The Netherlands had a live population database in the 1930s and Iceland achieved a full population register in 1953, followed swiftly by the other Nordic countries.

The argument for having such a register is essentially that it avoids the problem of the data going out of date. Even data which is one year or even one month out of date can be borderline useless, if it is very detailed public policy planning that you want to do. The other main reason for adopting a population register is that it creates a link between every single individual and the state. Although in the UK every birth must be registered, from that point onwards the government would have to go through a laborious process of searching different databases and figuring out exactly who you are among all the people who have the same name if it wanted to figure out where you were and what you were doing. For some people, this is precisely the argument for *not* adopting a population register.

When the declaration of war went out in August 1939, Registrar General Vivian was good and ready. Already nearly a year earlier, peers and MPs had started debating the merits of compiling a new population register and had been primed to expect one when war was announced. A National Registration Bill passed through Parliament without any real opposition at the start of September, with MPs agreeing that '[in] time of war up-to-date statistics as to man-power and as to the general population both on the producing and the consuming side of the nation's activities are absolutely essential'.[21] There was no need for vagueness on the part of government as to the NR's role, nor for conspiracy theorists to claim that it was a prelude to conscription: the day before, Parliament had passed the National Service (Armed Forces) Act 1939, which enforced full conscription for men between the ages of eighteen and forty-one.

Despite some MPs claiming they had 'not the faintest idea' what the NR would be for, the government had spelled out a clear justification for it this time around. Not only would such a register allow the country to 'make the best use possible of the man-power and the woman-power available', it would also facilitate 'the distribution of food, food supplies, and the preservation of contact between members of families which have been dispersed for example under the evacuation scheme'.[22] Behind the scenes, in Cabinet meetings to discuss the setting up of the NR, another argument was that 'it would furnish machinery, more effective than any now available, for rounding up defaulters'.[23]

Vivian had been working throughout the interwar period to advocate for an NR, and even for one which would continue during peacetime. He had strong convictions about the right way of compiling and maintaining one and could be described as a bit of a control freak. A problem, from his perspective, was that the government would not allow a register to be set up until war had been declared. It was too costly, they felt, and it would be too hard to maintain the public's compliance without the justification of an emergency. Besides, introducing compulsory ID cards was seen as sailing far too close to the wind of fascism.

Vivian had devoted a lot of time and energy to figuring out how an NR might work and achieve the maximum level of buy-in from the public. Given his experience in the First World War, he was adamant that the only way to ensure the public provided information – and, crucially, that they notified the registrars when they moved house – was to link it to food rationing. If the announcement was made in advance that the purpose of the register was to ensure everybody got their rations, people would see it primarily as in their own interest.[24] This was a little rich, given that Vivian and his colleagues had been discussing among themselves the use of the register to 'exercise pressure' on people who were trying to evade conscription.[25] He had even suggested in his Sub-Committee on Registration's final report to the government that it would be wise not to advertise 'the ultimate conscription purposes of the scheme'.[26]

After the National Registration Act was passed on 5 September 1939, the new NR was compiled with astonishing speed. The Minister for Health took to the radio to announce that a 'roll-call of the whole nation' would take place on 29 September and that people were encouraged to participate if they didn't want to be left out of the rationing system. Next on the airwaves was Vivian himself, calmly explaining how the enumeration of 'Britain's new Domesday Book' (an odd choice of phrase at the outbreak of war) would go. Households would each receive a registration form in the post before registration day and should fill it in carefully for each individual in the household. On 'Domesday' itself, an enumerator would call to collect the form and, after checking that no one had put their name down as 'Mickey Mouse' or 'Donald Duck', he or she would write out an identity document for each individual on the spot. Enumerators had also been primed to be on the lookout for instances of fraud, including persons who were leading a 'double life' and cases of 'imaginary persons' made up in the hope of trying to secure extra rations. If the enumerator called after hours, they would have to be invited inside, since the streets were already completely dark due to blackout regulations. The ID cards, it was recommended, should be kept on the person at all times, particularly if there was any risk that one might die and need to be identified.

The newspapers had been cooperative, on the whole, and many reminded and encouraged people to fill out their forms by the appointed day. Women were addressed specifically, in case they should feel the need to downplay their age. 'Ladies,' said one newspaper, 'your butcher, baker or grocer won't see your age staring at them from your identity card. It will be a secret, known to a very limited few, who are bound by oath to keep it "dark".'[27] You would have thought people had more to worry about than the butcher knowing their age, but it could be a generational thing.

Filling up National Registration schedules is a big item at many local institutions to-day. Here are some of the regular 150 lodgers at the local Salvation Army Hostel giving their particulars.

Within one week, the registration was all but complete and ID cards had been issued to forty-one million people across the United Kingdom.* A ration book was posted to each household, containing coupons which would be used to buy items which were in controlled supply. From January 1940, butter, sugar and bacon were rationed and, later, items such as tea, milk, eggs, cheese, meat, jam and cereals were added to the list. Some items disappeared almost entirely from the shelves for the duration of the war, particularly fruit that could only be grown abroad. The song 'Yes! We Have No Bananas' was a popular hit on this theme – and some children grew up unsure as to whether bananas were real or some kind of myth made up by adults to trick them.

In terms of information storage, the original forms were collected by the enumerator, who would also note down the ID number issued to each individual. Copies of the register were kept at the local and central level, and whenever an individual moved house they had to notify the local registration office. It was that or lose your next ration book to whoever moved into your old house. Ensuring all these records were updated was immensely fiddly and cumbersome work, which kept hundreds, if not thousands, of people busy throughout the war. Between 1939 and the closing of the register in 1952, over one hundred million changes of address were handled, a quarter of million of them taking place in just one week after a single spate of German rocket attacks.[28]

In 2015, the records from the original 1939 Register for England and Wales were digitised and made publicly accessible online for the first time. Not all of the digitised records are open to the public, most notably because entries for anyone

---

* Members of the armed forces were also registered and separately issued with ID documents.

confirmed or suspected to still be alive are redacted.* But those that have been released are now searchable through the services FindMyPast and Ancestry, which means we can see a snapshot of where and with whom people were living at that time, as we would with a decennial census. In what seems to have been an amusing coincidence, the very first people who appear on the register, with ID numbers AAAA1 and AAAA2, are a Mr and Mrs Start.[29] Eleanor Roosevelt makes a surprise appearance, staying at the Foreign Office that night. Her occupation is given as 'Wife of President Roosevelt'.[30]

In 2024, a record was opened up for a girl who would have been ten years old in 1939 and living in Elham, a small village in Kent.† Her name was Audrey Hepburn-Ruston – yes, that Audrey Hepburn. Better known at the time as 'the little Dutch girl', Hepburn had been sent to live with the Butcher family at Orchard Villa in Elham and attend a nearby private school. Meanwhile her mother, the Baroness Ella van Heemstra, was touring around Germany as a kind of fangirl to Adolf Hitler and an outspoken fascist sympathiser.[31] When war broke out, Audrey was bundled onto one of the last flights to Europe and taken back to Arnhem in the Netherlands. This turned out to be the opposite of a good decision because shortly afterwards the Netherlands was invaded and the family lived under Nazi occupation for years, enduring the 'hunger winter' which saw people resort to eating tulips to survive. Hepburn would go on to become one of Hollywood's most beloved stars thanks to iconic performances in *Roman Holiday* (1953) and *Breakfast*

---

* When an individual in the register reaches what would have been their hundredth birthday, their record is generally opened up, unless they are still alive. Records for people younger than this are generally only opened if the National Archives or FindMyPast sees proof that they are deceased, such as a copy of their death certificate.
† It was me, along with the help of genealogist Dave Annal, who discovered the location of Hepburn's record and had it opened up by FindMyPast in January 2024.

at Tiffany's (1961) and be among the most famous people on the planet, so it is a remarkable and charming oddity that she appears in our wartime register.

We can also see that on 29 September 1939, twenty-seven-year-old Alan Turing was enumerated in Hughenden, near Naphill in Buckinghamshire. His occupation was 'civil servant'. Also present was the owner of the house, Alfred Dillwyn 'Dilly' Knox and his family, and another civil servant named Hugh Foss. Turing, Knox and Foss were not just your standard pen-pushers, however. They were cryptoanalysts at the top-secret codebreaking facility at Bletchley Park. But they had signed the Official Secrets Act, and so had to keep mum even to an enumerator from the NR. All three men would already have been stationed at Bletchley and it's possible they were instructed to be enumerated at a domestic address so as not to draw attention to the facility via a random clustering of civil servants in a country house. The enumerator would have had no idea that he or she was standing among people who would be responsible for some of the most crucial intelligence breakthroughs that would help the Allies win the war.

Bletchley Park was the headquarters for British codebreaking from 1939 until 1945 and employed thousands of men and women who were responsible for receiving, collating, decoding and deciphering intelligence intercepted via all mediums, from all around the world. In July 1939, Polish codebreakers had shared information with Britain on the workings of Germany's Enigma machine, which was used to scramble coded messages. This meant that intercepted messages could be relayed to Bletchley to be deciphered in a matter of minutes. While the Polish spies had only been able to supply the code settings at one point in time, these would periodically change, putting the codebreakers back at square one. Turing developed a crib for figuring out what the code settings were each day and later developed this into a design for a massive system of machines which would work mechanically through all possible combinations with a minimal level of programming, making it possible to crack the code nearly every day. Another codebreaking machine invented by Turing, known as the 'Colossus', is considered to be the first working computer ever built. It was thanks to Bletchley codebreaking that on D-Day the Allies knew the precise location of all but two of the fifty-eight German divisions that were lying in wait on the Western front.[32]

Perhaps understandably, staff at Bletchley Park were not people who had been selected and 'rounded up' via the National Register. When the Government Code and Cypher School (GC&CS) realised in 1939 that it might soon need to dramatically scale up its codebreaking activities, it turned to the universities of Oxford and Cambridge. Classified memos were sent out to deans of colleges and faculties asking them to put forward the names of 'men and women of a professor type' – intelligent people with puzzle-solving skills. Turing came from the mathematics department at Cambridge; Dilly Knox was a papyrologist – someone who deciphers hieroglyphics. Other staff were recruited from the civil service, and GC&CS even compiled lists of chess champions and members of cryptography clubs to look for potential recruits. A lot of the codebreaking work was manual and suited small hands, so around three quarters of recruits were female. Some of the women came from the Women's Royal Naval Service: as one story goes, a group of newly recruited Wrens was told by an officer, 'Raise your hand if you like doing crossword puzzles', and those who did were sent to Bletchley.[33]

After demobilisation, one Wren who had been at Bletchley went to work at the House of Commons Library, causing some Members of Parliament great shock on discovering 'a girl' in the inner sanctum. The woman in question, Roseanne O'Reilly, devised an innovative card-file index to help answer MPs' enquiries which was probably inspired by the system devised at Bletchley to catalogue the huge volume of intercepted information for easy reference. O'Reilly's system had been replaced by a digital database by the time I came to work at the library three quarters of a century later.

It's hard to overstate the importance of data in war – especially in total war, where an entire country has to throw everything at a single focused and collaborative effort. Having precise information on your own population can give a huge boost to efficiency and planning, while having information on your enemy has obvious advantages too. The work of codebreakers at Bletchley resulted in a huge database of scraps of intercepted messages, which were all meticulously indexed (after being translated from anything from German to Japanese). Some snippets of information might not be comprehensible until a further message which gave it more context was intercepted. But this painstaking deskwork was absolutely vital to military success. After intelligence helped the British navy to victory over Mussolini's forces in 1941, Dilly Knox was moved to compose a couple of lines of poetry, which were unearthed when the Bletchley documents were declassified decades later:

> *These have knelled your fall and ruin, but your*
>   *ears were far away*
> *English lassies rustling papers through the sodden*
>   *Bletchley day.*[34]

*

Having very good data on your population can also work to your own disadvantage. In May 1940, German troops invaded the Netherlands and within four days had captured the whole of the country. After the city centre of Rotterdam was annihilated in aerial bombing, the Dutch were forced into surrender and the invaders took control of a highly advanced bureaucracy which was probably then one of the most efficient on earth. The Central Statistics Office effectively had a full population register, in the form of an individual card for each person living in the country, neatly stacked in boxes at the office of each municipality. Over the next year, all Dutch residents were ordered to come forward to collect a photographic identity card and the national register was centralised at an office in The Hague. Files relating to Jews were stamped with a large letter J, as were their identity cards. By requiring these cards to be shown for a range of mundane purposes, the occupiers were able to enforce complete Jewish segregation in everyday life: to shut Jews out of public places, to freeze them out of jobs, to corral them into smaller spaces and, finally, to deport them to prison camps and to their deaths. In total, more than a hundred thousand Jews were transported from the Netherlands to be murdered or otherwise perish in concentration camps.[35] The Frank family knew exactly what to fear when they received a letter from the authorities on 4 July 1941, ordering them to report for deportation.[36] There was no way to hide from a bureaucracy which had eyes in every private place, except to burrow like mice into the hidden spaces behind walls.

It was because of the importance of data that the RAF mounted one of its most audacious raids, in April 1944. A squadron of Mosquitos left RAF Swanton Morley in the east of England in the middle of the day and were flying towards the Dutch coast. In the squadron was a pilot for whom the flat coastline coming into view was a familiar sight. Robbie Cohen was Dutch refugee who had made an extraordinary escape in 1941 by paddling a canoe for fifty hours, all the way from Katwijk to the coast of East Anglia.[37] On arriving, he had joined the RAF and the mission now at hand was particularly close to his heart. In broad daylight, the squadron flew low over The Hague and dropped their payload of explosives and incendiaries onto the Kleykamp building, a relatively innocent-looking government block in the heart of the city. But the building, or rather what was inside, had been very carefully selected for destruction: the Kleykamp contained all the original records of the population register. In a cauldron of flames, thousands of ID cards, photographs, names and addresses were incinerated, and the information cage was partially lifted.

All across the areas occupied by the Nazi regime, information was used as a weapon with which to control people. In 1933, as soon as Hitler became Chancellor, Nazi officials had been appointed to the Central Statistical Office and preparations started for a national census in Germany. Birthplace, which had previously been removed from the census because of fears of discrimination, was reintroduced for exactly that purpose. The Gestapo went to extreme lengths to compile lists of Jews from census data on religion and birthplace, school enrolment records, election registers and even membership lists of Jewish organisations.[38] Data that was supposed to make life easier and even to establish a feeling of 'strength in numbers' through group membership was turned against people.

As well as the Kleykamp bombing, other data repositories were targeted for destruction by the RAF: one squadron in particular came to specialise in low-level precision raids on Gestapo headquarters and bombed targets in Denmark, Germany and France.[39] The Gestapo headquarters in Berlin was destroyed in 1943, and the control room for state surveillance was badly compromised.

Back in Britain, the war was treating ordinary people to a daily ration of tedium and fear. Throughout 1940 and 1941, the population was subjected to the terror of the Blitz, which destroyed residential and industrial properties and left thousands of people dead or injured. Some two million Anderson air-raid shelters were constructed in back gardens; in London people took to sleeping in tube stations once the raids became a nightly occurrence.

From the hundreds of Mass-Observation panellists who carried on observing and keeping diaries during the war, we get many candid reflections of what life was really like. The initial response to the air raids was one of suppressed hysteria. In a Stepney air-raid shelter, one diarist wrote of people screaming and huddling as 'tremendous crashes' shook the whole street, only to lapse into bickering as soon as things went quiet. Coming out after the all-clear sounded, everywhere were 'screams of horror at the sight of the damage', with houses destroyed and thick smoke pouring from the direction of the docks.[40] A few weeks later, half of Stepney's population had left the area altogether, and a 'cheeky sort of attitude' was emerging among the stoics who remained. An observer records a Jewish neighbour joking that the sound of bombs falling onto their shelter was just the sound of somebody dropping potato latkes upstairs.[41] Out in the countryside of Dorset, one woman who had taken up the call to 'dig for victory' by volunteering to work in a vegetable garden was almost giddy from the novelty of the whole situation. 'Here we should certainly not know there was a war on,' she wrote, 'if it was not for the fact that we have our butter on separate dishes with our names stuck on with stamp paper and our jam in jars likewise.'[42]

In Coventry, which was all but obliterated in a largely unexpected aerial attack, there was a sense of 'aching nothingness'.[43] In Southampton, which was targeted for its port, 'people seemed stunned and quiet but, on the whole, not really depressed'.[44] In Plymouth, another important southern port, people were also 'passive ... without any alternative outlets from the emotions which inevitably follow upon nights of random death'. People seemed to be too stunned to formulate any emotional response, with one Mass-Observation observer noting, 'they have no answer to their local disaster'.[45] When the weather permitted, some Plymouth residents slept outdoors in the darkness of the nearby moors, as did people from the targeted port area of Clydebank in Glasgow.[46] One observer copied out a sign observed in a shop whose owner was sleeping on the moors: 'In case of fire, please get drum of paraffin out. It is inside window. Also cat.'[47]

Evacuation took place from cities that were considered at risk of being bombed. Over the course of three days at the start of September 1939, one and a half million evacuees, mainly young children, were sent to the countryside to stay with host families.[48] Statistics from the NR, which was compiled only a few weeks later, show that some parts of London had been drained substantially by evacuation. The population recorded in Finsbury was more than 40 per cent lower than it had been at 1931 census; Holborn, Paddington and Chelsea were in a similar situation.[49] Outside London, some places had more than doubled their population in the space of a year, swelling with evacuees who had been sent to perceived safety in places like Kent and Northamptonshire.[50] A 'bomb census' was carried out in 1940, initially in London, Birmingham and Liverpool, so that the Ministry of Home Security could assess the damage caused by the German attacks.[51] Towards the end of the war, the RAF started producing public maps to show how many targets it had hit in Germany with its own bombing campaign, seemingly to make people feel better about what they were going through.

Somerset House, home of the General Register Office, was hit by a bomb just once during the Blitz.[52] It didn't matter too much from the perspective of the GRO, since the staff had already relocated almost entirely to Southport, a seaside town near Liverpool. Already as early as 1938, the Registrar General had been making plans to move his stash of over a hundred years' worth of paper census records out of harm's way by transporting them up the River Thames.[53] This was how they had eventually ended up at Hayes, where the 1931 records were later immolated by accident. Up in Southport, accommodation had been found to house 470 staff along with 13,000 cubic feet of paperwork associated with the NR and a lot of heavy machinery for sorting punch cards and calculating figures. In those days, we must recall, procedures which could now be done on a laptop required a room full of wardrobe-sized machines connected by a jungle canopy of hot wires.

The staff seemed to have been relatively settled at Southport, because when a rumour went around that they would be moving again, to Blackpool, it triggered 'strong feelings' among them. Relocation to a distant part of the country was, according to an angry staff communiqué, already 'soul-destroying' enough but the prospect of Blackpool was beyond the pale. At a union meeting, members agreed 'to resist by every possible means any move except back to London'.[54] 'We are prepared to do anything to "bust" this Blackpool scheme,' one employee told a local newspaper, while another claimed that 'loyal women workers' were 'so fed up that they were contemplating resigning and joining the ATS', the women's branch of the army.[55] 'Death before Blackpool' – put that one on a postcard. In the end, the move was abandoned, if it ever had been a plan at all.

When the war came to an end, almost six years to the day since it had started, Britain was left battered and bruised in every possible way. Over 366,000 people had been killed, one in six of them civilians, and around the same number had been wounded, a quarter of them civilians.[56] The economic damage from financing the conflict and from the destruction of industrial assets inflicted by German bombs was quite simply crippling. But we had resisted, we had fought back, and we had won.

It's unclear how much of a role the NR played in steering Britain to victory, because where would one even start in terms of trying to work that out? The GRO did try to calculate the contribution of the register in a post-war report, claiming that it boosted the war effort by 'securing the registration of over 100,000 men ... and of well over 500,000 women' who had not complied with the requirement to enlist for national service or offer themselves for employment.[57] We probably need to take this with a pinch of salt, since we really don't know that they wouldn't have eventually signed up during six long years of war. What the register probably did give us, and what is much harder to quantify in terms of benefit, is a clearer idea of where people were. We knew where all the evacuated children were, we knew how many rations would be needed in a particular place, and when someone died we knew right away where to find their next of kin.

This time after the war ended, the NR didn't disappear overnight. Because food shortages continued, so too did rationing, which meant the register continued to be updated until 1952. It became quite integral to some functions of government and by 1950 was being used by thirty-nine government departments.⁵⁸ It was also still a requirement to carry an ID card when out in public that entire time.

The door had been left ajar to consider carrying on a population register indefinitely. The benefits were certainly appealing to a nation embarking on the creation of the biggest public structure in its history (bigger even than the Victorian sewers): the welfare state. But ultimately counterarguments about civil liberties were too compelling to ignore. And who would not be wary of identity cards and public registers now that the truth was out about how such things had been used in the Third Reich to strip people of all privacy and protection? When the NR was introduced in 1939, some had already foreseen a slippery slope from ID cards to more dehumanising methods of tagging people. Some MPs had innocently suggested printing everyone's ID number on a metal disc that could be worn on a chain around the neck, like military dog tags, so that they could be identified in the event of a violent death.[59] 'You might as well tattoo people,' was the response of another Member, who was against the registration system as a whole.[60]

Sylvanus Vivian retired in 1945 and so didn't get to try to steer through his vision of a population register extending into peacetime. It's clear, though, that it was still very much the wish of the GRO to continue with the system as it was.[61] Statisticians crave order and simplicity (speaking for oneself) and so it's easy to see the appeal of a central population register as a database which is both simple and very versatile. It can provide an instant, current overview and can also be sliced and diced to produce statistics on very specific matters of interest. But it's precisely this power that also makes it so objectionable.

In February 1952, it was confirmed that the government had decided to abolish the requirement for people to carry ID cards. This news was largely greeted with ambivalence, except by a Mr Harry Willcock, of Hadley Wood, Barnet, who posed for press photographers ripping up his ID card. Willcock, 'the fighting Yorkshireman' (from Barnet) had been a vocal opponent of the cards on civil liberties grounds and had become a martyr to the cause after becoming the last person to be convicted for failing to produce their ID card when requested to do so by the police, in December 1950. Willcock suggested people post their old cards to him so that he could sell the 300 tonnes of waste paper to raise an estimated £7,500 for charity (£15,000 with the envelopes). It's unclear whether anyone did.[62]

11

First Born

Edna May Rees had been in labour for eighteen hours as the clock approached midnight on 4 July 1948. Finally, the baby was coming, and she was gearing up for a final push when instead of encouragement from the nurses and midwives, she heard 'Hold on, Edna, hold on!' She held – but then a minute later they were shouting 'Push, push!' and at one minute past midnight her baby girl was brought into the world, the first person to be born on the new National Health Service. At the stroke of midnight, the Amman Valley Hospital in South Wales, like thousands of others across the country, had come under the management of the NHS.

There was no formal changeover ceremony and no snipping of ribbons to open the new service. Medicine is a round-the-clock business, so people went into surgery under the old system and woke up in the new one; one minute Edna was pushing in a charity cottage hospital and the next she was the first maternity patient in a universal free healthcare system. The baby was named Aneira, after Aneurin Bevan, the Health Minister who had by that point become known as the architect of the NHS. It was fitting that the first baby born under Bevan's grand system was from South Wales – Bevan was born and had worked for much of his life as a miner in nearby Tredegar in the Welsh Valleys. Aneira herself would go on to work as a mental health professional in the NHS for twenty-eight years and to credit the service with saving her own life eight times.

The NHS was one of the radical and transformative social policy changes in the UK which happened immediately after the Second World War. There had been a mood shift during wartime towards a new consensus that the state should take on full responsibility for the wellbeing of its citizens. It had been 'the people's war', a full national effort which had dissolved class boundaries like never before. The 1930s had taken a great deal from the poorest sections of society and still they had come out to fight. It was now recognised just how much was owed to so many. The war years and those preceding them had also seen a renaissance of social research, which generated a compelling new body of evidence with which to justify major reforms. The high-profile civil servant William Beveridge, when he announced his proposal for a full 'welfare state' in 1942, made it clear that 'the plan is based on a diagnosis of want. It starts from facts.'[1] Data and big thinking had come together, in the words of Britain's wartime leader Winston Churchill, 'to bring the magic of averages to the rescue of millions'.[2]

Earlier in this book we saw how collecting evidence on the health of the nation gave us vital warnings about the way people were living and led to much-needed public policy reforms. But the vital statistics of the nation were initially quite limited. For a long time, causes of death were more or less the only pointers public health statisticians had to work with, and these could err on the side of unscientific ('sore legge' being, after all, one diagnosis). There was also life expectancy, an estimation of how long a person should on average expect to live, which was usually calculated separately for men and women. In the 1840s, life expectancy for boys at birth was forty years, but because the most dangerous age to be was newly born, boys who made it to the age of two could be expected to live to around fifty-one. By the 1920s, life expectancy at age two had risen to fifty-nine years, although continuing high levels of infant mortality meant life expectancy at birth was fifty-one.[3] Female life expectancy has consistently been higher than male, although the gap had widened from around two extra years of life in 1840s to five extra years in the 1950s.[4]

A century earlier, under the influence of William Farr, it had been proposed to use the census to collect and analyse more information about illness and disability in the population. A question on whether people were 'blind, deaf or dumb' was added to the 1851 census and showed that around 1 in 975 people in Great Britain was blind and 1 in 1,670 'deaf-and-dumb'.[5] In 1871, this question on 'invalidity' was expanded to capture whether a person was '(1) Deaf & Dumb (2) Blind (3) Imbecile or Idiot [or] (4) Lunatic'. These are terms which come directly from the census and seem quite shocking to us now. Even at the time it seems to have been acknowledged that they weren't particularly sensitive. In the 1851 census, it was speculated that the thirty thousand 'idiots or imbeciles' identified might have been an undercount of the true number because families were inclined to keep such information secret, owing to social stigma. Mental illness was regarded as humiliating, and the choice of wording on the census form – which was usually read to respondents by an enumerator rather than by the family in private – was likely not doing much to reduce feelings of shame. Later, in 1901, an alternative categorisation of 'feeble-minded' was introduced, which was supposed to be an improvement.

Policymakers were always keen to respond to information

on the health of the nation. But the measures they took to try to keep us healthier depended both on what it was possible to do at a given time and the prevailing theories as to why exactly our health was at risk. Up until the late nineteenth century – and beyond it, for many people – medical care was a frightful and haphazard offering. Our understanding of the human body was limited and sometimes guided by mistaken but compelling ideas, like the medieval notion that the body was sustained by the balance of four humours (blood, phlegm, black bile and yellow bile). Herbal remedies dispensed by apothecaries or local healers were the sole recourse for many of the poorest in the Middle Ages. Mint, camomile, marshmallow root, vinegar, liquorice and increasingly more exotic New World spices mixed into cordials and tinctures were the only kind of medicines people could generally get their hands on. Leeches were used for blood-letting; prayer and water cures were used if all else failed. Stronger remedies were developed without anything we would consider adequate testing in the eighteenth and nineteenth centuries. Morphine, cannabis, arsenic, tar and strychnine could be found in medicines recommended for relatively minor ailments. Ayer's Cherry Pectoral was a cough syrup which contained alcohol and opium. One spoonful of that and you'd have forgotten all about your symptoms.

An early example of an effective public health policy was the draining of marshland in Essex and Kent, which played a major role in eradicating malaria in the UK. In the 1670s it had been noted that mortality rates were twice as high in marsh areas: 60 deaths per 1,000 people per year compared with 30 in non-marsh areas. The solution – to transform marshland into non-marshland – had the effect of almost levelling the mortality rates by the 1800s, to 21 and 28 deaths per 1,000 people in the respective areas.[6] This was a case of 'environmental medicine', a type of treatment which became increasingly popular. As we saw in the mid nineteenth century, a core belief in the medical establishment was that disease spread itself by means of a miasma or cloud of some kind of evil-doing particles. The outlawing of cesspools and other public nuisances, the construction of sewers, the clearing of the slums and the focus on cleanliness and air flow in hospitals were all other examples of environmental measures.

The Victorian era was when the scale and ambition of public health policy really took a step up. Vaccines for smallpox, typhoid and finally cholera were developed and rolled out. Various Acts of Parliament formalised the medical profession and encouraged local authorities to invest in medical infrastructure.[7] At the beginning of the nineteenth century, there were very few hospitals, as we would understand the word now. People would seek treatment at a dispensary or apothecary – unregulated providers of medicine and minor surgery – if they sought it anywhere at all. The wealthy could call on a physician or surgeon to treat them at home, which was undoubtedly the safest place to be.

Public Health Acts in the 1860s and 1870s enabled local authorities to build hospitals for the people at large, with a particular focus on the poor.[8] Workhouses had also been able to construct their own infirmaries, although numerous reports into the appallingly under-resourced state of these and the experiences of patients made them places of horror rather than sanctuary. Specialist hospitals sprang up, including many which are still renowned within their field today such as Moorfields Eye Hospital and Great Ormond Street Hospital for Sick Children in London. By 1911, there were more than seven hundred hospitals in England and Wales which just specialised in infectious disease, with bed space for a total of thirty-two thousand patients.[9]

Within communities there was often some form of

healthcare provision for the poor supplied by charities and, less often, by community groups established by working people themselves. It was common and indeed fashionable for the wealthy and successful to set up charities, often in their own name. This was often done out of religious beliefs about the importance of helping one's neighbour and performing acts of selflessness; equally, it could be about demonstrating to one's neighbour just how superior one was. During the nineteenth century the number of charitable organisations swelled to a 'full, almost rankly luxuriant bloom', as one historian puts it, with London seeing the founding of at least 170 charities for healthcare alone.[10] In Bristol, five new charities opened in each year of the 1870s, which might not sound like many, but they did tend to have wide and ambitious aims like the 'rescue of prostitutes' and 'civilising the poor'.[11] The experience of people seeking help from these organisations would have varied greatly, depending on where they fell on the scale from serious enterprise to vanity project. Mutual aid groups, building societies, trade unions and support within minority communities (such as the Jewish Board of Guardians) were other options for an exclusive few.

By the turn of the twentieth century, philanthropy had become less fashionable and the provision of healthcare more jaggedly uneven than ever. The conversation turned away from what the wealthy few should be doing to sprinkle down good health and moral instruction, towards what workers could do for themselves. In 1911, national health insurance was introduced (alongside unemployment insurance), which provided compensation to workers who had to miss work due to sickness. At first the scheme covered nearly half of men and one in five women; by the eve of the Second World War, coverage had risen to nearly two thirds of men and under one third of women.[12] Clearly, large numbers of people – in particular women – were still without an official safety net when it came to health, and civil society was expected to pick up the slack. What national health insurance also started was an unofficial two-tier system of healthcare, whereby private patients paying in cash would go in through the front door of a practice while health insurance patients would go in through the side and be seen by the most junior doctor on the staff.

War brought with it a new urgency to address the nation's health. In recruiting soldiers for the Boer War in 1899, it had been noted that many men presenting themselves for enlistment were in very poor health, to the extent that 40 to 60 per cent of them were rejected as 'physically unfit for military service'. A government report from 1904, titled simply 'Physical Deterioration', noted this fact and recommended a wide range of public measures – including formal education on the dangers of alcohol, on cookery and on child-rearing – which targeted the public at the group and individual level. In a hangover of the Victorian idea of poverty as a personal failing, the upshot of this was to open several 'schools for mothers', which did nothing to address the underlying structural reasons why children from poorer families grew up with the worst health.[13]

The First World War had been a medical challenge like no other, with an unprecedented number of casualties and new mass threats to health in the form of chemical weapons. Wartime practices seeped back into British healthcare: blood transfusions, artificial limbs and plastic surgery, and therapies for shell shock and gas poisoning. The war also awakened the public consciousness (or at least that of the people in power) to the fact that infant mortality was still disturbingly high. In 1921, the infant mortality rate was estimated to be around 79 per 1,000 births, while medical experts argued that advanced communities should be capable of achieving a rate of 15.[14] The rate was much higher for the working classes, still sitting at around one in ten babies born to manual labourers. Despite the idea of schools for mothers, the provision of proper post-partum healthcare was extremely sparse. In 1917, two in five midwives had not received any formal training.[15]

Another problem was that the health system was overly complicated, with both too many overlaps and too many gaps. Seven central bodies were responsible for various aspects of healthcare; at the local level there were 1,800 sanitary authorities, 630 boards of guardians, 238 local insurance committees, 318 local education committees and 320 pension committees. The apparatus of social policy had become vast and unwieldy, and was not even delivering what it promised. In 1919, a Ministry of Health was established. A Maternity and Child Welfare Act, passed in 1918, was another turning point, introducing universal maternity care and healthcare for children under five for the very first time.

The Great Depression dealt a further blow to the nation's health. A 1936 study by the Pilgrim Trust of the impact of long-term unemployment uncovered some worrying evidence not only about the physical effects of being underfed and inactive but also about the psychological toll. Looking at the reasons for unemployment among a sample of one thousand sick insured people, it was found that in a third of cases the sickness was a form of mental illness.[16] Four in ten of those who had been unemployed for one to two years were suffering from 'psychoneurosis', which would have included conditions like depression, anxiety and even psychosis. By 1931, there were 446 asylums for the mentally ill in England and Wales which held 184,000 patients (or perhaps more accurately, inmates), up from 90,000 in 1901.[17] The population of people recognised as being severely mentally ill had grown six times as fast as the general population since the turn of the century.

The Pilgrim Trust's report also contains vivid accounts of families in Liverpool living in unheated houses (and some still in cellars) in the dead of winter and going short on food in order to clothe their children. One account described a man who had 'finally given up the unemployment club because literally every penny counted and it cost a penny a week'. The report concluded that 'structural unemployment' was in danger of creating 'an extensive pauper class'. When people could not afford health or unemployment insurance, even when it was offered, there was a significant problem.

By the time of the Second World War, our health system was complete pot luck. A National Survey of Hospitals, which had been done in preparation for the war, had exposed major gaps in provision, and during the war the government ordered a more in-depth survey of 'every institution that might be called a hospital' across the whole of England and Wales. The resulting mega-report, referred to as the 'Domesday Book' of healthcare, showed poor infrastructure, a shortage of beds, a lack of staff and a very uneven spread of specialists around the country.[18] There were still some GPs out there who were self-taught. There was no organisation or planning of specialisms, which had left the whole of Lincolnshire relying on just one gynaecologist.[19] A separate report on the quality of GP services found some 'a positive source of public danger'.[20] The mountain of evidence could no longer be ignored and in 1944 the wartime coalition government published the white paper 'A National Health Service', which set out its vision for a free, universal and standardised health system across the entire country.

At the start of December 1942, the Stationery Office in Whitehall, where official government papers were printed, had suddenly found itself very busy. *Social Insurance and Allied Services*, a paper by an inter-departmental committee formed to look at these subjects, had just been released and was absolutely flying off the shelves. Seventy thousand of them had sold in just the first week. In total, the Stationery Office would sell 250,000 copies of the full report, 350,000 copies of an abridged version and 42,000 copies of a special American edition.*[21] A Mass-Observation participant recalled being surprised at the queues when he turned up to buy one, and on the bus home he was asked by the conductor, 'I suppose you haven't got a spare copy of that?' People were picking up *Social Insurance* to put aside for light reading over Christmas.

It was both unprecedented and slightly surreal that a dry, 300-page government report should be an instant bestseller – but this was no ordinary report. Better known as the Beveridge Report, it was a revolutionary proposal for a full national social insurance scheme and a national health service which would provide a comprehensive cradle-to-grave safety net for all segments of society. In other words, it was the foundation stone of the welfare state and the NHS.

Beveridge was an economist who had been studying the problem of unemployment since well before the First World War, before others had really begun to take notice. He had been appointed to the civil service at the outbreak of the Second World War to work on the organisation of manpower. By this point, however, he was highly respected in academia and was also master of an Oxford college as a prestigious day job. As such he was never really integrated into the civil service culture and also seemed to be viewed by others as

---

* America's reaction was considered crucial because they were bankrolling us to a large extent after the war. Luckily, as early as December 1942 it was being reported that President Roosevelt approved of the plan and was already making arrangements to present similar social security reforms to Congress.

above the requirement to suppress the ego and refrain from partisanship. When Beveridge was tasked with drafting the *Social Insurance* report, it was not wholly anticipated that he would turn it into a manifesto for social revolution.

The report's recommendations were framed around the goal of defeating the 'five giants' of Want, Idleness, Disease, Ignorance and Squalor which would otherwise stand in the way of post-war reconstruction. Beveridge was a scholar and was well aware of the profusion of social research emerging in the 1930s on the subject of Want. The picture consistently emerging was that 'three quarters to five sixths' of poverty cases were 'due to the interruption or loss of earning power'.[22] The statistics also clearly showed an ageing population – this was before the post-war baby boom – which was a disaster waiting to happen unless far more resources were mustered for elderly care. The existing systems of unemployment assistance, poor relief and healthcare where threadbare to the point of disintegration. A 'revolutionary moment in the world's history', Beveridge declared, 'is a time for revolutions, not for patching'.

His proposal was to introduce a scheme of national insurance whereby every person would contribute a small flat fee every week via taxation and in exchange would have uncapped entitlement to a range of welfare benefits: unemployment benefit, medical treatment, widows', orphans' and old-age benefit, workplace injury benefit, and funeral costs. It was a fully costed plan for comprehensive social security. Housewives were not expected to pay national insurance contributions, since they were assumed not to have any income of their own.* Women who were working would be entitled to thirteen weeks' paid maternity leave. In addition, the report

---

* It's worth noting that the report has been criticised for an old-fashioned and sexist attitude towards women's agency.

called for the state to become responsible for achieving full employment (thereby skewering the giant of Idleness), meaning it should manage job creation and the distribution of industries around the country.

To accusations of it being a socialist vision, Beveridge responded that it was not socialism but a straightforward 'common sense' insurance scheme.[23] Not 'from each according to his ability, to each according to his needs', as Marx would have had it, but 'cooperation between the State and the individual' to weave together a strong safety net that would catch us all.

The public reaction to Beveridge's report was intensely positive, particularly among the working classes who were giving their all to the war effort. 'In peace time industry and the state did not need the masses: they were an embarrassment,' reflected one of the Mass-Observation participants. 'Now the need for them is very great.'[24] The Blitz had thoroughly ignored class distinctions and evacuation had thrown together people with very different backgrounds who could now quite literally see how the other half lived. Rationing had affected everyone who didn't have an extensive kitchen garden (it was said that even the royals ate Spam, although one suspects they probably did have a secret food stash), so social equality felt more like a touchable reality than ever. The public were greatly attracted by the idea of a universal social security system, which put dustmen on a symbolically equal footing with dukes.

Surveys commissioned by the government to gauge the scale of this reaction found that 95 per cent of people had heard of the Beveridge Report and that it was the most talked-about subject in the country in the week after publication. The surveys also revealed that the vast majority of people thought that its recommendations should be followed through – particularly the part about a nationalised health system.[25] Tellingly, however, the majority didn't actually think the proposals would come into effect. The *Sunday Mirror* predicted that it would be a 'fight to the last invested penny and the last shred of power' to have the plan implemented against the opposition of vested interests.[26] One woman wrote to her local paper, begging to know, 'How can my husband and I make sure that the Beveridge Report does come true?' The spirited response was that while they alone might have no power to do so, 'all the husbands and wives put together could make it a dashed certainty'.[27] A revolutionary fever was in the air.

Beveridge himself became an instant celebrity and was held in high esteem. Incidentally, he got married just three weeks later in a ceremony officiated by the Archbishop of Canterbury. The bride wore floor-length mink and the reception at the Dorchester Hotel was attended by a full who's who of the political scene.[28]

The government was a little overwhelmed by the public response to the Beveridge Report. Its significance as an 'epoch-making and epoch-marking document' was noted in Parliament, and it was advised that ignoring the revolutionary mood would be a risky move.[29] Nonetheless, the Cabinet went to some pains to distance itself from the report and to avoid making any commitments. The minister overseeing the committee which had produced the report ordered that no members other than Beveridge himself be allowed to sign it, and it was even referred to as a 'private and unofficial inquiry', which clearly it was not meant to be when government resources had been allocated towards it.[30] Initially, while the government worked out its response, the entire civil service was banned from even speaking to Beveridge.[31] The general impression was that he had become ungovernable, had gone well beyond his instructions and created something which now had a life of its own. In the background, however, the civil service had effectively been tasked with putting together early plans for a full welfare state. In 1944, two very important white papers were published, one proposing a national health service and the other agreeing with the proposition that the state should be responsible for achieving full employment.

In the 1945 general election, the Labour Party defeated the governing Conservatives and immediately set to work making Beveridge's proposals a reality, alongside a swathe of reforms including nationalising the railways, utilities and coal mines. In the same election, William Beveridge lost his seat in Parliament, which he had held for just six months. Yes, Beveridge the civil servant had been elected to Parliament in a 1944 by-election, to represent the constituency of Berwick-upon-Tweed for the Liberals. It was all right, though: shortly after he was defeated, he received the title of Baron Beveridge and took his seat in the House of Lords.

The year 1947 was a tough one. The winter had been very harsh, with freezing temperatures and weeks of snow, and the spring which followed it was so wet that farmers couldn't plant crops and livestock were washed away in floods. Food was still in short supply, even though the war was over, and rationing continued. For the first time, in 1947, bread was rationed, and the meat ration was reduced later that year. People were weary and in dire need of some good news.

Aneurin Bevan (pronounced 'A-nye-rin' hence its shortened form, Nye) had about as different an upbringing to William Beveridge as it was possible to have. While Beveridge had come from wealth to attend public school before cruising into Oxford, Bevan had been born to a working-class family in South Wales, had left school at thirteen to work in the coal mines, and had managed to secure a higher education in his twenties thanks to a scholarship from the Miners' Federation.[32] Bevan started agitating for workers' rights, became a union official and in 1929 was elected to Parliament as the MP for Ebbw Vale, a seat he would hold until his death in 1960. In speech he still came across as unpolished in comparison with more privileged politicians, after painstaking years of training himself out of a stammer and adopting a more English accent. Bevan had known the struggle of long-term unemployment first hand and had seen his own father die from lung disease caused by working in the mine, without being compensated because it was not a recognised workplace injury. When Bevan's party was elected to lead the country in 1945, he was the obvious candidate for the job of Minister for Health and for the role of midwife to the delivery of the new NHS.

On 5 July 1948, the NHS – and its first new patient, little Aneira – were born. On the same day, the National Insurance, Industrial Injuries and National Assistance Acts all came into force. 'Today the British people join together in a single national friendly society for mutual support during the common misfortunes of life,' announced *The Times*, commenting on the new system that enabled 'the masses to join the middle classes'.[33] 'World's biggest health army is yours today,' proclaimed the *Mirror*. 'Nobody in this world before has had such a powerful force ranged on his side than YOU do now.'[34] The country was in a romantic mood, basking in a 'sense of purpose and common humanity', notwithstanding a public outburst by Bevan the previous day in which he railed at 'Tory vermin'. Bevan had been reflecting on his long-held resentment at how mining families like his had suffered during the Depression, which, in his case, had included him being encouraged to emigrate when work in his local area dried up.

By December of that year, twenty-one million new patients had sought medical treatment and 13.5 million prescriptions were being dispensed per month, double the number under the old system.[35] 'I shudder to think of the ceaseless cascade of medicine which is pouring down British throats at the present time and they're not even bringing the bottles back,' reflected the stunned Bevan. The NHS would end up costing far more than planned and its funding structure would have to be revised through many difficult negotiations over the years. But since 1948, the NHS has delivered virtually all of the fifty-two million babies born during that time, provided care to most of forty million or so people who died, and treated the tens of millions of people who have come in and out of this country.[36] Medical research on the NHS led to the discovery of DNA, the birth of the world's first 'test-tube baby', and definitive evidence that smoking causes cancer. The massive roll-out of vaccines via the NHS has protected us from polio, diphtheria and, more recently, Covid-19.

That day in 1948 was also the birth of Beveridge's brainchild, the welfare state (a term he himself loathed, preferring the less catchy 'social security state').[37] It was, as Prime Minister Attlee proudly announced, the most comprehensive social security system of its kind ever introduced into any country. Half a millennium of the Poor Law had been brought to an end, to the vast relief of many. Under the new system, citizens were to be treated equally: there was to be no front door versus side door distinction and the stigma of being a 'pauper' reliant on the begrudgingly offered crusts of the wealthy was to be felt no longer. A new National Assistance Board took over as the one-stop shop for benefits, dispensing unemployment compensation, old age pensions, child benefit and various discretionary forms of lingering wartime assistance for refugees, people displaced by the bombing and the dependents of internees. Unemployment – the great scourge of Idleness – was vanquished almost instantly, dropping to just 243,000, or 1.2 per cent of the labour force, by 1949.[38] The workhouses were taken out of use, with some converted into retirement homes or homeless shelters. Many were abandoned to rot and eventually torn down, left only to haunt the memories of their communities.

The creation of a comprehensive national social security and healthcare system was music to the ears of the statisticians at the GRO, who in the 1940s were feverishly engaged in keeping alive their National Register. With the end of rationing on the horizon, the visceral incentive for people to keep updating the GRO as to their changes of address would be lost. In the new social security system, Sylvanus Vivian saw a new source from which the NR could draw its 'parasitic vitality'.[39]

The Cabinet and some government departments, on the other hand, had been falling further out of love with the NR for some time and were actively looking for reasons to scrap it. ID cards were becoming increasingly unpopular and the register was starting to be seen as an indulgent use of money in the country's post-war financial straits. The War Office was keen to continue the NR in order to carry on conscripting people to national service, although understandably this wasn't the kind of argument the GRO necessarily wanted on its side.[40] Vivian was replaced as Registrar General in 1945, after the war. His successor, George North, was unable to convince the Cabinet to keep the NR and even started to irritate them with these proposals for yet more grand national plans. As a compromise, a system of National Insurance numbers was proposed, and an office was set up in Newcastle employing thousands of staff to deal with the central administration.

But the GRO statisticians had been right about at least one thing: it would be very hard to coordinate NHS patient care across a national system without some central register in which patients had a unique identifier. National Insurance numbers wouldn't work because they had only been issued to the twenty-five million people who were paying National Insurance contributions – mostly those who were working – and so excluded children and a great many women.

It was decided, much to the GRO's vindication, that the NHS would use people's numbers from the NR to keep track of them. The GRO's Southport operation was partly taken over to run the administration of the new NHS numbers database, which it still does to this day. But a problem for this new system was that, at first, doctors' pay was linked to how many patients they had on their lists at GP surgeries, which created an incentive not to try very hard to shuffle people off them when they moved away or died. This became a major issue for the NHS, which found itself financially stretched in the early years partly due to these expanding lists. The database was eventually brought under control, although to this day it is not clear that it has ever achieved the level of accuracy the NR had, with its thousands of dedicated staff and rationing-related incentive for people to keep their own record up to date.

From 1952, when the NR ended, new patients on the NHS would get a new type of number and those who had a number from the NR would carry on with that. The old numbers, which linked people to the wartime register, stayed in use until the 1990s. By that point, to most people their NHS number was something completely arbitrary, if they were aware of it at all. But many elderly people knew their number by heart, and to them it meant a great deal.

12

Calculating Change

In 1951, London was in a fairly bad state, architecturally speaking, with large areas condemned to the wrecking ball after being destroyed beyond salvation in the Blitz. The loop of the river around the Isle of Dogs in the east resembled a boxer's grin with half of the teeth knocked out. The East End neighbourhoods of Poplar, Stepney and Limehouse had been the hardest hit, due to being closest to the heavily targeted area of the docks, and the London Council decided it was best to start completely afresh when it came to the rebuild. It was because of this that one rubble patch in Poplar became the site of an unlikely tourist attraction in 1951 – a 'live architecture' exhibit, showcasing an innovation which town planners insisted would be the way of the future: the council estate.

The exhibition was a side attraction to the Festival of Britain, a celebration of British invention, design, the arts, science, history and technology along the same lines as the Great Exhibition a hundred years earlier. London's South Bank was transformed into a wonderland of architectural oddities, including a colossal dome housing exhibitions on the theme of discovery, which was to be mirrored another fifty years later by the Millennium Dome. As well as browsing the displays, visitors could see concerts, watch a film in a 3D cinema and take a short boat ride down the river to a funfair in Battersea Park. They could also, if they wanted, visit the live architecture exhibition in Poplar, where they could marvel at a crane (the first to operate in London), see a demonstration of a 'jerry-built' pre-war house being utterly unsuitable for habitation, and be inspired by the fresh and stylish modern dwellings of the newly built Lansbury Estate. There was a special café, the Rosie Lee, serving up egg and chips and cockney kitsch. Being so far out of the way for most people, however, the exhibit was a bit of a flop. But the Lansbury Estate is still inhabited today and would have a cosy feel to it, were it not for the towering glass backdrop of Canary Wharf which drifted up next to it like an iceberg in the 1980s.

The post-war vision of Britain was ambitious and promised a clean break from the past, which many people found appealing. They didn't want to look backwards to the bad memories of unheated houses and the fearful strictness of the Victorian age. But ten years on from the Festival of Britain, some sections of the population started to experience the nagging discomfort of cold feet. Yes, there had been consensus at the end of the war that things couldn't go on as they were, but they were now changing so rapidly that nothing could be taken for granted as solid or sacred. There was anxiety in some quarters that our way of life had changed *too* fast, faster even than we could grab hold of it or make sense of it.

That was why in 1963 the government made a radical suggestion: instead of waiting for the next decennial census in 1961, they proposed to hold one in 1966, after just five years. When this was announced in Parliament, one member of the House of Lords questioned why the results of the census were expected to take a year to come out, when 'Gallup polls and the national opinion polls come out in about a week', to which the government's representative tartly responded, 'My

Lords, I could not say that a census is really comparable with a Gallup poll.'[1] But in many ways – in this particular case – that was exactly what it was. The state was carrying out its own market research. The real Gallup polls, meanwhile, were offering some candid insights into people's behaviour and opinions. In June 1951 a poll found that only 5 per cent of people reported having been to the Festival of Britain exhibition on the South Bank, and a slim 58 per cent majority had been left with a favourable impression.*[2]

It was true that life had changed in some fairly radical ways in the decade or so since the end of the Second World War. The NHS and the welfare state were not the only grand projects of the post-war era: the landscape of the UK was also changing via huge building initiatives. The Lansbury Estate was just one constellation in a galaxy of new housing developments in the 1950s. Already during the war a feeling had begun to take hold that if we were going to have to rebuild large parts of the country, we should go at the job with maximum effort. We could also use it as an opportunity to repair problems with our housing situation that were nothing to do with visits from the Luftwaffe. The 1946 Land Acquisition Act enabled local authorities to compulsorily purchase land if it was for housing development and the 1947 Town and Country Planning Act reduced 1,400 planning authorities across the country to just 145.

Central planning was the order of the day. A Ministry of Town and Country Planning was also established, and with that cement mixers were fired up all across the land. While a large part of the plan was to rebuild and expand existing

---

* Overall, the Festival of Britain was not as successful as the Great Exhibition of 1851 had been. Around 8.5 million people attended the Royal Festival Hall exhibition, or around 17 per cent of the population, compared with one third of the population who were estimated to have visited the Great Exhibition.

towns and cities, an ambitious other side to it was the construction of whole new towns. The first were a ring of eight dormitory towns around London – including Stevenage, Hemel Hempstead, Bracknell and Crawley – and in total fifteen new towns sprang up in the 1940s and 1950s.

By 1961, the new towns were a success, with the total population of the first twelve growing by over four hundred thousand people between 1951 and 1961.[3] Some areas had gone from being essentially hamlets to reasonably sized towns, such as Peterlee in County Durham, which grew from three hundred to thirteen thousand residents in ten years. The village of Harlow in Essex went from under six thousand to fifty-three thousand residents by 1961.

In much the same manner as the Saltaires and Bournvilles of yore, and the early twentieth-century garden cities movement, the focus of these projects was not only on providing more spacious, modern and comfortable living quarters but on promoting an idealised way of life. The footprint of new towns was intentionally sprawling, with trailing suburbs of semi-detached or detached houses. Planners wanted to avoid at all costs the dense, chaotic clustering that urban areas had all naturally tended towards in the past: places of filth, demoralisation and associations with cholera. The focus was on scale and simplicity, and the concrete poured.

The reconstructed centre of Plymouth (which had been destroyed by bombing) represented an alternative vision for the future. Through the middle of the newly developed shopping and business centre the planners cut an ostentatiously broad avenue stretching almost a mile from the train station to the sea, fringed by minimalist shopfronts in grey Portland stone. This 'monumental' feature, as the planners intended it to be, was supposed to be a place of inspiration and restoration of the soul for Plymouthites, as well as somewhere to pick up a few household bits.[4] Early 'brutalist' developments were constructed with the same kind of intentions. Clean lines, monotone colouring and the absence of frills were supposed to provide a kind of classless, timeless environment in which communities could thrive with calm focus instead of friction and stress. Planners started favouring high-rise blocks of flats in cities, to reduce the visible clutter of life at ground level. The Barbican Estate in London, built in the late 1960s, was the same idea but repackaged for the upper middle classes, where luxury-flat living was combined with an onsite concert hall and art gallery.

A noticeable change in many people's lives was that they could afford a lot more consumer goods than in the past. A whole host of new materials had been introduced to manufacturing in the 1930s and 40s which had changed the possibilities of production. Cutting-edge but affordable new products like Tupperware containers, plastic bags, Lego bricks and Barbie dolls were rolled out to the masses in a very short space of time. No longer would working-class and middle-class families have to live years behind the curve of technology. By the 1950s, refrigerators, freezers, toasters, televisions and motor cars were not just being made in small batches for a privileged few – they were being churned out and could be afforded by most of the people working in the factories which made them. Synthetic, inexpensive fabrics also opened new frontiers for clothing and interior design, and high street fashion started to become available to the masses.

By the 1950s, every home – and in some cases every room within a home – had a wireless and a fair proportion of houses had a television set. Instant mass communication was possible and had been essential during the war to relay instructions and warnings, and to generally encourage keeping calm and carrying on. On 6 February 1952, the nation had listened as the shock news broke that King George VI had died and that his daughter Elizabeth had succeeded him to the throne at the age of just twenty-five. The coronation in June of 1953 was watched on television by twenty-seven million people in the UK and an incredible eighty-five million in the US.

But radio and television were not just there for royal announcements: one of the main things they did was to establish and spread pop culture. And this new vibrant culture involved a furious shaking-off of the strictness and conservatism which had defined British life for a very long time. Through the war, Britain had soothed itself with mawkish, nationalistic ballads and drinking songs along the lines of 'Knees Up Mother Brown', which could be easily bashed out on the piano. Suddenly there was a new sound in the air, and it was electric. From America came twelve-bar blues and rock 'n' roll, along with swagger and sex appeal. People whose primary concern for the past decade had been making sure they had enough coupons for tea could barely cope with the spectacle of Elvis Presley and his swinging hips. Some broadcasters refused to air footage of Elvis unless it was only from the waist up. In 1962, the Beatles burst onto the scene with their ironic take on the suited and slick boyband quartet. The bowl-cut hair, the unsmiling, awkward poses and the raucous feel of some of their hit singles expressed the essence of youth in the early 1960s: individuality straining against convention, a lust for life blooming in surroundings which were otherwise rather strict and grim.

The sense of a very fast pace of change was most noticeable in the lives of the young. They were the first generation who hadn't had to do national service (or be sent immediately to fight in an actual war) and who didn't necessarily need to have jobs until they left school at the age of fifteen. Teenagers were starting to have something their ancestors had never known:

heaps of free time. Pop culture also meant they had a unity with one another, which stretched far beyond their social circle. When it became possible to produce vinyl records and record players at low cost, there was scarcely a teenager in the country who wasn't being told to turn down that racket as they blasted the Rolling Stones, the Kinks, the Who and Jimi Hendrix. The times they were a-changing; the future was bright, liberated and in Technicolor.

The 1950s had seen the start of a shift in the lives of women. Perhaps the most significant material improvement was that the NHS provided free maternity treatment, including hospitalisation if necessary, which dramatically increased the level of health security that women felt. By the 1960s, contraception was widely accepted for use on medical grounds and, increasingly, as a means for a woman to simply control her fertility. Female sexuality was gradually becoming an acceptable topic in public conversation too, despite a great deal of continued pearl-clutching by older generations. The contraceptive pill came onto the private market in the 1950s and was made available on the NHS from 1961 (although not free of charge until 1974). There was some discussion as to whether the pill should only be made available to married women, although the Minister for Health was forced to conclude that the only fair way to dispense it was for doctors to decide based on medical requirements, not marital status.[5] To borrow a slogan that would be adopted by feminist groups towards the end of the decade, the personal had become political.

All the while, the government was flying blind for long periods of time in between censuses when it came to data, and needed more help with navigation. During the war, and until 1947, a large-scale Wartime Social Survey had been used to plan public policy. Starting out as a scientific project, it morphed into a rolling programme of public opinion polls on a variety of war-related policy issues. It is revealing that the survey came to be carried out from within the Ministry of Information, which had been set up to control communications from government to the public. The idea of an information flow going in the other direction was still rather new at the time.

The Wartime Social Survey had involved asking a sample of the population – typically one or two thousand people – to report their behaviours and to give their opinions on a number of topics. These ranged from seemingly trivial questions like how many times a week people baked or bought a cake, to finding out what people were intending to do for work after the war. Some of the more serious surveys – such as whether children had been immunised against diphtheria – were clearly intended to be used to evaluate and, if necessary, reconfigure public policy. A sizeable number of the surveys were the Ministry of Information checking whether people had seen its communications. Yes, 97 per cent of people had seen its suggestion to eat more potatoes instead of bread; however, only 43 per cent thought it would be possible for them to comply.[6] After one survey asked female manual workers what undergarments they were wearing, the project became known as 'Cooper's Snoopers', since evidently the Minister of Information, Duff Cooper, seemed to want a little too much of it.

During and after the war, more large-scale government social surveys were established, including the National Food Survey in 1940, the Family Expenditure Survey in 1957 and, in 1961, the International Passenger Survey, which was the country's only means of measuring migration to and from the

UK until 2021. These surveys were rolling market research processes, by which the government gathered insights into the personal realm.

It was in the context of all this that the 1966 census was proposed. Given the feeling that the country was in a state of 'rapid change and development' which required us to have our eye on the statistical ball, the fact that 1961 census results ended up badly delayed only increased politicians' anxiety. For the first time, a computer had been used to process the census results and it hadn't gone entirely to plan.[7] In the meantime, the government had been told off for making policy decisions based on speculations rather than data. One such critic was the MP Judith Hart, a trained sociologist, who schooled them that 'the duty of the Government is now much greater than it was to issue ... factual information so that we may attempt ourselves to judge what kind of society we are moving towards. Facts must obviously be the basis of social and political judgments.'[8] In the era of mass polling, advanced statistical techniques and computer power (when it worked), there was no excuse for airing mere opinions as if they were facts.

One big worry was people were moving around a lot more than before, and so basic population statistics could go out of date very quickly. 'A relatively small percentage migration into a populous area or a relatively small change in the make-up of its population may seriously affect the amount of land and the amount of money required for housing, schools, hospitals and other services,' the Minister of Health reported to Parliament.[9] The GRO also worried that 'extensive population movement' meant that the 1961 census figures were already out of date when it came to planning.[10]

It wasn't that the government had a problem with people wanting to move – quite the opposite. After the war, it had been noted that the population was in danger of shrinking, if recent trends weren't actively reversed. In fact, the fertility rate had lowered from just over three live births per marriage at the start of the century – and nearly six per marriage half a century before that – to just over two in the late 1940s.[11] Clearly wartime austerity had put a dent in some people's plans. A Royal Commission on Population was convened to see what was going on, and in 1949 they concluded that couples were putting off having children (or more children) until they had a bigger house. Overcoming the current housing shortage was of 'fundamental importance' to dealing with 'the population problem'.[12]

We were still in the heady days of the post-war consensus, with huge public policy ambitions in the pipeline, like the mass building of council housing, new towns and big improvements to schools and hospitals. 'In a nutshell,' a GRO press release about the 1966 census declared, 'orderly planning must be geared to population changes ... and the Government have decided that ten years is too long to wait.'[13]

The rhetoric made it sound a bit like citizens of the UK were consumers and that the government, as the supplier of services, was focused on trying to make their experience as comfortable as possible. What a turnaround from the government's attitude towards the people only a few decades earlier. As recently as the 1930s, governments had refused to get involved in matters of job creation, even when unemployment stood close to three million and hunger marchers streamed into London. As recently as the 1940s, there had still been sections of the population who were grudgingly shunted between workhouse, asylum and charity because they were not eligible for any insurance scheme, and many people avoided doctors at all costs because they would expect them to cough up money they didn't have.

What was interesting too was that the government acknowledged that the 1966 data would be 'of value to users outside government – to those engaged in research in the social sciences, economics and medicine and to industry and trade'.[14] A press release later added 'market researchers' to the list of parties who would no doubt be interested in the results.[15] Although the questions weren't quite on a par with those in Gallup polls about magazine-reading and thoughts on atomic weapons, censuses had effectively become a giant form of market research for the state, part of their suite of public research tools which also now included social surveys.

What was crucially different about this census was that only *10 per cent* of the population would be included, making it a 'sample census'. The idea was to sample one in ten dwellings across the whole of the UK and collect details for each person who lived there. These findings could then be scaled up to represent the country as a whole with a reasonable degree of accuracy, even for local areas the size of small towns.*

The benefit of the 10 per cent approach was that it was only expected to cost £2 million, rather than the £5 million for a full census, a large proportion of which would go towards acquiring a second-hand IBM 705 machine for tallying up the returns. This was no laptop computer – it took up an entire room and resembled somewhere from which you might control a nuclear power station. Thankfully the GRO reassured the public that 'the Department's staff are conversant with the

---

* In Scotland, where big industrial plans were taking shape in more sparsely populated areas, six 'special study areas' were chosen in which 100 per cent of people would be counted. These records will be a treat for genealogists in 2066.

computer's "language"' – as if we statisticians needed more reasons for people to call us massive dorks.[16]

As for what information we needed so rapidly, the sample census included a few new questions which reflected what was considered important at the time. Because it was thought that the population was migrating more than before, the questionnaire asked for people's address five years previously, as well as where they currently lived. New questions were added about car ownership and where people kept their car ('on the street', 'in a garage' and so on), how they travelled to work, whether they had more than one job, and whether they had any academic, professional and vocational qualifications. These kinds of questions reflected both the need to get a grip on the new phenomenon of commuter traffic and the government's ongoing commitment to organising the economy so that everyone could be fitted to a job.

A lengthy debate also went into whether people should be asked if they used their kitchen to eat breakfast or any other meal. It was decided that this line of questioning was useful in order to 'give a rough idea of the size of kitchens'.[17] This was clearly for the benefit of architects, housing developers and planners, who were itching to know whether people would be expecting a dining room when they walked through the door of their new council house or suburban semi, or whether they would be content with a large kitchen.

The public were, of course, familiar with filling out censuses, but this 10 per cent census was a slightly different beast. It was speculated early on that the tenth man selected might resent the fact that he was being asked to respond to intrusive questions while 'the other nine chaps next door are not being asked the same'.[18] The solution of the GRO was an ingenious publicity offensive which made it seem like being chosen as a 'Ten Per Center' was to have won the lottery for this most prestigious role. From fourteen million addresses, a computer had selected in a mere 150 hours a random 10 per cent sample on whose answers the whole nation depended. 'Five million vital seconds will be capsuled into Sunday's stroke of midnight,' read one rather confusing press release, reminding people to fill in the form on 5 April 1966.[19] The form-fillers in Britain's 'Ten Per Cent households' should record, 'like diarists', whoever was present in their house on that night. This was definitely reminiscent of Mass-Observation, in which participants' most banal reflections were treated as a valued historical record. 'Form haters' need not despair, because the questionnaire had been tested on a notoriously reluctant 'London plumber', who had grumbled his way through it in thirty-five minutes.

As the day of the enumeration approached, press conferences were held, posters went up ('Are you a Ten Per Center?') and various publicity stunts were arranged by the GRO. *Woman* magazine – the largest women's magazine in circulation – ran two features on the census, while influential business magazine *The Director* had a four-page illustrated story. The BBC was all over it, covering the live dispatch of enumerators' record books from the new census headquarters in Titchfield in Hampshire, recording a special television mini-series, *The Newcomers*, about the need for enumeration, and covering it on radio programmes such as *Woman's Hour* and *Today*. Soap operas *The Archers* and *Coronation Street* sought to break the stigma by featuring households who came out as Ten Per Centers. A census form was conspicuously delivered to 10 Downing Street, leading to feverish speculation as to whether the prime minister was a Ten Per Center too.[20]

On the day of the launch, the press assembled in the vaults of Somerset House, where a family of Ten Per Centers were presented with a copy of the form by the Registrar General himself, and a boy born on census day in 1961 was paraded before the cameras to remind us what an incredibly long time ago that was. In a final flourish, 'two attractive girls' from the GRO staff were enlisted to pose wearing model dresses of 1961 and 1966, the earlier style looking inconceivably frumpy next to the playful miniskirt combination of the newer look. 'The *Daily Mail* ran this as a half-page illustrated story,' the GRO reflected with pride. 'The *Sun* gave it a whole page.'[21]

The results of the 1966 sample census were released with comparatively less fanfare, and what they showed didn't generate much of a buzz. This might have been because when the computer had done its speedy work of tabulating the figures and the GRO statisticians had cast their hungry eyes over the results, there was nothing particularly remarkable there at all.

Migration within the UK, which had been repeatedly described as 'extensive' and unusually 'rapid' in justifying the need for the survey, was at exactly the same level that it had been according to previous statistics. Around one in ten people had moved house in England and Wales in the year leading up to April 1966, which matched with the claim that 'something like 10 per cent of the whole population moves every year' which statisticians had already been making.[22] Sure, it confirmed existing estimates but this scale of population shifting could hardly be termed unusual. The country had coped with much higher levels of mobility during the Second World War, as evidenced by the blood, sweat and tears of those having to continuously update the National Register, and society hadn't collapsed. The 1966 figures did show that a higher proportion of people – nearly a third (309 in 1,000) – had moved house within the past *five* years.[23] Again, this didn't appear to have caused any earth-shattering repercussions, and we had no previous statistics with which to judge whether it was an unusually rapid pace of change.

Some areas had seen fairly large changes in the overall size of their populations as a result of migration within the UK. Many of these were places where new suburbs, housing developments or even new towns had been constructed – Bletchley, Grimsby, Lichfield, Canvey Island.[24] In other places, far more people had moved away from the area than into it. High on this list were the old centres of Victorian industry – Manchester, Newcastle, Burton upon Trent, Birmingham, Rhondda and the Welsh Valleys – which were still seeing the tail end of their decline in terms of job opportunities and reasons to stick around. Scotland was the only part of the UK which had shrunk overall in terms of its population, although only by a fairly small amount.

The sample census also didn't give the impression of a society which had suddenly achieved lift-off and was now orbiting the planet in silver jumpsuits. Overall across Great Britain, one in eight households didn't have any access at home to hot running water. Nearly one in seven didn't have a fixed bath and one in six households only had use of an outside toilet.[25] The picture was one of continuing inequality between areas and of some places where housing conditions were evidently still pretty dire. In Poplar – scene of the live architecture exhibition a full fifteen years previously – over a third of households had no hot water. More than half of dwellings in parts of Manchester only had an outside toilet, and in some parts of the Scottish Isles around one in five households didn't have access to a toilet at all, however that worked. This was in a country which had just put satellites into space; which had been visited by Marilyn Monroe. The future clearly had not yet arrived for many people – and there was certainly work to do for housing planners.

Meanwhile it was evident that parts of the country which had already benefited from new housing estates and developments were living the modern dream. In the London suburbs of Harrow and Ealing, over 94 per cent of households had hot running water and their own indoor toilet. Across Great Britain, 45 per cent of households had a car, and an impressive 6 per cent (over a million households) had two or more cars.[26] Again there was variation across the country, the lowest level of ownership being 36 per cent in Scotland and the highest 53 per cent in the south-west and East Anglia. Car manufacturing had become a major UK industry, employing around a million people or 5 per cent of the workforce. Nearly a quarter of British vehicle manufacturing went on in Coventry, where nearly one in three working men was employed in the making of Triumph Heralds, Jaguar E-Types and other iconic cars of the age.[27]

The census did pick up some interesting new developments in what women were up to. Thirty-eight per cent of married women were economically active but nearly half of these women were working part time.[28] This was a large increase on the situation in 1961 and suggested that the number of married women working part time had gone from around 1.5 million to 2.2 million in the space of five years (although there was major doubt as to whether these figures were perfectly comparable).[29] The proportion of married women who were working part time was by far the highest in the south-east of England and the outer London area. Some of this was women switching from full time to part time because this was now widely accepted; in other cases, married women who wouldn't otherwise have worked were finding that homemaking was no longer a full-time job, thanks to the wonder of electrical appliances. The most common types of roles for married women to do part time were in the service industry and in clerking, jobs which typically put them in shops and offices. It had become very normal to see women staffing the cash register in shops and the front desk in hotels, and in offices a female secretary was a given.

The statistics also acknowledged that around two thirds of divorced women were economically active and that three quarters of them worked full time.[30] This was clearly quite different from married women, who were generally not employed or, when they were, were as likely to work part time as full time. The fact that divorced women had their own row in tables about employment activity testified to their considerable growth in numbers. In 1931 there had been around twenty thousand women recorded in the census who had had their marriage 'dissolved'; in 1966 this figure was over two hundred thousand. The fact that we were now specifically considering divorced women as contributors to the economy was acknowledgement that life does go on after divorce and a person shouldn't merely scuttle away in shame. Sadly, the times had changed too late for Princess Margaret, who had triggered a constitutional crisis in the 1950s by becoming engaged to a divorced man, whom she eventually had to give up.

While the 1920s and 1930s had seen some attempts to restrict women's participation in the job market – not to mention banning them from playing football – the post-war anxiety for women to go back to the kitchen was a comparatively faint shout in the wind. With the welfare state and the government committed to finding a job for everyone who wanted to work, what need was there for men to hoard sections of the economy for themselves? Women were still paid less than men for doing the same jobs, but now that the general feeling of disapproval towards women's work was reducing, they felt emboldened to push for improvements. The rule that women had to quit the civil service when they got married was lifted in 1946, although it lingered in the Foreign Service until 1973. In 1970, the Equal Pay Act made it illegal to pay women and men differently for doing the same job, a milestone that was reached thanks in part to high-profile protests by female workers at the Ford car factory in Dagenham.

The 1966 sample census was undoubtedly useful to housing planners and industry, although whether it was essential is another matter. In the decade or so after the census, seven further new towns (including the radical Milton Keynes) were built across Great Britain, and the construction of new suburbs and high-rise blocks in existing towns and cities continued apace. It's hard to argue that projects like that couldn't have still been planned using localised surveys rather than one at the level of the whole country. From the 1970s, more social surveys were added to the government's information-gathering apparatus, including the New Earnings Survey in 1970 (later the Annual Survey of Hours and Earnings), the General Household Survey in 1971, the Labour Force Survey in 1973 and the Family Resources Survey in 1992.

All supplied the state for decades with more regular, timely and in-depth information than a census could provide, and at considerably lower cost.

Over time the momentum went out of the post-war public planning drive. An enormous act of national exertion had reached the end of its strength, and the country had to sit back and take stock of what it had: lives that, for the majority of people, were freer than they had ever been, a great weakening of the structure of social class which had caged many a previous generation, a safety net from the cradle to the grave, and a heck of a lot more concrete on our skylines.

13
Divisions

It was a warm August night in Nottingham, 1958, and there was a crackling tension in the air of the St Ann's neighbourhood. But the start of the evening had been full of laughter and fun, as groups of young women headed out in their glad rags for a drink and a dance. Couples walked arm in arm, and young men leaned on the corner of the St Ann's Well Inn pub, hair neatly greased, cigarette smoke curling slowly upward. Some of the men there were self-styled Teddy boys, part of a sub-culture that involved colourful dinner jackets, stiff collars, hair combed forward into a peak and a general air of violent unpredictability.

It never became clear who started it. Some said afterwards that the Teddy boys had kicked off after witnessing a Black man flirting with a white woman. Others said a group of young Black men had assembled in the pub and launched an orchestrated attack on the Teddy boys, in retaliation for weeks of threats and bullying. Either way, the pub erupted into a maelstrom of kicking and punching, razor blades and broken bottles wildly slashing through the air. The place was a 'slaughterhouse', with one man left bleeding on the floor from a throat wound that would require thirty-seven stitches. By the time the police intervened, it was said that around a thousand people had joined in the bloody brawl. A policeman was run over and at least eight people ended up in hospital.[1]

In the aftermath, rumours circulated that American white supremacist group the Ku Klux Klan had been behind the escalating tension and triggered the eventual blow-up.[2] Other onlookers condemned both white and Black Nottinghamians for letting their aggressive, gang-like behaviour boil up to this point. Some Nottingham pubs put up signs banning 'coloured persons' from their premises, and white hooligans issued a warning in the press to their Black neighbours: 'Don't walk in groups or you will be attacked. Tell your friends.'[3]

A week later, riots broke out in the similarly named location of Notting Hill, west London, which were even more intense and widely publicised. What seems to have started with a group of around 350 white youths attacking the homes of Black residents continued into a 'race war' that lasted for five days.[4] Molotov cocktails were thrown through windows, buildings were vandalised and groups of young men skirmished in the streets with iron bars, broken milk bottles and bin lids as makeshift weapons. Britain looked on in sincere horror. To some it was a sign of how far teenage hooliganism had spiralled out of control, but others saw it for what it really was: Britain could no longer fool itself that so-called 'race relations' were just fine.

The riots followed ten years of post-war migration to the UK which was different in character from the migration flows seen before. In 1946, the Cabinet's Manpower Working Committee had sat down to start planning the epic task of post-war reconstruction – as well as improving what was still there from before – and concluded that we needed a great many more workers than we had. Around a hundred thousand Polish men and their families were allowed to settle, and tens of thousands of famished and miserable refugees from the United Nations camps in Germany and Austria were recruited and brought over to help with the rebuilding. But this was a mere drop in the ocean when the committee had concluded that in the order of 1.3 million workers were needed.[5] What was not the plan at that point – although the possibility had been discussed – was to recruit manpower from Britain's colonies in the Caribbean, Africa and Asia. Nonetheless, the message got around that there were jobs going in Britain, and in 1947 110 Jamaicans arrived in Liverpool on the ship *Ormonde*, keen to take up any kind of work. Employment prospects for Jamaica's Black and mixed-race population had been deliberately stifled for longer than anyone there had been alive and a hurricane in 1944 had dealt severe damage to the country's infrastructure. When the *Ormonde*'s passengers were absorbed into the British population with a minimum of fuss, people across the West Indies started applying for passports in their thousands.[6]

At the end of May 1948, the majestic white steamboat the *Empire Windrush* left the docks of Kingston, Jamaica, bound for London, with around one thousand passengers onboard, half of whom were West Indian men migrating to the UK. Half of these passengers already had jobs (in the armed forces) and others were responding to a general manpower recruitment drive. Somewhat bizarrely, there were also sixty Polish refugee women onboard who had already made a head-spinning journey around the world in search of sanctuary.[7] The crossing was slow, and passengers amused themselves with songs, boxing contests and gambling. As they neared British waters, it became apparent that they were being tailed by a British warship. An official communiqué went up on the noticeboard: 'Conditions in England are not as favourable as you may think ... If you think you cannot pull your weight, you might as well decide to return to Jamaica ... No slackers will be tolerated.'[8] The *Windrush* arrived at Tilbury Docks to a swarm of press photographers and crowds of curious onlookers, before the passengers were whisked away to hastily arranged accommodation in the tunnels of Clapham's underground bomb shelter.

For a brief moment, it looked like we were willing to pull out all the stops for these West Indian arrivals, who were full British subjects and whose right to migrate to the UK would be confirmed in the British Nationality Act which was passing through Parliament at that very moment. 'Welcome Home!' read the front page of London's *Evening Standard*, which had chartered a plane to greet the 'sons of Empire' who were now clinging to the comfort of mother's apron. Life was certainly not easy, though, for many of the Windrush arrivals or for the hundreds of thousands of others who would migrate to the UK from its colonies over the next decade. Prejudice made it hard to find work and acceptable wages in some industries, and exploitative landlords charged them a fortune for damp and dilapidated lodgings. As more people followed the *Ormonde* and *Windrush*'s trajectory, open hostility started to flare towards the new arrivals in some quarters, culminating in the violence in Nottingham and Notting Hill.

In terms of numbers, the scale of migration was nothing out of the ordinary. The UK had absorbed hundreds of thousands of French, Germans, Poles, Belgians and Italians over the years without making a particular fuss (a notable exception being intolerance towards Jews). It was also barely a ripple in comparison with the millions of British people who had flowed in the other direction over nearly two centuries of imperial expansion. But it obviously wasn't about numbers, and it wasn't about country of origin. It was about race.

In 1962, after lengthy Parliamentary debates about the unrest in multi-ethnic communities, the Commonwealth Immigration Act passed into law. It split what had previously been a single tier of citizenship of the UK and its colonies into a hierarchy. From then on, only British citizens whose passports had been issued in the UK could travel unrestricted to and from the motherland. Inhabitants of the colonies and of the independent Commonwealth countries (Australia, Canada and so on) could come if they had recognised qualifications or a job offer but were subject to a quota and had to wait in a lengthy queue if they did not. In practice, as opponents of the Bill foresaw, the 'net effect' was that 'a negligible number of white people will be kept out and almost all those kept out by the Bill will be coloured people'.[9] It was not explicitly introducing a 'colour bar', but indirectly the effect was to shut out British citizens in the colonies who were overwhelmingly Black, Asian or mixed race.

Before the drawbridge was yanked up in 1962, British subjects in the Commonwealth got wind of these proposals and many realised it might be their last chance. In 1961, at least 113,000 Commonwealth migrants arrived, which was double the figure for the whole of 1960 and more than five times that for 1959.[10] The year before the Act came into force was the fourth in a row with positive net migration, and the net gain (170,000 people) was considerably higher than recent years.[11] Historian Robert Winder has pointed out the astonishing fact that in the three years up to the 1962 Act, 'more migrants arrived in Britain than had disembarked in the whole of the twentieth century up to that point'.[12] The Home Secretary, in what would become a familiar refrain, warned that 'over the past ten years the population here has increased by 2½ million ... [and] immigration is becoming an increasingly important factor in this problem'.[13] In the grand scheme of things, this number was not high – the population increase was larger in every ten-year period from 1871 to 1911 – but it certainly sounded alarming without that context.[14]

What this wave of migration meant was that by the 1960s there were undoubtedly more people of colour living in the UK than ever before.* Even in 1954, a Gallup poll revealed the somewhat surprising result that 42 per cent of people said that they 'personally knew or had known any coloured people'.[15] Black and Asian faces were certainly not unknown in the UK prior to that. In the early and pre-colonial era, Black people, including children, had been transported from Africa to the UK, sometimes to be pet-like servants to fashionable households, sometimes as exotic specimens to be gawked at by the public. Some had come of their own volition as merchants, businessmen, diplomats, sailors and entertainers. In the later nineteenth century, as we saw, some fugitive and freed slaves made it to the relative safety of Britain's shores, and other Black castaways of the colonial machine settled in England's port cities of London, Liverpool and Bristol. There was already a long history of Indians and other Asians being integrated at all levels of British society – including as Members of Parliament – and the same went for Jews, who were in some cases regarded as being of a distinct race and sometimes as white.

The UK was already an ethnically mixed, multi-racial society; that was no secret. What the British didn't have, despite increasingly loud talk about the subject, was any data on how

---

* One time before this when there would have been anything near as many people of colour present in the UK was when several hundred thousand US troops were stationed in the UK during the Second World War, a large proportion of whom were African American. These African American troops were warmly received by the British, according to many accounts, and the British were proud of pointing out that there was no 'colour bar' for them here as there would have been at home.

many people were actually in the category which was at the time referred to as 'coloured'. No data on the UK itself, at least.

It was a different story in some of the places Britain had colonised, where collecting data on race or skin colour was a matter of routine and, in some cases, conducive to public policy. While UK censuses had never asked about race – instead using country of birth and nationality as proxies – some of the colonial censuses recorded information on race, caste, 'colour', religion or tribe as a matter of course. The designations were not standardised across countries, so while in Gambia there was a breakdown of 'colour' into Black, white and 'mulatto', in Basutoland (now Lesotho) the population was divided into white, 'natives' and 'other coloured races'.[16] In New Zealand the distinction was between Europeans, Māori and 'half-castes', while in Australia 'full-blooded Aboriginal' was contrasted with 'half-caste'.[17] In Canada they employed the terms 'half-breed' for people who were mixed race and 'Indian' for the indigenous population.[18]

The tendency, when space was tight in a census report, was always to separate out the white population and lump all others together under a heading such as 'coloured', even when the latter outnumbered the white population by a hundred to one. 'Broadly speaking,' concluded a 1901 census of the British Empire, 'the 398 million persons residing within the Empire may be divided into two classes – "Whites" numbering approximately 54 million or 13.6 per cent of the population, and [the] "Coloured" population numbering about 344 million.'[19] When listing religions, colonial census reports focused in detail on the Christian denominations while combining the religions practised by most of the non-white population into categories such as 'pagan' and 'Mohammedan'. The 1901 Sierra Leone census contains such detail on the white population that we can count individual Hungarians and Swedes, and see that there were thirty practising Presbyterians. On the other hand, there is a large single category for 'Natives, i.e. children born of strange tribes' and a third of the country's population is recorded as practising paganism.[20]

The categories imposed in these official statistics were likely not, for the most part, designations people had chosen themselves. Attempts to categorise the population were often simple hierarchies intended to separate out the white element so as to monitor their welfare. The idea of caste appealed to colonial administrators in some contexts because it somewhat resembled the British notion of class, although the true significance of caste was poorly understood (and indeed the 'theory' of castes was scoffed at by the British as having 'no basis in fact').[21] Attempts to record caste, tribe or nation often resulted in mistranslations or reflected the prejudices of the local people who had been enlisted to do the counting. A misunderstanding in Bengal resulted in people having 'Chandala' listed as their caste, which was really just an insulting term used to describe people in the so-called 'untouchable' castes.[22] 'Gypsies' became a catch-all term for nomadic people in Europe because it was once rumoured that the origin of the Romani people was Egypt.

By the 1970s, when 'race relations' had become a topic of discussion – and of legislation – there was much more sensitivity and understanding when it came to labelling people according to race. The theory of white or, more specifically, white British superiority over the Black, Asian and Indigenous people they had subjugated had waned to the point of being a historical embarrassment. Those who might have flirted with eugenics in the past wouldn't have touched it with a barge pole after the horror of what had gone on in Nazi Germany. Britain had also watched the racist violence in 1960s America with deep disapproval – despite having had its own race riots – and had been appalled by the assassination of civil rights leader Martin Luther King in 1968.

But although the UK had no official form of racial segregation, racial stereotyping and low-level hostility towards people of colour was a fact of life. It is not overnight that a nation is weaned off centuries of believing that some form of innate superiority lies in the colour of the skin. In the 1970s this was expressed in pop culture, where caricatures and exaggerated send-ups of racial stereotypes were stock forms of entertainment. *The Black and White Minstrel Show*, which ran on the BBC for twenty years until 1978, was considered a cosy, mawkish Saturday night staple (although many did also accuse it of racism at the time). People had been raised on what we would now consider insulting caricatures in children's books such as *The Story of Little Black Sambo* and Enid Blyton's *The Three Golliwogs*. Robertson's marmalade, which sat on millions of breakfast tables, had a golly as its mascot from the 1930s until 2002, and children lovingly assembled collections of golly enamel badges and figurines which could be obtained by sending off jam labels.

By 1971 there were 3.3 million people in the UK who had been born abroad, of whom 1.2 million had been born in the 'New Commonwealth or Pakistan' (NCP), which was the new terminology for the UK's former colonies.[23] As a pamphlet on the 1971 census results pointed out, this meant that the UK's foreign-born population had gone from one in fifty people in 1951 to three in fifty people in 1971.[24] The 1971 census had also included a – somewhat controversial – question on people's parents' country of birth. Using this information, we could see that three quarters of people who had come from the NCP had parents who had also been born there, which indicated there were nearly 900,000 'first generation' NCP migrants living in the UK. Of these, 115,000 were from

Africa, 210,000 from the West Indies, 240,000 from India and 128,000 from Pakistan.

There were also 323,000 people who had been born in the UK to parents from the NCP across the past twenty-five years, eight in ten of whom were under ten years of age.[25] These were second generation migrants born to parents who had come from Africa, the Caribbean, America and Asia in the post-war 'Windrush' wave. In fact, the 1971 census showed that more children were being born to migrant parents than ever before: for nearly one in eight children born in the UK in the past four years it was the case that at least one of their parents had been born abroad. One in twenty-five children born in the UK in those years was born to parents who had both been born in the NCP.

The UK had recently enacted the Race Relations Act of 1965, which banned racial discrimination and made inciting hatred on the grounds of 'colour, race, or ethnic or national origins' a criminal offence. This had been partly in response to the violent scenes in Nottingham and Notting Hill.

But by 1969, seven in ten people were identifying 'immigrants/coloured persons' as a 'very serious social problem' in response to a Gallup poll.[26] The previous year, Enoch Powell, MP had made his 'Rivers of Blood' speech which implied that catastrophic consequences would result from allowing migration to continue in its current form, and a poll showed that 58 per cent of the population agreed with him.[27] The 1971 Immigration Act closed the door even further to NCP migrants and limited their 'right of abode', unless they could demonstrate that they had been living in the UK before the Act came into force. There was a way to register one's presence with the Home Office but, perhaps understandably, few people chose to do so. This lack of documentation 'set the trap for the Windrush generation', who would be accused of being illegal immigrants if they could not produce this kind of evidence nearly five decades later.[28] Despite the Race Relations Act and government attempts to placate the public with tighter immigration controls, by 1976 six in ten people thought that 'the feeling between white people and coloured people' was getting worse. But, interestingly, only one in fourteen people considered that they had a 'colour problem' – which might have meant a failure of 'race relations' – where they lived.[29]

There had been some official steps in the right direction to protect communities from discrimination and violence, but real and unaddressed tension was still very much alive. What didn't help was that while a lot of hot air was circulating about 'race, colour and ethnicity', the UK didn't have any comprehensive data on different ethnic groups within its population and what their lives were like. An attempt to collect some would soon end up opening a whole new can of worms.

The need for data not only on people's countries of origin but on their ethnic background had not escaped the notice of the government. In 1978 a white paper acknowledged 'a need for authoritative and reliable information about the main ethnic minorities' for 'developing effective social policies'.[30] Statisticians at the newly created Office of Population Censuses and Surveys (OPCS), which had merged the GRO with the government's statistical service, also insisted that 'any study of community relations must start from a knowledge of the demographic, social and economic characteristics of the ethnic minorities'.[31]

The question on parents' country of birth in the previous census had been an attempt to gather data on race or ethnicity, the idea being that even if a person had been born in the UK, having a parent from, say, an African, Caribbean or Asian country made it relatively likely that they were a person of colour. This was rather a rough indicator if the goal was to conclude anything about race, given that millions – likely tens of millions – of white British people had dispersed themselves around the globe in the centuries previously. Nevertheless, on the evidence of the 1971 census, the OPCS statisticians felt bold enough to claim that one in twenty people in the south-east of England and in the West Midlands was 'of New Commonwealth ethnic origin', while across the rest of the UK the figure was around one or two in a hundred.[32] It was surely not very accurate to take this as evidence of skin colour or even of cultural affiliation. The empire had by this point almost entirely disintegrated and Britain had received back a generation of foreign-born colonial administrators whose ethnicity, as we understand the term now, was white.

The issue now, in the government's words, was that 'there has been public interest not only in the immigrants themselves but also in their families born in the UK'.[33] Ethnic minority children born in the UK were hard to identify in the statistics, and the country was also on the cusp of a 'significant' rise in the number of third generation New Commonwealth migrants.

'Why did this matter?' you might ask. Well, because in addition to problems of hostility and violence targeted at ethnic minority communities, there was a growing body of evidence that some of them were facing considerable levels of material and social disadvantage. Concerns had been voiced by politicians, the media and charities and campaign groups such as the Runnymede Trust and the Commission for Racial Equality that children from ethnic minority backgrounds were faring badly in school and faced limited employment prospects when they left. A report by the Select Committee on Race Relations and Immigration found that one in four children whose parents had been born abroad needed special tuition in English reading and writing, and one in nine of these pupils still needed extra tuition at school-leaving age.*[34] Even when ethnic minority children attained high grades, prejudice from prospective employers made it harder to find skilled work.[35]

There was also a perception that housing and living conditions for some recent immigrant communities were very deprived, although when had that ever not been the case? It was speculated that the prejudice against people of colour made it harder for them to escape from these 'run-down and twilight areas' via what we might now call social mobility. A 1977 report on 'the West Indian community', which was estimated to number over half a million people or 1 per cent of the UK population, painted a very gloomy – and rather patronising – picture of a sub-community that was socially alienated and culturally lost.[36]

In light of this, it was proposed to include a direct question on ethnic origin in the 1981 census and the OPCS set to work establishing how this could work in practice. The first question tested was simply 'Race or ethnic origin: Please tick the appropriate box' and then a list of options: White (European descent), West Indian, 'Indian, Pakistani or Bangladeshi' (all one option), West African, Arab, Chinese, or 'any other race or ethnic origin'.[37] There was also a requirement to describe ethnic origin if one was of 'mixed descent'. One of the main objections came from South Asian respondents, who did not feel that a single tick-box for 'Indian, Pakistani or Bangladeshi' was an accurate reflection of their race or ethnicity. In a follow-up test, the question was extended so that having ticked the 'Indian, Pakistani or Bangladeshi' box, one could then select

---

* It is worth noting that problems with English reading and writing may have been over-diagnosed among ethnic minority children, due to prejudice, or rather under-diagnosed in the white pupil population by comparison.

from another list to indicate religious background: Hindu, Sikh, Muslim or Other. This approach was ultimately scrapped over the 'intrinsic awkwardness of asking only one group in the community to do this', plus the fact that some Turkish people were ticking the 'Muslim' box when they shouldn't have been. A general question on religion had not featured in the census since 1851 and was itself considered highly controversial.

The other problem which kept coming up in the tests was that West Indian respondents would give answers which the statisticians considered to be 'incorrect'.[38] More specifically, they found that a 'significant minority' were 'content to classify themselves as "West Indian" etc., but were reluctant to classify their children who were born in the United Kingdom in the same manner'.[39] When the form included 'White (European)', some would tick this, seemingly to identify their child as 'European'. When 'European' was removed from the form, to try to discourage this, people refused to fill it out at all. The judgement as to whether answers were incorrect was based on follow-up interviews with a sample of people who had filled out the form, in which 'the interviewer made her own assessment of the person's ethnicity and if this was inconsistent with what had been recorded, she checked it with the respondent'.[40] Although these interviews were trying to extract reasons for people responding in unintended ways, the disconnect between the statistics office and some members of these Black communities rings loud and clear from reflections such as the following: 'It was often difficult to determine whether this resulted from misunderstanding of the question or from a real objection to describing their children in this way. West Indians experienced far greater difficulty with *all* the questions on the forms ... than any other group.'[41] Did they experience greater difficulty, or did they just have more objections?

The final test of the ethnicity question took place in north London at the end of March 1980. Haringey was selected for its 'wide mix of ethnic groups' but the fact that the testers had deliberately 'targeted' a multicultural area would not turn matters in their favour.[42] Forms were delivered to fifty-six thousand households, to be collected later by census enumerators. A local census office was established, as well as a telephone hotline for questions, and Haringey Community Relations Council organised an all-day meeting with representatives of local ethnic minority groups to explain the purpose of the test.[43]

Despite this effort to get the community onside, the response rate was dire. Only 54 per cent of households returned their forms; 7 per cent had refused to accept them in the first place, 15 per cent had managed to avoid any contact at all, and 25 per cent had received the form but refused to hand it back.* Some local organisations had been actively discouraging cooperation and their objections to the test had been widely publicised in local media. One leaflet which seemed to have had a lot of influence claimed that the census was linked to plans for new nationality laws which 'would make nationality depend on your parents' nationality and not where you were born'. The pamphlet's authors warned: 'If we say now who is and is not of British descent, we may one day be asked to "go home" if we were born here or not.'[44] A follow-up survey (employing the same eye-balling method of checking whether people's responses were 'incorrect') found that nearly nine in ten West Indian and two in three Asian households had done what was expressly forbidden and identified their children as 'English' or 'European'.[45]

---

* The percentages are the result of rounding.

| Panel 3 | Direct ethnicity and parents' countries of birth questions tested in Haringey in 1979 |

11 Parents' country of birth

Write the country of birth of:

a the person's father

b the person's mother

This question should be answered even if the person's father or mother is no longer alive. (If country not known, write 'NOT KNOWN').

Give the name by which the country is known today.

a Father born in (country)

b Mother born in (country)

11 Racial or ethnic group

Please tick the appropriate box to show the racial or ethnic group to which the person belongs.

If the person was born in the United Kingdom of West Indian, African, Asian, Arab, Chinese or 'Other European' descent, please tick one of the boxes numbered 2 to 10 to show the group from which the person is descended.

1. ☐ English, Welsh, Scottish or Irish
2. ☐ Other European
3. ☐ West Indian or Guyanese
4. ☐ African
5. ☐ Indian
6. ☐ Pakistani
7. ☐ Bangladeshi
8. ☐ Arab
9. ☐ Chinese
10. ☐ Any other racial or ethnic group, or if of mixed racial or ethnic descent (please describe below)

This was a disappointing result for the census-takers but an entirely understandable one given what life was like for many people of colour in the UK – and especially in London – at the time. The 1970s had seen an escalation in the activities of violent anti-immigrant groups, most notably the National Front, which had provocatively moved its headquarters to east London. In June 1978, a group of 150 youths stormed down Brick Lane, a predominantly Bangladeshi part of Whitechapel, smashing shop windows and daubing the walls with swastikas and National Front logos. The behaviour of racist hooligans seemed to have become more brazen and menacing, and the police were perceived as being overzealous in shutting down peaceful counterprotests. Distrust of the police among people of colour, particularly the young, also grew in the years around the census test. A Select Committee report which collected views from the West Indian community found that the police were feared and seen as being a menace to Black young people rather than providing any justice or protection and warned of 'violence on a large scale' if the situation did not improve.[46] This was in 1972. The situation reached fever pitch in 1981, when furious riots broke out in Black communities from Liverpool to London over new 'stop and search' police tactics which disproportionately targeted Black people. As the historian David Olusoga puts it, 'There was a terrible symmetry to the fact that the most serious and sustained of the 1980s riots took place in the cities from which the slave traders had set sail ... Liverpool, Bristol and London. Cities that had been enriched by the slave trade and the sugar business saw fires set and barricades erected by young people who were the distant descendants of human cargo.'[47]

Going back to Haringey, when follow-up surveys were done with some of the census test households, something interesting emerged. What West Indian respondents really wanted to be able to put down as their children's ethnicity was 'Black British'.[48] In fact, many people were 'very reluctant to see themselves as anything other than Black British'.[49] Yet this was never among the options given to them. The census designers baulked at the idea of using the term 'Black' because they objected to 'any reference to colour in a census question' for reasons of possible controversy.[50] But what else was the question really about? There was some hypocrisy to this too, since test questions had repeatedly featured the term 'White'.

If they put their foot down about using the term 'Black', then 'White' had to be out of the equation too, meaning English, British, European and so on would have to be substitutes for whiteness – and that was clearly not a universal interpretation. The ethnicity question was deemed unworkable and too controversial. Announcing that it would not be included in 1981, the government noted that 'there was a real risk that the inclusion of an ethnic question could jeopardise the census as a whole'.[51]

The sticking point for the statisticians and the government was that they refused to countenance using 'Black' because it was seen as being too on the nose in terms of pointing out colour. But this squeamishness led them to do the opposite of what they had intended with all the question tests and consultations, which was supposed to be to listen to how people wanted their identities represented.

It also seems like a slightly old-fashioned view in 1981 to consider 'Black' to be a needless and perhaps even offensive reference to colour. For decades the term had been being reclaimed via civil rights movements and reappropriated as a positive identity, as captured in the notions of Black Power and Black Pride. In the United States, the campaign group Coalition for a Black Count had formed to encourage Black citizens to 'make Black count' by participating in the 1970 census and taking ownership of how they were represented in statistics. One of their sayings was 'On census day say it loud and clear: I'm Black, I'm proud and I'm here. Be counted, baby!'[52] How different might the next decade have been in terms of having useful information on racial disparities if the statisticians hadn't panicked at the use of a word the British had imposed millions of times before when people hadn't been asking for it?

The tests clearly also raised the issue that 'ethnicity' meant different things to different people, if it meant anything at all. It was and still is a fuzzy concept. Ironically, surveys in America had found people with British ancestry to be the 'difficult' ones when it came to giving consistent answers to ethnicity questions because hardly any of them were 'full-blooded' anything and they kept changing their minds.[53] The 1981 census test episode also stretched the thread between what people wanted to be able to record in terms of identity and what the people in charge deemed useful or appropriate. Social policy wonks wanted data on skin colour; people from some ethnic minorities wanted official recognition of their Britishness or, better yet, to not have their race be a subject of conversation at all. And people in the free country that was the United Kingdom would no longer tolerate being labelled with politically loaded terms they didn't agree with.

The campaign for ethnicity data was kept alive by a cross-party Sub-Committee on Race Relations and Immigration, as well as civil society pressure. One of the most persuasive arguments was that having solid data was the only way to counter misinformation about ethnic minority communities. The House of Commons' Home Affairs Committee, after trying to look into the issue of 'racial disadvantage' and rueing the lack of hard data, called for a direct ethnicity question in the 1991 census.[54] And their wishes were granted, with the OPCS agreeing that such a question was essential. After carrying out more sensitive testing this time around, they concluded that there was no avoiding the terms 'Black' and 'White'.

When it comes to counting people according to race or ethnicity, while there is no denying the social significance of such distinctions, categorisations of this kind are inherently loose and not fixed over time. Neither biologists nor geneticists have ever been able to pinpoint exactly what 'race' is in scientific terms, and some would consider it to be an entirely social construct. The current classification we use for ethnicity, in the 2020s, has not moved on a great deal from the 1970s census tests, in that it is still a mixed bag of references to skin colour ('White'), nationality ('Black British', 'Bangladeshi'), place of origin ('Asian'), and broad sense of cultural belonging ('Roma', 'Arab').[55] But though they may not hang together very consistently, the point is that they are based on how people wish to identify themselves. One person might identify as being of Pakistani ethnicity while another might describe themselves as Asian British – does it not seem fair and right that the choice should be theirs? But how many choices should there be? Who should decide which identities we collect data on? More on this in the next chapter.

The important issue that enumerators discovered in the 1979 census test, and in the ultimately successful ethnicity question in the 1991 census, is that public buy-in is everything when it comes to collecting data by consent. Yes, you can compel people to answer questions with threats of fines and imprisonment, but try to do that en masse and see how far it gets you.

South Africa provides an extreme cautionary tale of consent versus compulsion. Between 1911 and 1991, censuses were generally taken every five years and in many cases only included the white population. Even when they did count the full population, which was done more or less by force, census reports were heavily skewed towards whites (in 1960, only 5 per cent of the census tables included the whole population).[56] When the 'full' population was included (and there were still large numbers of people in the pseudo-ethnically segregated zones known as 'homelands' excluded from the count), the classification of race was central to the operation. During the apartheid years, censuses formed the basis of a population register and a person's race, as recorded therein, determined everything about their social and economic rights. But race was not self-declared. It was assigned according to a visual inspection by census-takers, with people dumped into the simplistic categories of 'White', 'Indian', 'Coloured' or 'Black African'. If people felt they had been categorised incorrectly, they could appeal to be re-inspected by the statistical bureaucrats, who would sometimes apply the 'test' of threading a pencil into a person's hair. If it fell out easily, they were deemed 'White'.[57]

The taking of the South African census became a five-yearly reassertion of the cruel system of segregation, and so communities began to resist being counted, sometimes with violence. By the final apartheid census in 1991, the neighbourhood of Soweto was completely inaccessible to enumerators and its population had to be estimated by counting houses from the air.[58] When apartheid ended and the race classification lost its legal significance, an early order of business was to count the people. While you might be forgiven for thinking people had had enough of being counted and classified at that point, the response rate for the 1996 South African census was the highest ever, at over 90 per cent (it has since sunk to 70 per cent). People were now being counted on their own terms, and the result was that ten million more Black Africans were counted in South Africa than just five years previously.[59] People will not hand over sensitive information if they don't believe you have good intentions – but they will happily if they believe you do.

14

All Equal

Iqbal Sacranie was said to consider himself a shy man.[1] But in June 2000, he found himself emboldened as he drafted a letter from the Muslim Council of Britain (MCB), the organisation he represented, to the then prime minister, Tony Blair. The letter carried a simple request: that a question on religion be added into the upcoming 2001 census. 'It would be the single most important step taken by the Government to recognise not only the needs of the faith communities but also clear recognition of religion as a living force in our society,' the letter argued. Not to do so would leave a generation of British-born Muslims 'invisible, unaccounted for and inequitably provided for' – merely a 'blur on the fringes' of the census snapshot. 'It is saddening [and] desperately frustrating,' it complained.[2]

As Secretary General of the MCB, Sacranie was in the fortunate position of having contacts in some fairly high places. Along with sending the letter, he placed a series of frantic phone calls directly to the prime minister's office. Blair had promised the previous year that the government would support including a question on religion in the census. Yet the clock was ticking for the census questions to be finalised and the legislation needed to add a religion question was not yet in place. The government had neglected to introduce a Bill itself, so everything was riding on a Private Member's Bill, which was stuck in a logjam of legislation thanks to filibustering MPs. But Sacranie's request went all the way to the top. The issue regained Blair's personal attention and the government provided its own time for the Bill to be heard.

In 2001, a religion question entered the main census form for the first time ever. But it had taken more than a few well-placed phone calls – the full story had been a saga more comparable to a modern-day *Canterbury Tales*, and which we shall come to momentarily.[3] But why on earth, we might be wondering, hadn't there been a religion question on the census before?

The first censuses, as we saw, were relatively sparse in terms of the information they collected. Just going to the trouble of collecting any basic information about people was enough, but once the census format was established, other questions did start to be added in. Collecting data on hitherto neglected groups was often done as a precursor to developing some kind of public policy to deal with a real social problem: poverty, dreadful housing conditions, the management of labour, disadvantage felt by certain groups. Other times, it was as a not-so-subtle means to monitor the scale of goings-on that may or may not have been real problems, like women stubbornly having fewer children, rising levels of lunacy or the presence of foreigners. When it came to religion, the fact that it didn't make it onto the census form for two hundred years in some ways reflects a lack of a perceived policy need.

But perhaps the more persuasive reason was that religion was a very sensitive topic. Although monotheistic on a surface level, the UK had always contained a multitude of different Christian denominations and sects, and, as everybody knew, there was a very real pecking order. Catholics had long been on the receiving end of persecution and throughout the nineteenth century other groups such as Dissenters, Baptists, Quakers and Presbyterians joined them in the corner of suspicion and disapproval. Because it was feared that the Churches of England, Scotland and Ireland might be losing their sway, the government did argue for including a religion question in the 1851 census. The idea was rejected by the House of Lords on the basis that it was not right to compel people to answer this on pain of imprisonment, as was the case for the rest of the census, and the compromise was a census of congregations, the results of which were published in 1853. As well as tallying up the followers of mainstream denominations, it catalogued some congregations which were bravely trying to make a point: 'Teetotallers', 'Free-thinking Christians', 'Gospel Refugees' and the 'Doubtful' are all listed.[4] Not quite succeeding in the aim of being non-judgemental, Mormonism is described as the practice of 'very peculiar doctrines' and Druidism as 'a creed of mingled mystery and terror well adapted to impress the uncultivated intellect of an almost savage race'.

At times, of course, in the UK and in its colonies, the making of lists of religious minorities (or simply the population which was not Protestant) was done to intimidate and control. Religious superiority was also a key ingredient in Britain's attitude and approach towards its empire. Indigenous people were often described as 'pagan', as if they were the direct parallel of the 'savage' population of Britain before its Christian conversion.[5] The threat to small and rebellious religious minorities was that exposing their weak numbers left them vulnerable to being targeted or taken advantage of.

Being the dominant religion, in terms of numbers, often means having the edge in terms of political power, so it is perhaps surprising that the census of Northern Ireland has included a question on religion since it began in 1926. The question had always been included in the census of Ireland and the Irish had made a point of noting that Great Britain was the odd one, by global standards, for *not* asking about religion.[6] But during the Troubles in Northern Ireland, the census became a flashpoint, with republicans calling for people to boycott the religion question to protest what they saw as the unequal treatment of Catholics in comparison to other Christians and to signal distrust in the state's intentions when it came to holding 'sensitive' data. In 1981, nearly one in five people refused to answer the religion question, making the remaining data 'virtually unusable'.[7] Protest spilled out into the streets, where census forms were publicly burned. Enumerator Joanne Mathers was on her way to collect forms in Londonderry when she was shot and killed, in an apparently political murder. Her killer has never been identified.

Although this was relatively recent history in the mid-1990s, the story of the movement which succeeded in getting a religion question onto the 2001 census form is one of determination completely unafraid of a backlash. With ethnic minorities now being recognised in official statistics, the question became 'Who else is currently being missed when it comes to data?' The distrust people in Haringey had felt when being asked about ethnicity back in 1980 was a faded memory. There had been immediate interest in the ethnicity data when it was published, and terms like 'Black British' were firmly in the lexicon.

The Haringey census tests had also made it clear that some people felt a strong desire to record their religion, as a more important characteristic in some cases than ethnicity or nationality. Some respondents had objected to having to record themselves in the broad category of 'Indian, Pakistani or Bangladeshi' but, rather than having insisted on separating out these nationalities, they had expressed a wish for a further breakdown where they could record whether they were Muslim, Hindu or Sikh.[8] By the 1990s, with the notion of 'ethnic minorities' now in common currency, there was a feeling in some camps that we needed data on religious minorities, not just so that Indian Hindus and Pakistani Muslims could signal a different identity from one another, but to be acknowledged as part of the population as a whole.

It was also felt that the country might be operating on an outdated model of what role religion played in people's lives. Despite a lack of data, it was no secret that Christian churchgoing in the UK had irretrievably declined over the latter half of the twentieth century, and day-to-day life in the UK was now a largely secular experience for most people. At the same time, recent decades had brought the largest migration to the UK in its history of people who belonged to non-Judeo-Christian religions. Indians, Pakistanis and Bangladeshis had arrived in large numbers, some on the wave of 'Windrush' migration when the door was briefly open to the Commonwealth. Many came afterwards as family migrants and, sometimes, refugees. Britain had always been, to some extent, a haven to people fleeing persecution, even if never particularly keen to advertise itself as such. At the turn of the millennium, we had recently absorbed hundreds of thousands of people in total from Iran, Somalia, Sri Lanka, Iraq and the former Yugoslavia, most of whom had been propelled by targeted discrimination or war.[9] And while much of the British population was quietly letting go of its Christian faith – or at least not feeling the need to warm up a church pew several times a week – these newer arrivals often held religion at the heart of their communities and were much more committed to demonstrations of piety.

While religious minorities in the UK had, in the past, often tried to avoid drawing attention to themselves, by the 1990s proudly and publicly claiming an identity was a way to gain society's respect and even its protection. The language of 'multiculturalism' had come into the mainstream, along with the idea that that allowing distinct cultures to coexist in one country signalled that it was a healthy liberal democracy. The world had seen many a recent humanitarian disaster stemming from the illiberal desire to stamp out cultural, ethnic or religious differences. Several ethno-religious conflicts occurring in the 1990s – in Sri Lanka, Rwanda, Serbia and Sudan – were commonly being described as genocides. For some religious minorities in Britain, recognition became about demonstrating strength in numbers: a tallying for the record so that their existence could not be denied. The Muslim community was particularly keen to gain control of its own narrative, having recently been eyed with suspicion and alarm following the extreme reaction abroad to British author Salman Rushdie's novel *The Satanic Verses* (1988), and the positioning of Islam as an existential threat to the West in Samuel P. Huntington's influential bestseller *The Clash of Civilizations and the Remaking of World Order* (1996).

The push to get a religion question on the 2001 census form started in a meeting of Christian church leaders in 1996, as noted by Jamil Sherif, who chronicled this episode in a contemporary journal article. That year was to see the birth of the UK's new official statistics bureau, the Office for National Statistics (ONS) – which is the producer of our statistics to this day – and the church leaders decided to use that opportunity to start lobbying for a religion question in the next census.*[10] The ONS's initial reaction could not have been described as keen but they did agree to consider it in their census tests.

But figuring out exactly what the question on religion

---

* The ONS was formed by merging the Central Statistical Office (CSO) and the Office of Population Censuses and Surveys (OPCS).

should be turned to be neither intuitive nor straightforward. The first census test in March of 1997 asked people 'Do you consider you belong to a religious group?', followed by a series of tick-boxes, the first of which was for 'No', followed by the various broad religious groups. Although people tended to cooperate with the question, the ONS didn't feel it had hit the nail on the head. It formed a Religious Affiliation Sub-Group, including some of the church leaders who had started the campaign, as well as representatives of other faiths, to formulate a better wording of the question. Like the *Canterbury Tales* pilgrims, they were an unlikely grouping brought together through common purpose and represented a full diversity of beard lengths and a kaleidoscope of religious attire.

What came out of this was a framework within which religion could be conceptualised in three ways: belief, practice or affiliation. Belief would be too personal, and practice was not necessarily useful for getting at the idea of identity, so affiliation was the aspect of religion that the ONS needed to try to capture. Armed with this insight, the ONS carried out testing in which it asked people explicitly about their 'religious affiliation', with the result that many respondents said that they would go and look up the term when they got home.[11] In Scotland, testing led to the different approach of asking two questions: 'What religion, religious denomination or body do you belong to?' and 'Which one were you brought up in?'

Aside from problems over the question itself, the ONS had also committed itself to producing a business case for each newly suggested question and religion was deemed to come 'about two thirds of the way down the list of priority topics' in terms of quantifiable benefit.[12] Out of the 'sensitive' topics ONS was trialling – including a new version of the ethnicity question and a question about income – it was the weakest in terms of business case. The Religious Affiliation Sub-Group was disbanded, and its pilgrims scattered to the winds.

In parallel, the Muslim Council of Britain, which had formed in 1998 to represent the interests of British Muslims, had been doing some tactical schmoozing. In 1999, Tony Blair attended one of its receptions and the issue of religion and the census had come up. On the spot, the prime minister announced that 'one way of ensuring that the Muslim voice is heard is our decision to include a question on religion in the 2001 census', which was taken to mean that it would be on there after all, statisticians and business cases be damned.[13] But as the deadline approached for the census form to be finalised, the government had still not introduced the needed legislation to make this happen. It took more lobbying by the MCB, including the eleventh-hour phone calls from Sacranie to the prime minister's office, to get the ball rolling again. The government made the rare step of giving up its own Parliamentary time for a Private Member's Bill to bring in the new religion question and, just in time, it was signed into law.

For Muslims, and in all likelihood for many others from religious minorities, being able to tick a box representing their faith was a moment of pride and contentment at this simple act of recognition. There were 1.5 million Muslims recorded in England and Wales in 2001 and forty-three thousand in Scotland.[14] In England, they were concentrated in London, Birmingham and in the north-west; in Scotland, more than two in five Muslims lived in Glasgow. The MCB had run a publicity campaign in the weeks before census day, calling on believers to 'tick the box marked "Muslim"' in order to make the most of this historic opportunity. Overall, the question had received quite a good response – around 92 per cent – and testing showed that people were answering accurately and honestly.[15] For the most part, that is. When it came to the write-in responses that people could provide for 'other' religions, the ONS got far more than it had bargained for.

In England and Wales, 259 'religions' were identified in addition to the six named categories, and this was bearing in mind that the tick-box for 'Christian' was already supposed to capture all denominations within that faith. In Northern Ireland, a further 148 'religions' were dutifully assigned their own code in the statistics, based on what people had written in. The people of the UK represented faiths from all over the world, from Shintoism to Syrian Orthodox to Raja Yoga and to West African Vodun.[16] People had also clearly used the opportunity to record allegiance to very specific sects with intriguing names like 'Highway of Holiness' and 'Infinite

Way'. But what also inevitably happened was that the definition of 'religion' was interpreted in a loose sense by many people and ended up capturing various worldviews, ideologies and lifestyles that would tend not to be considered religions in any official sense. Responses like 'New Age', 'Spiritualist', 'Universalist', 'Mysticism', 'Occult' and 'Free Church of Love' were arguably ways for people to signal rejection of traditional and organised religion. 'Internationalist', 'Realist', 'Straight Edge' and 'Neo-Platonism' captured ideologies or lifestyles rather than religions per se. And some responses were either plainly not serious or intended as acts of sabotage. Whoever wrote 'Stalinist' was hopefully having a laugh, and it's hard to take 'Follower of Ra', 'Juju Black Magic', 'Heathen' or 'Way of the Leaf' seriously.

But of course the most famous example of this kind of sabotage was that so many people wrote down 'Jedi' as their religion – a fictional religion in the *Star Wars* films – that it emerged as the fourth largest religion in England and Wales. In fact, the 390,000 Jedi surpassed the number of Sikhs (330,000) and trounced the Buddhist faith in terms of followers (Buddhists numbering around 144,000).[17] The Jedi campaign was a light-hearted joke spread partly by a chain email which encouraged people to 'do it because you love Star Wars ... or just to annoy people'.[18] There was also a myth going around that if enough people responded with 'Jedi', it would become an 'official religion', whatever that was supposed to mean. Dedicated seats for Jedi knights next to the bishops in the House of Lords? Proponents of this highly successful practical joke took the trouble to reassure people that the threat of prosecution for filling out false information on the census form didn't apply to the religion question. In any case, how could one prove that a person's report of religious affiliation was false? The Jedi faith was not as popular in

Scotland, it turned out. There was, however, a sizeable following there of 'Terry's Old Geezers and Gals', more commonly known as TOGs – who were devotees of a radio programme presented by Terry Wogan.[19]

Muslims in Britain did not have much time to bask in the contentment of having been counted before events took a significant turn. On 11 September 2001, two hijacked commercial planes were flown at full speed into the Twin Towers of the World Trade Center in New York. The stunned world watched live on television as, within hours, both towers collapsed in a fountain of dust. The attacks – which included a similar attempt on the Pentagon and a further hijacking, and collectively killed nearly three thousand people – were swiftly identified as being the work of the militant Islamic organisation al-Qaeda, whose ultimate goal was the destruction of the West. The UK became gripped by a new fear of terrorism. The memory of bombings by the Irish Republican Army (IRA) was still very fresh – as recently as 1996 the IRA had detonated its largest ever bomb in Manchester, injuring two hundred people – but this threat had an unfamiliar and unsettling new flavour. New words entered common parlance: *jihad*, *radicalism* and *Islamism*, the last a fusion of evangelical religiosity and political activism.

A year on from 9/11, half of British Muslims were reporting that the public was 'less sympathetic' towards them than before the attacks, and nearly two thirds were reporting a perceived increase in hostility or abuse towards them as a community.[20] The full census results were not released until 2003, by which point suspicion towards the Muslim community had only increased and the government had embarked on a counter-terrorism strategy which even it acknowledged was disproportionately focused on detecting radicalisation in British Muslims.[21] The announcement that, based on the census data, Luton was the UK's 'most Muslim town', with a fifth of its population identifying themselves as Muslim, did not necessarily go down as well as those who had advocated for the religion question might have hoped.[22] A backlash appeared, in the form of the British National Party (BNP), which fielded candidates for election on an anti-Muslim platform as early as 2002, and the pressure group the English Defence League (EDL), many of whose early anti-immigrant protests were focused on its origin town of Luton.

Had it been considered by campaigners for more data on Muslims – and data on religion in general – that achieving this could work against them? Published census data can be used to make rankings of the highest concentrations of religious minorities, down to relatively small local areas. The unpublished raw data of course identifies where religious minorities live, to their exact house, and we know that some prominent Muslim voices did express concern at the theoretical risk of such data being used by a surveillance state.[23] Only around ten years earlier, this misuse of census data on religion was exactly what had happened in Serbia to target Bosnian Muslims, with grim effectiveness.[24]

But such voices were faint in comparison with the louder clamour, which had been for the recognition of identity. And despite the questionable benefits, it would set a precedent for similar campaigns demanding data for validation.

In 2001, almost by accident, the census gave England and Wales a windfall of data on another minority group within the population: same-sex couples. In a redesign of the census form in 1991, members of a household were now able to identify themselves not only as 'husband or wife' but to indicate that they were 'living together as a couple'. This change was supposed to be more in service of acknowledging unmarried heterosexual couples and it must have come as a surprise to many same-sex couples to discover this option on the form. There was certainly no campaign to encourage them to declare their same-sex couple status loud and proud, along the lines of 'tick the box marked "Muslim"' (or, for that matter, to declare oneself Cornish). Some people might have been wary of doing so or interpreted the question as being not for them. The data on this from 1991 appears never to have been published but we do know that in the 2001 census roughly seventy-nine thousand people identified themselves as living together in a same-sex couple, which was a data milestone for the population.[25]

It's not an exaggeration to say that before this we had virtually no collection of records in which lesbian, gay or bisexual people had identified themselves willingly. We can probably assume that homosexual desire has existed as long as humanity itself and yet there is just nothing out there to reliably tell us how common it was for people to act on it. Of course, such relationships were forbidden for centuries by church and law, so did that mean these desires were for the most part suppressed? Or were there hidden lives numbering in the thousands, hundreds of thousands or millions which didn't leave a single trace?

Sex between men was punishable by death until 1861 and for more than a century after that it was still a criminal act which could result in imprisonment. In 1806, more men were executed for homosexual acts than for murder.[26] In 1967, the Sexual Offences Act decriminalised sex between men aged twenty-one and over in England and Wales (Scotland and Northern Ireland followed suit in the 1980s) but it was not until 2001 that the age of consent was equalised with that for heterosexual pairings. Sex between women was not specifically criminalised, although it was generally considered unacceptable from a moral standpoint. For obvious reasons, the richer and more powerful segments of society could push the boundaries with less fear of punishment. This allowed Oscar Wilde to write sensual depictions of male romantic relationships into his novels and the writer and socialite Vita Sackville-West to openly pursue a career of lesbian affairs, including with the writer Virginia Woolf. But in the end even Wilde's fame and money couldn't protect him from being convicted of 'gross indecency' and sent to prison.

In fact, when almost nobody seemed to be volunteering the information that they were gay in general settings, one place in which some evidence of their existence was being picked up was in the statistics on police-recorded crime. Between 1930 and 1949, the police in England and Wales recorded an escalating number of crimes of 'indecency between men', from an annual average of 540 at the start of the period to nearly 2,200 per year by the end of it.[27] Records of 'buggery' and 'attempted buggery' also rose and, together with 'indecency', over thirty thousand of these crimes were recorded across the whole twenty-year stretch.* It is true that the police were recording more crime of virtually all kinds as time went on and policing became more sophisticated. So what the statistics tell us is that either homosexual encounters between men were becoming more visible and perhaps more common or that the police were getting 'better' at nobbling people for engaging in these acts.

By the 1950s, the UK was still no place in which to be openly gay, although the gradual fading of the taboo towards

---

* It should be noted that 'buggery' and 'attempted buggery' were crimes which could also include a female victim.

discussions about sex meant that it was deemed time to have a public inquiry into the nature of what we might now call the gay community. The resulting Wolfenden Report, which was published in 1952, noted the huge data gap at the core of the inquiry. It simply wasn't possible to say whether 'homosexual behaviour is much more frequent than used to be the case', as was widely believed at the time.[28]

After Wolfenden, the recorded crime statistics suggest that the policing of 'indecency between males' gradually lost its zeal, with cases falling from 2,300 in 1955 to around 950 in 1966.[29] But it would take until the 1980s for there to be anything like a critical mass of acceptance towards gay men and lesbians in society at large. A flashpoint was the HIV/AIDS crisis. Initially the disease which seemed to be disproportionately affecting gay men was labelled 'gay-related immune deficiency' or GRID because it was assumed to originate from a failing in the constitution of the sufferers. You are forgiven for having déjà vu to the 1850s, when the poor were told that getting cholera was the result of their own moral and genetic failings. When the AIDS virus was discovered, the stigma and victim-blaming started to drain away. But homosexuality itself was still considered taboo and a legal provision known as Section 28 which prohibited 'the promotion of homosexuality' by local authorities – and which all but silenced any discussion of the topic in schools – was in place from 1988 to 2003.

At the end of the 1980s, only 14 per cent of people responding to the new British Social Attitudes Survey agreed that 'same-sex relationships [were] not wrong at all' and though this proportion did gradually rise, we would not reach the point at which more than half of people felt that way until 2013.[30] In that year, same-sex marriage was legalised and a great unthawing of the stigma around homosexuality was well under way. By 2021, the proportion of the public who considered same-sex relationships to be wrong had dropped quite astonishingly from over half (53 per cent) in 2012 to around a quarter (26 per cent).[31]

It was all, sadly, far too late for Bletchley Park codebreaker Alan Turing. In 1952, Turing was convicted of 'gross indecency' following a consensual same-sex encounter and was made to undergo chemical castration, in which oestrogen was regularly injected into his body. In 1954, physically and mentally broken, Turing took his own life. It would be another two decades before the veil of official secrecy over Bletchley was lifted and the public would discover the astonishing feats he personally had achieved in service of his country.

What had changed by the 2000s was that being gay or bisexual had come to be accepted as characteristics of a person which occurred naturally and which it would be unfair to expect them to deny. The idea that people should be judged on their merits and talents rather than on personal characteristics or circumstances outside their control was not new, but it found new articulation in the late twentieth century thanks in part to new language to do with human rights. The UK had been an active party in establishing global aspirations for a more equal world via the United Nations, the European Union and a host of other international projects, and had continuously made a loud point throughout the Cold War about standing up for freedom and democracy. The strictness had also drained almost entirely out of British life by the twenty-first century so that, on a surface level, some social markers like class had ceased to have such a defining effect on life. Conversations about 'equal opportunities' became a staple of political discourse.

The Equality Act 2010 was brought in to enshrine this idea that a society in which people were free from discrimination would be more cohesive and have benefits for all.[32] The Act condensed all the piecemeal legislation that existed already on equalities – consisting of nine pieces of primary legislation, more than a hundred regulations and over 2,500 pages of guidance – into a single law. It created a duty for public bodies to work towards reducing socioeconomic inequalities, and one mechanism for doing this was to outlaw discrimination on the basis of a list of 'protected characteristics' which were (in alphabetical order): disability, gender reassignment, marriage and civil partnership, pregnancy and maternity, race, religion or belief, sex, sexual orientation.

Why these characteristics? Because, quite simply, those were the ones on which legislation already existed. As people have continued to point out, they are a motley assemblage of characteristics, some of which could be said to be entirely beyond a person's control (age, race) and others which could be said to include an element of choice (religion, pregnancy), some of which pose direct conflict with each other in terms of rights (sex and gender reassignment and, in some cases, religion and homosexuality). People have argued that other characteristics are as worthy of inclusion, notably social class.[33] Caste, speaking the Welsh language, homelessness and genetic factors have also been suggested, along with accent, weight, hair colour, hair style, baldness and overall attractiveness – with there being strong evidence that conventional good looks provide an unfair advantage in life.[34] And what about charisma or intellect? Uniqueness, nerve and talent? Although Parliament could expand the official list by way of simple amendment, nothing further has yet made the cut.

What the Equality Act 2010 also did was introduce the requirement for public bodies – and in some cases private companies – to collect a whole lot of new data. 'We cannot tackle inequality if it is hidden ... Transparency is essential to tackling discrimination,' declared the Bill, calling on employers to start reporting on their gender pay gap and proportion of ethnic minority and disabled employees.[35] From 2010 onwards, an industry developed around collecting and monitoring equalities data – sometimes known as diversity and inclusion data – its output a mountainous spoil heap of very personal information. As of 2024, the government held no fewer than 275 mass datasets including information on protected characteristics, which, although the data itself is quite patchy, is remarkable in terms of scale.[36]

Despite this, there remained no reliable estimate of the number of people who considered themselves as belonging under the LGB umbrella. A government survey in 2016 had tried to gather some new data but had run into problems of representativeness, since almost all the people who responded were under the age of thirty-five.[37] The ONS decided there was nothing for it but to pull out the big guns and introduce a question on sexual orientation at the 2021 census. But they wouldn't stop there. They would also try to count another population which had never been systematically counted before: people who were transgender.

The ONS set to work testing different versions of possible questions to capture the lesbian, gay, bisexual and transgender (LGBT) population, and would eventually complete nineteen rounds of testing, while National Records of Scotland (NRS) carried out separate testing of its own.[*][38] An issue with the sexual orientation question was that, as with many identities, there was no universally agreed-upon list of categories or acceptable terms. The NRS initially proposed to have an auto-filling response box for the online version of the sexual orientation question which contained twenty-one options

---

[*] The census in Northern Ireland also asked about sexual orientation but did not include a question on gender identity.

including 'androphilic' and 'skoliosexual' but it was suggested this might be collecting too much information that was a little too obscure.[39] As with the categories for ethnicity, the end result was a somewhat inconsistent list which included 'heterosexual' and 'bisexual' but not 'homosexual', instead offering 'gay or lesbian'. It often comes down to gut feeling as to which terms seem appropriate in a particular place and time.

The statisticians had even more difficulty when it came to devising a way to ask people whether they were transgender. The first challenge was deciding how to instruct people to fill out the question on sex. The ONS initially proposed that people should fill out the sex question according to how they identified, rather than in accordance with their legal sex. But this was successfully challenged in court on the basis that data on sex was a necessity and something distinct from a sense of one's identity at a given time.* The ONS also encountered a backlash when it proposed to add a third, 'other' response category to the sex question and ultimately shelved this idea for fear that a significant number of people would boycott the question or even the whole census in protest.[40]

Adapting the sex question was not going to get us any closer to counting the transgender population, so it was proposed to add a new question about 'gender identity'. In England and Wales, this question was 'Is the gender you identify with the same as your sex registered at birth?' with the response options 'yes' and 'no (write in gender identity)'. To some people, this came across as slightly 'underhand'.[41] People who had legally changed sex, as was made possible by the 2004 Gender Reassignment Act, were now being asked to present

---

* There was also a challenge made along the same lines in Scotland, which was dismissed.

this as a 'gender identity', which had more of an air of transience about it. There was also the fact that although most people were surely aware and accepting of the idea that people could be transgender, the specific concept of gender identity was rather new. The framing of the question ('Is the gender you identify with the same ...') implied that one would have a sense of one's gender identity as a matter of course, when in fact this was far from certain.

The question was also criticised for being too wordy, as well as not particularly intuitive by asking people to affirm in the negative if they had the characteristic. And when the census results came in, it did appear that the question might have confused some people. The ONS found that 'there were clear patterns of trans identification being higher for people born outside the UK and people with lower proficiency in English', which was unexpected to say the least.[42] In fact, people who rated themselves as poor English speakers were six times as likely to say that their gender identity was not the same as their sex at birth. We could certainly come up with arguments as to why this should be taken at face value, but the more likely explanation is that quite a few people misunderstood the question. The local authority where the highest proportion said that their gender identity was different from their sex at birth was Newham in east London, which also had one of the largest populations of recently arrived migrants. Brighton and Hove, regarded as 'the LGBT capital of the UK' and which anyone would have expected to have had one of the largest shares of transgender inhabitants, only ranked twentieth.[43] After the Office for Statistics Regulation reviewed the evidence and concluded that 'people may have found the question confusing' and that the question 'did not work as intended,' the figures were stripped of their accredited status.[44] It was the first time in the census's

220-year history that any of its figures had been officially downgraded.

Would it have been too blunt simply to ask people whether they were transgender? In England and Wales, testing suggested that the question 'Do you consider yourself to be trans?' had low public acceptability.[45] This was not the case in Scotland, however, and a question of this kind was the one finally selected for their census form: 'Do you consider yourself to be trans, or have a trans history?'

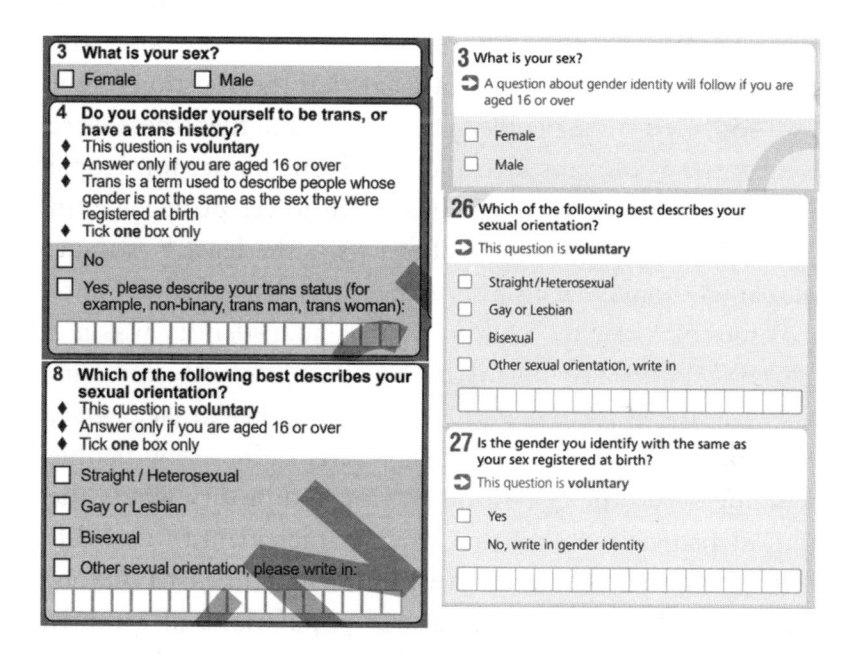

3 What is your sex?
☐ Female ☐ Male

4 Do you consider yourself to be trans, or have a trans history?
♦ This question is **voluntary**
♦ Answer only if you are aged 16 or over
♦ Trans is a term used to describe people whose gender is not the same as the sex they were registered at birth
♦ Tick **one** box only
☐ No
☐ Yes, please describe your trans status (for example, non-binary, trans man, trans woman):
▯▯▯▯▯▯▯▯▯▯▯▯▯▯

8 Which of the following best describes your sexual orientation?
♦ This question is **voluntary**
♦ Answer only if you are aged 16 or over
♦ Tick **one** box only
☐ Straight / Heterosexual
☐ Gay or Lesbian
☐ Bisexual
☐ Other sexual orientation, please write in:
▯▯▯▯▯▯▯▯▯▯▯▯▯▯

3 What is your sex?
⮕ A question about gender identity will follow if you are aged 16 or over
☐ Female
☐ Male

26 Which of the following best describes your sexual orientation?
⮕ This question is **voluntary**
☐ Straight/Heterosexual
☐ Gay or Lesbian
☐ Bisexual
☐ Other sexual orientation, write in
▯▯▯▯▯▯▯▯▯▯▯▯▯▯

27 Is the gender you identify with the same as your sex registered at birth?
⮕ This question is **voluntary**
☐ Yes
☐ No, write in gender identity
▯▯▯▯▯▯▯▯▯▯▯▯▯▯

In the end, 1.5 million people (3.2 per cent of the population) in England and Wales identified with an LGB+ sexual orientation, and 184,000 in Scotland (4 per cent). In England and Wales, notwithstanding some confusion over the question, 144,000 people gave a specific gender identity which was different from their sex at birth, and a further 118,000 said they had a different gender identity but without giving specifics (totalling around 0.5 per cent of the population).[46] In Scotland, despite a different question being asked, the number of people identifying themselves as transgender was very similar, at 0.4 per cent of the population (around twenty thousand people).[47] The figures for the transgender population were a bombshell in terms of statistics, given that the only previous official figure, which had come from the Government Equalities Office in 2009, had estimated an adult transgender population of 6,800 people across the UK as a whole.[48] It was not perfect, but finally the LGBT community had something to say with conviction about its own size.

Identities are moving targets and require us to keep rethinking the terms and the methods we use to hit the bullseye. Kevin Guyan, who has written a history of 'queer data', recommends that we think of data collection processes not as 'reveal[ing] the existence of fully formed LGBTQ identities awaiting discovery' but rather 'partly forg[ing] the identities they claim to locate'.[49] In other words, devising statistical classifications is not a dispassionate, technical process but an act of creation which can have substantial real-world influence. Because classifications can become meaningful to us, whether we would have necessarily chosen them as they are or not, through every repetition of ticking the same box that we 'belong' to on a diversity form. For all their slipperiness, the categories into which we arrange ourselves for the purpose of being counted often end up being passionately defended and deeply cherished. And these categories can also change over time. To a gay person in the 1970s the term 'queer' would have been an insult, while young adults in the 2020s will happily self-identify in that way.

And what's remarkable is how big a role collecting data has played in influencing how importantly some identities are treated in relation to others. The Equality Act used the term 'protected characteristics' to quite literally seal off a selection of personal attributes, and part of the 'protection' involves monitoring via statistics. The greater the effort made to collect data on a population, the more attention it will receive because there is simply so much more that can now be said. And although the list of protected characteristics has not been changed since 2010, who is to say that we won't think of other socially significant identities in future that are worthy of adding to that hallowed list? In 2021, the Law Commission weighed up the idea of adding further groups to those who could be, legally speaking, the victim of a hate crime. It considered sex workers, homeless people, adherents to certain philosophical beliefs and people in 'alternative subcultures' such as 'goths, punks, metallers, [and] emos'.[50] Some police forces had already started recording data on crimes against goths and emos as early as 2013, although the official hate crime laws have never been changed to include them.[51]

Will questions about clothing and hairstyle or affiliation with a particular subculture ever be added to diversity monitoring forms or even the census? When considering what information to collect on equalities, Guyan suggests we ask ourselves, 'What is the goal?' Is it a person's innate characteristics, their presentation, their behaviour, or something else which we think might put them at risk of disadvantage or persecution? That might guide us towards what exactly we need to capture in statistics.

Although the last few decades of data collection on identities have been somewhat messy and fraught, they represent a work in progress. If nothing else, we can say that our census has been doing what it has always done and catching us with the overly bright flash of a Polaroid camera: not necessarily looking our best but as we really are.

15

A New Order of Magnitude

In 2003, dog walkers on the hills around Cheltenham in Gloucestershire were treated to a highly unusual sight. A huge flying saucer seemed to have made a permanent mooring on the Cotswold plains below them and now glinted intriguingly in the sun. It was not an alien vessel, however, but the end product of what had been the largest building site in Europe at the time: a striking aluminium ring, containing seventeen football pitches-worth of open-plan office space and a central courtyard big enough to contain the Royal Albert Hall.[1] The building was the new base for the Government Communications Headquarters (GCHQ), the UK's vast intelligence-gathering operation which at that point employed over five thousand staff. It was a comfortable, modern new office space for these government spooks, some of whom had been working for decades in 1950s huts reminiscent of Bletchley Park.

The fact that the UK's communications espionage operation was going to be housed in a futuristic doughnut which not only lacked any hint of secrecy but could quite literally be seen from space was calculated to have a certain effect. It showed off to the rest of the world the sheer scale of resources we were willing to throw at communications interception. It was also designed to attract young, more glamorous recruits who might not have identified with the stereotype of bespectacled boffins who didn't mind working in a fifty-year-old Portakabin. But most of all, it was to respond to the fact that the flow of information around the world had changed in a way that had pushed our old systems well beyond their limit. Largely because of the internet, we had now entered the age of mass information, and were blasting further into it at warp speed.

By 2013, however, GCHQ had gone into damage control mode. A whirlwind of controversy was sweeping through the open-plan floors and, with the nation's eyes fixed upon them, some staff were likely rueing the fact that their workplace had made such a glittering effort to draw attention to itself.

In June of that year, at a secret meeting in Hong Kong, a contractor for the American equivalent of GCHQ, the National Security Agency (NSA), had met with British journalists and handed over a huge stash of classified documents revealing the extent of communications interception on both sides of the Atlantic. After dropping this bombshell, the whistleblower, Edward Snowden, fled to Russia and claimed asylum, while the journalists returned to the UK and delivered these revelations with an enormous public splash. GCHQ, with the aid of telecoms companies, had been intercepting virtually all internet communications, including private messages via email and social media from the public at large, not just those who were under suspicion of anything.[2] Not only this, but a network of information-sharing meant any person's messages, browsing history – everything they did online or via their phone – was visible to spooks at both GCHQ and the NSA.[3] Snowden's most extreme claim, that from his desk he could 'wiretap anyone, from you or your accountant, to a federal judge or even the president' only using an email address, was forcefully disputed by the agencies in question but nonetheless created profound public shock and disapproval. There had, of course, already been public awareness that anything put on the internet was not exactly secure – but still we realised we had been naive.

The revelations fired civil liberties campaigners into action, some of the most prominent of which at the time were the groups Liberty, Big Brother Watch and the Open Rights Group. A string of court cases against the lawfulness of the powers in the Regulation of Investigatory Powers Act 2000, which had been used to justify the mass surveillance, went all the way to the European Court of Human Rights, which ruled that it had been an illegal breach of privacy. A law brought in to smooth over this wrinkle, the Investigatory Powers Act 2016, was immediately challenged on the same grounds and was still making its way through the UK courts as of 2024.

Surveillance of the population is nothing new and may have been just as invasive in the distant past as it is now, albeit via different means. The historian Edward Higgs has noted that 'in some ways, public surveillance in early modern England was more intense and wide-ranging than anything experienced in Western societies today', although admittedly that was before the GCHQ revelations.[4] In the Tudor times, for example, social control operated at the parish level, with the clergy, justices of the peace and overseers of the poor laws forming a moral and legal web that clung to people the more they struggled to escape. The liberty to roam freely around England was preserved for very few. The further back we go, the more confined people were in geographical and behavioural terms: in the thirteenth century it would have been very unwise to wander far from one's village without carrying written identification.[5] Straying outside of these norms and restrictions could cost a person their life.

Surveillance means watching. Information-gathering simply means collecting and storing data. And one does not automatically imply the other, although they do have a symbiotic relationship.

GCHQ in 2013 was doing what the secret services have always done, which was to comb through any and all available data, looking for red flags. In the age of the internet and social media, the amount of data that is out there is simply so much bigger and more personal than ever before. And the GCHQ revelations raised an important issue adjacent to the matter of whether it was acceptable to be spied on. The possibility exists now for the state to gather and store quite a lot of data on us without our conscious input – and even if it is being done for a more benign public policy purpose than spying, is this what we want?

The period from 1939 to 1952 when the National Register was being kept constantly up to date was the time when the government had the most information on the largest number of its citizens at its fingertips. But, as we saw in Chapter 11, seven years after the war had ended was deemed long enough to have kept maintaining this 'emergency' database and the idea of having a peacetime population register was thoroughly shut down. This was not for want of lobbying by the Registrar General George North, who tried to argue for the benefits of a single identification number for the new welfare system, only to be dismissed as being a proponent of 'socialist card-indexing'.[6] There had also been the influential case of Harry Willcock, mentioned earlier, who had appealed against his conviction for not presenting an ID card when asked to by the police and used the occasion to protest against the card-carrying requirement on the grounds of civil liberties.

Although Willcock's conviction had stood, the High Court judge in the case had questioned the justification for an ID requirement which 'tends to turn law-abiding subjects into law-breakers' (notwithstanding the fact that Willcock himself had been asked to present his card upon being caught driving over the speed limit).[7] Rather poetically, poor Willcock died suddenly in the middle of giving a public speech with the title 'Why I am not a socialist' in 1952, just ten months after it ceased to be compulsory to carry a card.[8]

Perhaps the most pressing reason for ending ID cards and the NR was the ongoing cost of the whole operation, which was estimated to be an unnecessary half a million pounds per year. The academic Christine Bellamy has gone as far as to say that the key constraint to carrying on the NR was money.[9] Had the Treasury not been so worried about post-war debt repayment, the register may well have continued for decades longer before the chipping of civil liberties complaints might have finally brought it down.

It was in the 1960s that a sustained line of questioning started up about the government's right to collect and store private data on its citizens. The campaign group the National Council for Civil Liberties (NCCL) drew attention to the amount of data being collected (and even computerised) by government departments as well as big business. This was at a time when the Cold War hung like a creaking glacier over daily life, threatening to come crashing down at any minute. Britain was on the side of liberty in this fight, the alternative being a very real curtailment of individual freedom which saw people living like feudalised peasants in the USSR and under the constant eye of the totalitarian Stasi regime in East Germany. Dystopian novels like *Nineteen Eighty-Four*, *Fahrenheit 451*, *Lord of the Flies* and *A Clockwork Orange* – and their respective film adaptations – resonated with a public disturbed by the prospect of authoritarianism and fearful about the corruptibility of human nature. The rise of digital technology was also providing us with new nightmare-fuel about man versus machine, a powerful depiction of which was operating system HAL coldly turning on its master in the 1968 film *2001: A Space Odyssey*.

In parallel, however, the UK government was collecting more data than ever before, and questions were being asked in Whitehall about how to manage it all. This led to the GRO and the Department for Education and Science drafting a green paper, innocently titled 'People and Numbers', in the summer of 1969 which proposed a system of common numbers to identify people across different government datasets.[10] Some other departments, including the Cabinet Office, were initially in favour of the idea, even if it involved a population register. But practical though it might have been, the government feared the suggestion to be dangerously out of step with the way the public mood was going and by November of that year all further discussion of it had been personally forbidden by Prime Minister Harold Wilson. When the idea of having a population register was floated in relation to the collection of the community charge ('poll tax') twenty years later, any mention of such an idea by ministers was again banned.[11]

In the meantime, data privacy had become the concern *du jour*. After Right to Privacy Bills were tested in the House of Commons in 1967 and 1970, the government instated committees to look at the issues of data privacy and data protection. The latter of these, the Lindop Committee, audited the number of records held by individual departments, uncovering an astonishing number of records that were already held on computers in 1978. There were records for the majority of people in the country on matters from national insurance to vehicle ownership and employment.[12] Some local authorities were keeping computerised databases of 'illegitimate' births, possibly without the knowledge of the parents concerned.[13]

All of this was being held with essentially no legal framework to ensure privacy or govern the way in which it could be shared across the public sector. In 1984, the Data Protection Act finally established such a system, although it did include a clause allowing the authorities to use any data in its holdings if there was a security-related case for doing so. This exception is still a key feature of privacy laws and even census records and other statistical survey data can be handed over for security purposes, which has worried privacy campaigners the more personal census questions have become.[14]

By the time the 2000s came around, 'national security' was the buzzword on the lips of the politicians, whispered continuously to soothe the passage of £330 million of public funds on the new GCHQ doughnut. At the same time, around 2002, the government published a green paper on 'entitlement cards', which suggested bringing back a population register.[15] Although the main argument and emphasis was on the idea of a physical identity card as a means of apparently tackling terrorism and other types of crime, it was also argued that a central register could be beneficial to all manner of administrative processes as well as the creation of statistics.[16] Despite some misgivings within and outside government, the proposals morphed into a Government Bill which became law as the Identity Cards Act 2006.

The remarkable scale of the vision in the Identity Cards Act really cannot be overstated. The government had legislated, in peacetime, that a full population register – the National Identity Register – was to be built, which would contain, 'in relation to every resident of the UK aged sixteen or over, his or her birth date, gender, names (present and past), addresses (present and past), nationality, entitlement to remain in the

UK and "external characteristics of his that are capable of being used for identifying him".[17] Had it been fully built – spoiler alert: it was not – and had people registered in their millions, it would have been the most extensive population register in the world, containing not only written but biometric personal information.

It was perhaps because the plans went so far down the road towards aiding law enforcement that the scheme became the target of protest by civil liberties campaigners. The campaign group Liberty was the loudest single opponent; director Shami Chakrabarti appeared regularly on TV and radio to condemn ID cards as an act of state overreach. A pamphlet produced by Liberty in 2005 argued that making registration compulsory turned citizens from 'volunteers to conscripts', 'tagged conscripts of the state' and 'traceable numbered entities' like cars, and placed innocent members of the public in the same category as 'paedophiles, murderers out of prison on licence, and suspicious characters monitored by the security services'.[18] It suggested that introducing a register and ID cards in the age of nanotechnology risked putting us on a slippery slope to more invasive means of tagging. Should people repeatedly keep forgetting their ID cards, the Liberty pamphlet speculated, 'a very tiny chip ... will be easily and painlessly inserted in an earlobe or under the skin of the wrist, carrying all the personal and biometric information the authorities would need'.[19] These were not the ramblings of a tinfoil-hat conspiracy theorist, mind you – the pamphlet was written by respected philosopher A. C. Grayling, then a professor at Birkbeck College, University of London.

Grayling's less sci-fi inspired objection to ID cards – and the National Identity Register – was on the basis of principle. It was not right, he argued, that the authorities should have 'permanent open access to private facts' about people, into which they could dip if a security need ever required it.[20] Just as the state must prove the guilt of a defendant in a criminal trial – rather than it being on the defendant to prove innocence – the state should come looking for information only when it had the need, as opposed to people being required to keep information about themselves on record all the time.

Other criticisms were along the familiar lines of objection to any apparatus that resembled that of totalitarian states. Another prominent critic of ID cards, the then MP Peter Lilley, accused the government of 'creating a system which could be abused in an oppressive manner by a future government of an (even) more authoritarian disposition than New Labour'.[21]

But although many defenders of 'liberties' mythologised Britain as a place which had never seen the kind of grim freedom restrictions as behind the Iron Curtain, it couldn't completely play the innocent. Britain had, of course, had a population register throughout both wars and compulsory ID cards in England and Wales during the more recent one. And some of its colonial administrations had operated regimes of exactly the kind that were now being condemned as 'un-British'. More recently in Northern Ireland, during the height of the Troubles in the 1970s, the army had conducted local censuses to establish a population register of certain areas. Using what is believed to have been an extensive network of covert surveillance, they built up an index within this of suspected terrorists and their extended families. It is estimated that by 1974, there were computerised personal records on 40 per cent of Northern Ireland's population.[22] Can we really call that innocent until proven guilty?

Initially, it looked as if the National Identity Register would be constructed regardless of this clamour of objection. At the end of 2008, foreign nationals started to be added and issued with ID cards. From 2009, residents of Greater Manchester, then everyone in the north-west, and then sixteen- to twenty-four-year-olds in London were invited to register. Uptake, it seems, was minimal, with only fifteen thousand cards ever being issued. The new coalition government which came to power in 2010 promptly abandoned the whole scheme and made a point of confirming that all records had been destroyed.[23]

As in the case of the 1939 National Register, a major factor in the decision to scrap the Identity Register was its apparently unjustifiable cost. The initial cost of running the scheme for a few years had, perhaps unrealistically, been estimated at as little as £1.3 billion, which later estimates revised to almost £20 billion.[24] The 2008 financial crisis had created anxiety about the level of government debt and politicians had even started to invoke wartime rhetoric about 'keeping calm and carrying on' and the need for austerity. It was an uncanny parallel of the 1950s that we were again talking about shedding a registration scheme in order to tighten our belts. The public had also not been thrilled at the idea of having to pay up to £93 to obtain a card under the scheme, which had been described as a 'plastic poll tax'.[25]

Trust in the state's ability to handle such a scheme had also been damaged by a series of large-scale IT failures in virtually all main government departments during the 1990s and 2000s. The failure of an online casework database to manage asylum applications had caused by far the biggest backlog of claims the country had ever seen.[26] Outsourced IT systems to manage criminal court records, welfare benefits and the fire and rescue services had ended up going way over budget and obstructing public service delivery.[27] We now know that, at the very same time, a glitching IT system used for Post Office book-keeping was inexplicably making money disappear from branches all across the country. More than nine hundred sub-postmasters were accused of theft and wrongfully convicted in what was later exposed as possibly the most extensive miscarriage of justice in UK history.[28] So, naturally, confidence in IT systems was not high. But it was also slightly pathetic that the Identity Register should be defeated by fear that the technology could not cope, given that the wartime NR had operated successfully on pieces of card.

But that persistent tendency for the state to want more data didn't switch off just because the Identity Register went out of the window. The fact is, the British state can collect and store more information on the population than ever before, and it does. The irony from a civil liberties perspective is that it is now amassing data in a less overt way than by requiring everyone to submit some details to a central register.

Information has been a source of power to governments since the days that William Petty coined the notion of 'political arithmetic' and, indeed, before. The systematic keeping of records on people living in the UK, as we've seen, began with records of births, deaths and marriages, and of taxpayers and military recruits, before progressing to ten-yearly censuses and regular surveys. The amount of data held centrally really took off as the state started to become more rationalised from the 1910s onwards. The creation of the old age pension and unemployment insurance meant the details of millions of people had to be collected and stored in a way that it could be easily retrieved. In 1910 there had been a grand total of twenty-seven people employed to manage pension records, six of whom were children; by 1946, the operation was employing four thousand staff. The high level of unemployment in the interwar period meant that in the mid-1920s, one fifth of the Ministry of Labour's staff were employed just to manage the scheme's records.[29] During the Cold War, for all its examples of overzealous surveillance, all countries had drifted towards a consensus that having more information was generally a good thing. The apparatus of the modern state is vastly more complex and far-reaching than ever before. By the end of the twentieth century, we had become a different beast entirely: what historian Edward Higgs calls the 'Information State' – a giant information-churning machine.

Administrative statistics are one thing, but where governments have really managed to capture the spice of life has been through large-scale surveys. Long-running initiatives like the Family Resources Survey, the Annual Survey of Hours and Earnings and the Crime Survey have given governments precious insight into people's real behaviours and preferences. It is not an exaggeration to say that these kinds of survey have been vital to public policy up until the present day. And between them they have generated millions of records of sometimes extremely personal information on members of the public who have volunteered it in the name of research. But the times in which people would respond obediently appear to be fading.

The Labour Force Survey (LFS) has been particularly badly hit by falling response rates. The idea behind the LFS is that eighty thousand people are randomly selected from the UK population each year to answer questions relating to employment. They continue to be followed up with for five years and the responses they give are supposed to be representative of the population as a whole. At its peak in the 1990s, 84 per cent of people who were asked to fill out the survey complied.[30] This went into a gradual downward slide, hitting just 28 per cent in 2023, with a mere 13 per cent continuing to respond to the survey for even one further year.[31] In 2023, the ONS had to admit that it couldn't use the data any more without having to make a lot of assumptions, which introduced uncertainty.[32] In other words, even though tens of thousands of people were still responding to the survey, the picture wasn't big enough to be of any use.

It isn't just the UK's problem that the public have mostly stopped responding to social surveys – the same thing has happened across Europe and North America. And there are two parts to the explanation as to why this is the case. Firstly, it is getting harder to make contact with people even to ask them to take the survey, of which much has to do with the fact that many people don't have a landline phone and that it has become less likely that someone (most often the woman of the household) will be at home during the day to open the door to an enumerator.

But the second and more influential factor is that, even when people are successfully contacted, people are no longer as willing as they once were to participate.[33] Even when the rationale for the survey is explained, more people than ever refuse to take part. Is this a sign that we feel less of a civic duty to respond to surveys simply for the sake of research? Or that we no longer trust the authorities to handle our data in an appropriate way? Perhaps we feel that our time is too precious nowadays to be spending hours on a survey without generous compensation. Or is it that we have reached the point of survey fatigue and feel like we already give more than enough through the information-gathering which now accompanies access to virtually any service? The answer is likely all of these. But the irony is that when we don't volunteer our data on request, those seeking to gather information will look for ways to obtain it – or at least a workable alternative – which don't really give us the option to say no.

In the case of the LFS, the statisticians have turned to two alternative sources: scouring the internet for clues about the labour market from job advertisements and taking data from administrative records.[34] The first of these is quite self-explanatory, except that it is done in a more systematic way than you might be picturing. The second involves asking His Majesty's Revenue and Customs (HMRC) for 'real time information' on the number of people employed in different sectors. These are records of people who are currently in payroll employment and could include whatever other information is attached to a person's tax record, notably age, sex, address and marital status. This is a case of data being transferred across departments and used for purposes other than the one for which it was originally collected.

The idea now, as of the mid-2020s, is that administrative data is the way of the future, not surveys and censuses. In 2014, at the peak of post-financial crisis austerity, the government was alarmed by the fact that the most recent census had cost nearly half a billion pounds and that the cost of the census undertaking seemed to be spiralling every time. In a letter to the UK Statistics Authority, which oversees all data-gathering by the state, it expressed its view that 'the census in its current form is outdated and – with modern technology – could be delivered more effectively and more cheaply'. The ambition was that 'censuses after 2021 will be conducted using other sources of data', by which they meant doing away with the census survey altogether and switching to administrative sources.[35] This was not a sudden whim – already in 2008 the Treasury Select Committee had recommended that the 2011 census be 'the last census in the UK where the population is counted through the collection of census forms'.[36] It was not, and a census went ahead in 2021 (2022 in Scotland). But more recently, the ONS has itself proposed an end to the census and a gradual move to a fully administrative system.[37] At the time of writing, it is not clear whether a full census will go ahead in 2031, although it seems unlikely.

While the idea of getting rid of the census might horrify historians and genealogists, it is not such a crazy idea from a practical perspective. Data from administrative records is often more accurate than people's responses to surveys. Just think of the fact that women misrepresenting their age on the census was once such a common problem that there were public information campaigns to get them to stop doing it. The census can also pick up some oddities because it is a snapshot on one single night, for example if people happen to be away on holiday, in hospital, temporarily between jobs or hiding in a broom cupboard in the Palace of Westminster. It is also potentially less burdensome to the individual. Some countries, including Denmark, Sweden and the Netherlands, stopped doing traditional censuses decades ago and permanently rely on administrative sources – such as payroll earnings, tax and welfare benefits, education and health department records – when they want to generate statistics on the population. The people concerned are none the wiser while this is being done: it is unobtrusive. Danes don't feel a shiver pass through them every time the eyes of statisticians scan across their data.

But the key difference between countries which do this and the UK is that those countries have population registers and we do not. They have what our Identity Register was supposed to be: some basic information on every person, held in a central repository, with a unique number attached to each person which is the same across all government services. This type of system would have seemed like a data utopia to someone like William Farr, and certainly to Sylvanus Vivian.

In our case, because we don't have this one number per person system, even compiling a central administrative dataset which includes most people is an almighty faff. Trying to join records across different departments' databases is also intensely laborious, compared with how easy it would be if we all had our own unique ID number. The National Audit Office has estimated that 60 to 80 per cent of government data analysts' time is spent cleaning and merging data – in some areas, the equivalent of hundreds of people working full time.[38] Moving to a purely administrative-based system without a population register is unprecedented anywhere. It is not clear how to link people without ID numbers in a country which has over thirty thousand John Smiths alone, nor whether doing so will cost less than a traditional census.[39] We are now in uncharted territory. And it is a turning point for the relationship between the people and the state.

The trend towards administrative data over surveys and censuses comes with a number of implications for us as citizens. Opting out of a social survey can be done at no cost or consequence, and opting out of a census may land you with a fine and a criminal record, but you cannot ultimately be forced to give up your information. Opting out from appearing in any government-held databases, on the other hand, is nigh on impossible. To not appear at all in payroll and tax records, in the benefits system, in National Insurance records or in the NHS's database would be quite a feat. You would basically have to live off-grid or be a very accomplished criminal.

Another implication concerns civil liberties. The fact that records currently can't be easily linked across government datasets means there are firewalls in place. If an oppressive, totalitarian government were to take over tomorrow, it would have a relatively hard time singling people out with accuracy – unlike the experience the Nazis had when they seized control of the Dutch central records bureau. This is clearly a point in favour of our traditional system and what some people argue should have been enough to justify keeping it entirely as it was. Although we never did the mass biometric data collection envisaged in the Identity Cards Act 2006, it did become compulsory for everyone issued with a visa to submit biometric information. The fact that most people have passports also means there is a huge repository of pictures of our faces attached to our personal information. The only real constraint to matching people across different databases, once we remove any legal partitions, is resourcing.

On principle too, as A. C. Grayling would have it, civil liberties are threatened by the very idea of government stitching together pieces of personal information collected for specific purposes and using it for something else. The ONS's proposals for how to estimate the population by ethnicity without a census includes harvesting data from the NHS's Talking Therapies dataset.[40] This is data from diversity monitoring forms people have filled out when referring themselves for counselling. Another suggestion is to use data provided by prisoners to make estimates about national identity.[41] It's easy to see an ethical case against using data that people have provided in circumstances where it might seem compulsory to do so (even if it isn't) and where they might naturally expect it to stay private. Diversity monitoring is carried out in a lot of settings nowadays and can sometimes feel gratuitous. Does my optician really need to know my sexual orientation? If we suspect this private data might be shared and used for other purposes, we may be tempted to stop providing it at all.

This brings us to the question of whether we want this level of disconnection from the state when it comes to information-gathering. Sure, it saves us half an hour every ten years if we don't have to complete a census form. But there is something about that moment of volunteering our information that resets the power balance between people and the state. The state needs us, in our millions, to give up private facts, and in exchange we expect functioning public services and some level of central planning. That moment is also one of negotiation. As we've seen, times when individuals have started to be included in a counting exercise can be powerful acts of acknowledgement and even liberation. Through lengthy campaigns to acknowledge the living conditions of the poor, the working conditions of the low-paid and of children, the reality of women's lives, and the plight of the sick and unemployed – in all these cases and many more – the gathering of public data was the oil in the machine. And even though the response rate to social surveys has slipped, censuses have continued to attract a very high level of cooperation. The fact that such concerted lobbying has taken place for questions on ethnicity, religion, sexual orientation and gender identity in recent decades confirms that many people see it as a type of ceremonial occasion to make their mark.

Most importantly, removing moments where we are asked to consciously volunteer our private information removes opportunities for protest – which is, in some ways, a necessary health check for governments and the legitimacy of the state as a whole. How can we make the same point that the suffragettes did – 'if we don't count, you don't get to count us' – if the state already has information on us, just from our participating in everyday life, and doesn't need to ask for more?

Censuses and surveys have been a rich arena for protest for the past two hundred years. As early as 1811, evidence suggests that there was mass avoidance of the census in Newcastle and Gateshead over opposition to the perceived possibility that it could be used for conscription.[42] Lone protesters often defaced their forms, gave false information to trip up the authorities or, in the case of Rolling Stones drummer Charlie Watts in 1991, declared publicly that 'those who fill in the forms are sheep' and accepted a £350 fine. In 1951, women from the British Housewives' League attempted to light their census papers on fire in a frying pan in front of the Houses of Parliament in protest against continued rationing. A photograph captures one of the housewives looking slightly perturbed as her form goes up in flames right under a policeman's nose.[43] Liberals protested the 1971 census on the grounds of civil liberties and fears that computerising the returns – which was being done for the first time – was a step too far in an Orwellian direction. The *Sunday Mirror* led a campaign against it, which conveniently featured women stripping naked to illustrate how the census would lay people's private lives bare.[44] In 2005, a group staged a naked protest in Parliament Square to make the same point about ID cards.[45] These protests were performative and generally benign. But important nonetheless. And as the government collects and holds more personal information on us than ever, is it not more important than ever that it is given and used by consent?

Or are we being too precious about privacy? Ripping up identity cards and burning census forms in frying pans now seem slightly quaint as ways of foiling the authorities' attempts to collect our data. Every moment that we use our smartphones we are releasing a cloud of data spores into a digital environment which is only in the early stages of regulation. Private companies have a huge amount of digital data on us, and we allow them the free use of it when we sign up to their terms and conditions. And there is now precedent for government departments to use this digital data from private companies such as Google in aggregate form to generate statistics. The ONS did this during the pandemic to analyse the impact of social distancing regulations.[46] As citizens we don't yet know what our boundaries are with the harvesting of our data via these unobtrusive methods, partly because there is an air of aloof technicality to the way the authorities go about it. We let our data be collected because we don't feel we have an alternative and we don't know whether or not to feel any apprehension about the way this is going.

But in the UK in particular, our tradition has been to hand over information to the state at discrete moments in time and to cherish what we see as respect for our privacy in this arrangement. This is different from a country like Norway, where people are used to the government having their data permanently on file. There they have had a population register for the entirety of most people's lifetimes and they also have a system whereby people's individual salaries are public information and have been since 1814. For one thing, we do not have the same culture of civil obedience in the UK as in Norway. We might think of ourselves as rather culturally and socially restrained – indirectness, formality and politeness are all part of our national stereotype – but in reality we are rather difficult and disruptive as a nation. F. Scott Fitzgerald once wrote that the English 'live on a concentrated essence of the anti-social', and while this is obviously rather unflattering, it catches at a truth which is that there is an antagonism at our core – and dare I say it, that of the Scots, Welsh and Northern Irish as well.[47]

Whatever the future holds when it comes to collecting data on the UK population, a power-sharing arrangement between individual citizen and state will always be part of the story. As A. C. Grayling would have it, '"who I am" is one central feature of the private domain of my liberty'.[48] Freedom is the right to withhold; democracy is cherishing this right while offering up the truth.

Summing Up

Statistics condense the complex lives of a multitude into a few basic numbers on a page. But over the course of two hundred years of producing statistics, we've ended up with a truly enormous volume of numerical information. We are talking warehouses full of census and survey returns, archives of birth and death records, and libraries full of statistical publications, not to mention the digital databases being constantly updated at a pace the statisticians of old could scarcely have imagined. At a certain point, the quantity of all this becomes far too much for an individual person to comprehend. As a society, how can we make sense of this mass of information? Our history is captured within that vast tangle, if only we can find a way to tease it out. Is there any way to pull out a central thread?

In the mid-1990s, academics Danny Dorling and David Atkins at Newcastle University were pondering these same questions.[1] They were trying to come up with ways to visualise population change in Great Britain over the past ninety years and one of their experiments led them to the elegant and pleasingly simple idea of pinpointing Britain's 'population centre of gravity'. This was the place on the map which would represent the centre point of the British population if each small area across the country was weighted according to its population size. If most of the population was concentrated in the south, the population centre of gravity would be south of the geographical centre of the country, and so on.

In 1991, this centre of gravity was just south of the town of Swadlincote in Derbyshire. But looking back over time, using historical data, Dorling and Atkins discovered that it had not always been there. Since the start of the twentieth century, it had been moving rapidly south-eastwards and had covered a total distance of just over sixteen miles as the crow flies.

Thirty years later, James Gleeson at the Greater London Authority tried the same exercise again, but going all the way back to 1801.[2] To go back that far, the data had to be limited to England only. And adding in this extra hundred years revealed a strikingly different trend. In this England-only version, the population centre of gravity had also moved south-eastwards since 1911 but prior to this it had been travelling consistently north. The result was that more than two hundred years of historical population movements told the story of an enormous U-turn. We had started out in 1801 on what would later become the A428 road to the west of Rugby in Warwickshire and had ended up in 2021 on the other side of Rugby, just off the A428 going east. Two hundred years of history and we were almost right back where we had started.

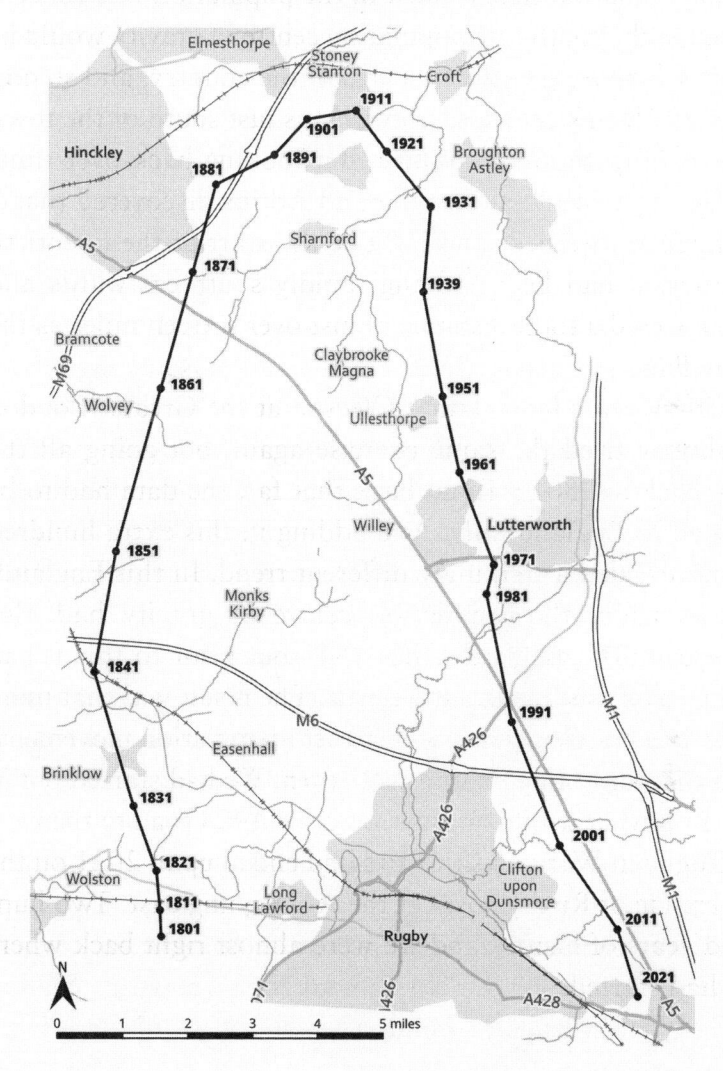

England's population centre of gravity, by decade

But, of course, it's not about the destination so much as the journey. At first, between 1801 and 1841, the population's centre had travelled north-west, as Lancashire and Merseyside swelled with workers busily engaged in the production of cotton textiles, wool and steel. After 1841, the population started to move north-eastwards towards the coal mines and heavy industries which were raising the fortunes of Yorkshire, Durham and Tyneside. It was not to last. In 1911, the population reached its most northerly balancing point, with the centre of gravity coming to rest in Stoney Stanton, a small village in Leicestershire which can trace its history all the way back to the Domesday Book. Around the same time, the shipbuilders in Jarrow started to get the first inkling that their livelihood's days were numbered. After the First World War, their industry collapsed and manufacturing downsized all across the country, hitting the north the hardest. Over the following decades, the drop in demand for factory workers and coal miners sealed the fate of many northern villages and towns, and power shifted to the suburbs of the Midlands and south. We went into a relentless southward plummet which doubled in speed once we hit the 1980s.

As of 2021, England's 'heart' in population terms was on a patch of scrubland between a new housing development and one of the country's largest distribution centres, in Northamptonshire in the Midlands. Some historians have speculated that nearby river plains might have been the site of Boudicca's final battle against the Romans, in which the Celtic Britons were defeated.[3] For the past few decades, our population centre of gravity has been more or less exactly tracing the line of the old Roman road known as Watling Street, which leads to London via the Watford Gap. If the trend continues, England's centre of gravity will pass that symbolic dividing line between north and south in the 2040s.[4]

The very last point in that journey, in 2021, represents us at a very unusual point in time. In January of 2020, Covid-19 started spreading across the UK and by the end of March the virus was killing several hundred people per day and the whole of the country was in lockdown. The pandemic would drag us across ragged peaks of mass infection for two years until we subdued it, by which point it had caused the deaths of nearly a quarter of a million people. In the midst of the general disruption, there were doubts as to whether the census which had been planned for 2021 should go ahead. In Scotland, the conclusion was that it should not – and so there it was postponed until 2022.

In England, Wales and Northern Ireland censuses were held in 2021, and what they give us is a historical snapshot of just how out of the ordinary that time was. In an echo of the evacuation of children during the Blitz, London's population came up around three hundred thousand (3 per cent) lower than expected, with some boroughs' populations being depleted by almost a quarter.[5] There were also nearly a million more people living in households consisting of parents and their adult children than there had been in 2011. In March 2021, around 5.6 million people were furloughed from work, and although they were instructed to fill out the census to reflect what they were doing previously, it's fair to assume that many never went back to those jobs. The census in England and Wales also showed that a staggering 8.7 million people or a third of the workforce was working from home, reflecting the fact that a 'stay at home' order was in place at the time.[6] Hybrid working became the norm for many, even after the pandemic subsided, and the long-term effect of these changes on population movements has yet to be seen.

The pandemic also generated an explosion of new data, both medical and social, and was a time of creative experimentation for UK statisticians. Some of the discussions at the level of high government resembled those of a War Cabinet and, as in the First and Second World Wars, data was given a prominent seat at the table in conversations about resources and manpower. Timely statistics were central to planning our response, from deciding where to build 'Nightingale' overflow hospitals to allegedly at one time considering a cull of all pet cats if it emerged that they could transmit the virus.[7] Luckily the latter measure was not needed, and in any case our official data on pets is thankfully very poor. Unlike in previous national emergencies, though, it doesn't seem anyone used the occasion to advocate for a population register. Had Sylvanus Vivian still been around, you can bet he wouldn't have let the opportunity pass.

In this book we've looked back over more than two hundred years of history through the moments in which we have counted ourselves. And there are a few key reflections that sum it all up, the first being that taking the trouble to collect all this data has been immensely worthwhile. Had it not been for the determination of Victorian statisticians to track and make sense of disease outbreaks, it could have taken much longer to understand and fight back against cholera, typhoid and other illnesses we have all but eradicated today. Snow, Farr and Nightingale might have been operating in the dark when it came to understanding why disease spread, but their data illuminated patterns which at least suggested what could be done to stop it. Without the creative efforts of social scientists like Rowntree and Booth, how much longer would the elites have gone on dismissing poverty as the result of people's moral failings, as opposed to recognising it as primarily the result of low wages, bad luck and the absence of any real safety net? It's doubtful that we would have been able to imagine, let alone pull off, some of the centrally planned projects which drove social progress in this country without accurate population data, from council housing to the NHS. 'Power may be localised,' wrote the Victorian reformer John Stuart Mill, 'but knowledge, to be most useful, must be centralised.'[8] If it hadn't been for times when we decided to lay aside our preconceptions and collect data that described our lives honestly, who knows how much longer governments would have gone on believing misconceptions: that the population was shrinking, that women didn't tend to work outside of the home, that the population mainly lived in the countryside, that we were being overrun with foreigners, and that the UK was still a vast majority Christian country.* More recently, we have embraced the idea that there is value in collecting data on people's personal characteristics for the sake of validation alone.

We've also learned is that there is no straight answer to the question of how much data is enough – or, for that matter, too much. When should we stop counting? While we have continuously added to the range of things we try to count, there have been far fewer examples of us ceasing to collect data once we have started. Yes, it's true we no longer use the census to record 'lunatics' and the 'feeble-minded', but only in the sense that we have sensitised and indeed vastly expanded the way we classify mental conditions. We have kept adding questions to the census, and they have tended to veer further towards the personal. The future holds some possibilities we already know about, in terms of where data collection will go, with the trend towards the personal likely to continue. Statisticians have started experimenting with using 'digital trace data', which refers to the breadcrumbs dropped by private individuals moving through the online world, for policy purposes. The use of biometric data is another frontier which public policy is slowly edging across. As critics of the National Identity Register pointed out in the 2000s, at that time we already collected

---

* Incidentally, the 2021 census of England and Wales showed that, for the first time, less than 50 per cent of the population identified as Christian. In Scotland's 2022 census, 51 per cent of the population identified as having 'no religion' – a substantial change even from 2011, when over half of the population said they were Christian.

biometric data from criminals in the form of fingerprints, mugshots and sometimes DNA. In the 1990s, the Home Affairs Select Committee suggested that we should have a national database of everyone's DNA, although this was never acted on.[9] But the government does now hold biometric data on anyone who has migrated to this country in recent years on a visa and it has a repository of photos of practically all of us through our passport applications. Scotland Yard detectives have started dipping into the DNA repositories held by private genealogy services to try to track down criminals in cold cases. No one is suggesting that the government is going to harvest all of our DNA or that we're going to be microchipped – put the tinfoil down – but this is an area of data management which is only going to become more significant in future.

With this in mind, something else we've learned is that public trust is important. Even when we're not indulging in conspiracy theories, the idea that data held by the government could be used to target people should still always be acknowledged. Because, of course, governments do use what they learn from data to target us with policies which are intended to improve certain situations. And there are examples of the reverse, even in fairly recent times. As circumstances escalated in the run-up to the First World War, a central registry was made of Germans and Anglo-Germans, which was used to bring them in for questioning. The same was done during the Second World War, aided by the machinery of the NR, except this time Germans, Austrians and some Italians living in the UK were classified as 'enemy aliens' and sent to internment camps. For some this meant a rather bleak five years on the Isle of Man; others were sent to the Australian Outback.* The NR itself was, of course,

---

* Incidentally, one of those internees, German-born Claus Moser, went on to become head of the Central Statistics Office (a precursor to the ONS) despite being initially denied a job there as a former 'enemy alien'.

used to assist military conscription for British men. Earlier, the fact that eugenics was briefly treated as a legitimate science meant that detailed and intrusive questions about fertility made it into the 1911 census. And statistical records were used for decades to manage racial segregation in some of Britain's colonies, notably in South Africa. It's no wonder people in Haringey were suspicious when an ethnicity census was tested in their diverse area in the 1970s, and seemingly nowhere else. Historically, the safest option was generally to avoid being on a list of any kind and, on some level, we still carry this instinct.

But a final takeaway from looking at history through this lens is that, in some ways, it's surprising how little has really changed. Yes, we've just heard a story of continuous radical upheaval in how our country looks as a whole. And sure, no one in 1801 could have dreamed of washing machines, cars and microwaves, of 'remote working', of dating apps and holidays to Thailand. They had never even seen a bicycle. But looking at the records from Mayhew, from Rowntree and Booth, and from the fragments in censuses and surveys, there is much to recognise in people's characters and behaviours. What we want from life stays essentially the same. We work, we attend to our responsibilities outside work, we seek joy, and we try to find meaning in our lives. We adapt and we make do in the most punishing of circumstances. And although poverty looks very different nowadays, its power to demoralise is exactly the same. What statistics must do is keep changing along with the way society looks on the surface, so that they stay accurate in capturing what really matters.

Our story can be told through data but is there anything unique about that? Yes and no. The UK has followed the typical pattern of advanced modern democracies in terms of how we've gone about enumerating ourselves. We were certainly not the first to do censuses; in fact, we were rather late to the party compared with the likes of France, the USA and the Nordic countries. We made up for it by being at the forefront in the nineteenth century when it came to social research through surveys and set the standard in this area for other countries to follow.[10] In its time there was nothing in the world that compared with Booth's study of London poverty for its sheer size and level of detail. But with the same basic methods being used in all similar countries, it's hard to point to anything particularly innovative about how we got our data.

We do find evidence of our own unique stamp, though, when we look closely at what information we decided to gather and store. Perhaps what reveals this even more clearly is what we decided *not* to do in this regard. Except in times of total war, we have never had a full population register and this has been the result of considered choice. We have also been extremely slow and reluctant to consolidate data in many areas where policy is managed locally, like policing, justice and healthcare, even despite having a health service which is national. Contrast this with countries such as Denmark, Norway, Sweden, Finland and the Netherlands, which have had full population registers for decades and national bureaucracies which penetrate all the way to the local level.

Can we take this further and say that this history through data reveals or reflects something about our national character? At times in this story, it has come naturally to point out how choices made were typical, or stereotypical, of some form of Britishness. Often the only way to make sense of things that happened and decisions that were made has been to recognise the molasses-like coating of British culture which clung to every part of our lives. Our tendency towards personal secretiveness is one characteristic that stands out, and which has been more of a restriction to data-gathering here than in some other contexts. Some might frame this differently and say that the British put a higher value on privacy in some areas of life than other cultures. We have never asked people in the national census about their income (although questions have been trialled in recent census rounds) and it took us two hundred years to find it acceptable to ask people about their religion. Outside wartime we have never required people to own a form of ID or even a valid passport. Sweden passed a form of freedom of information legislation allowing people to find out what information the state had on them in 1766 – we passed our own version of this in the year 2000.

Something else that stands out as peculiarly British is that while our central government machine has grown consistently bigger by the decade, the touch of the state in people's lives has continued to be comparatively light. This was no accident or coincidence – no more so than the development in other countries of very deep bureaucracies or even totalitarian states. In the UK, it was the result of centuries of politicians, activists and thinkers who were strongly committed to the idea of individual liberty. Of course, true liberty has been very unevenly felt, but the *idea* of resisting totalitarianism was, and still is, part of our national creed. 'Britons never, never, never shall be slaves.' This has influenced the way we have collected data on ourselves: almost always through the volunteering of information through censuses and surveys, with fairly minimal penalties for non-compliance or protest.

The irony is that while making a point of resisting state overreach at home, we ruled centrally from a small archipelago over an empire which stretched all the way around the globe and contained a quarter of the world's population. British civil servants were frequently tasked with making decisions about places they knew very little about and may not even have known existed until moments prior. Oftentimes going in and collecting data – with a complete lack of sensitivity to the context – was the only way they knew of coming to believe they had understood a situation well enough to make decisions about it.[11] We imposed reductive and often offensive classifications on people and gave no consideration to their own choice in self-identifying in a way that we would scarcely have done at home. A double standard applied to the UK and its colonies when it came to considering people's rights to liberty and privacy and when it came to allowing them a say in how they were enumerated. This is also evidence of what our national character was like for a very long time – acting from a grossly inflated sense of superiority – painful though that might be for us now to accept.

Our character also comes through in the way that data collection instruments were used to establish moral norms and confirm taboos. We didn't ask about women's work outside the home for the first five decades of censuses, not necessarily because it wasn't believed to be a thing but because the very idea of it was frowned upon by the class of people in charge of numbering the population. The 1911 fertility census was only concerned with children born within wedlock, which was meant to signal disapproval of 'illegitimate' births even if counting them had meant more accurate data. It only became possible to indicate on the census that you were living in an unmarried couple in 1991, for similar reasons of not wanting to legitimise the arrangement. We have never very effectively managed to collect data on social class, in this case because the idea of asking about it directly has always seemed too audacious for words. We didn't ask about race or ethnicity for a long time, dancing around what was undeniably a pertinent issue with proxy questions about where people's parents were from, because it was considered vulgar to ask. This is a little different from the approach taken in France, where to this day it is forbidden to collect official data on ethnicity, the point being to send out the official signal that it is (or should be) irrelevant.

Eventually we grew out of our moral disapproval towards women having lives outside the home and, more recently, towards extramarital sex and homosexuality. And we developed ways of asking about religion and ethnicity, with our own somewhat inconsistent set of categories for people to sort themselves into with the least amount of objection. Although we might not realise it, there are probably many things now that are considered taboo or overly invasive which we might one day find it acceptable to ask people about. Let's not forget that once the very idea of a census itself was viewed as a scandalous invasion of privacy, while now we see it is as not much more than a cosy cultural tradition. One recurring theme is that our curiosity has often got the upper hand over moral objections. The urge of private individuals to investigate social problems has been allowed to express itself in this country in a way that it could not in many parts of the world. It is not everywhere that Booth and Rowntree would have been permitted to carry out and publish their life studies of whole classes of people that both the state and the economy at large had catastrophically failed.

In the end, counting ourselves has been an important part of nation-building. It fits into what the political scientist Benedict Anderson has called the idea of 'imagined communities', which are shared clusters of cultural references that create the impression of a cohesive community. By going through the ritual of numbering ourselves every ten years (and volunteering our information much more often in the modern day), we have constructed something which represents us and is shared.

Common references can create a sense of national identity, even when there is little to hold people together in any real kind of joint endeavour. So too can the simple act of encircling people within the same counting exercise. The first time that census-takers ventured to the outermost corners of the United Kingdom, they had no idea who they would find or what reception they would receive. It wasn't until 1851 that enumerators first reached the wind-blasted island of St Kilda in the Outer Hebrides, where a community of 110 people survived by collecting seabirds' eggs from cliffs above the booming waves of the Atlantic.[12] In 1921, the final time that St Kilda was enumerated before it was evacuated for good, the Scottish Registrar General travelled there in person to deliver the census forms.[13]

To count people is to define the boundaries of who is in and who is out. Every act of counting tests the legitimacy of the classifications, the groupings and the divisions that are supposed to represent us. The rooms full of census reports and records in obscure government archives and the warehouses full of census and survey returns (and now servers keeping our digital information stored) contain the story of us. And every entry was a negotiation of sorts.

There are some characters who stood out in this story, firstly those who we have to thank for moving events forward. William Farr, regarded by some as the most accomplished medical statistician of his century, is an obvious one.[14] Dr John Snow, his more physically daring counterpart who ventured into the heart of disease to make sense of it through statistics, is another, along with lamp-lady Florence Nightingale, who could not accept that statistics were a man's work. John Rickman, who established the British census tradition in the face of a mountain of difficulties, and Sylvanus Vivian, whose dedication to the wartime population register can only be described as love, also cannot be forgotten.

But who else stands out? The fugitive slaves Ellen and William Craft come straight away to mind, sitting in a stranger's house in Leeds, reeling from another close escape from death while their host fills in the 1851 census return. We remember Mayhew's watercress girl, hawking her frozen wares on a winter's morning, eyes wide with disbelief at the notions of parks where children go to play, and we recall the anonymous families living five people to a room in depths of squalor that surveys and censuses could not describe. We remember the young servant who refused to give her details in the 1911 census 'because women have not got the vote', even if it meant breaking the law and her employer knowing it. Such a private act of dissent was arguably much higher-stakes than some of the census stunts undertaken over the years by people from the middle and upper classes. And we also remember the Mass-Observation participants, dutifully noting down mundane details of their lives for the sake of social study and pausing to draw the curtains as air-raid sirens started up. The nearly four hundred thousand Jedi who responded to the 2001 England and Wales census stand out too, if only for the heartwarming scale of their mass act of tomfoolery.

They live on in these records, as do all we individuals who make up a greater whole. Statistics are not dry or cold; they are bursting with life. And data is so much more powerful when it is honest, and represents us fairly, and is the result of mutual give and take. We get the most from trying to count not just some but all of us.

Appendix

Population on census day, 1801 to 2021, United Kingdom and its constituent countries

Year	UK	England	Wales	Scotland	Ireland	N. Ireland
1801	.	8,305,291	587,245	1,608,420	.	.
1811	.	9,490,916	673,340	1,805,864	.	.
1821	20,893,584	11,206,082	794,154	2,091,521	6,846,949	1,380,451
1831	24,028,584	12,992,397	904,400	2,364,386	7,784,536	1,574,004
1841	26,709,456	14,867,882	1,046,266	2,620,184	8,175,124	1,648,945
1851	27,368,736	16,764,470	1,163,139	2,888,742	6,552,385	1,442,517
1861	28,927,485	18,779,901	1,286,323	3,062,294	5,798,967	1,396,453
1871	31,484,661	21,299,683	1,412,583	3,360,018	5,412,377	1,359,190
1881	34,884,848	24,402,734	1,571,705	3,735,573	5,174,836	1,304,816
1891	37,732,922	27,231,095	1,771,430	4,025,647	4,704,750	1,236,056
1901	41,458,721	30,514,967	2,012,876	4,472,103	4,458,775	1,236,952
1911	45,221,615	33,649,571	2,420,921	4,760,904	4,390,219	1,250,531
1921*	.	35,230,225	2,656,474	4,882,497	.	1,256,561
1931*	.	37,359,045	2,593,332	4,842,980	.	1,279,745
1939†	47,856,000	41,552,000		5,008,000		1,296,000
1941	No census	.	.	.	.	.
1951	50,225,224	41,159,213	2,598,675	5,096,415	n/a	1,370,921

* 1926 and 1937 in Northern Ireland.
† Population estimated from the wartime National Register at the end of September 1939.

1961	52,708,934	43,460,525	2,644,023	5,179,344	n/a	1,425,042
1971	55,514,600	46,018,371	2,731,204	5,228,960	n/a	1,536,065
1981	55,099,911	45,771,956	2,749,640	5,035,315	n/a	1,543,000
1991	56,496,144	47,055,204	2,835,073	4,998,567	n/a	1,607,300
2001	58,789,194	49,138,831	2,903,085	5,062,011	n/a	1,685,267
2011	63,182,178	53,012,456	3,063,456	5,295,403	n/a	1,810,863
2021**	66,937,005	56,489,800	3,107,500	5,436,600	n/a	1,903,105

Notes

1. There was no census in 1941, because of the Second World War.
2. Censuses before 1981 recorded population present, rather than usual residents.
3. From 1981, statistics relate to usual residents, which from 2001 onwards include estimates of those not counted.

Sources

Census reports from the General Register Office/Office for National Statistics, National Records of Scotland, and Northern Ireland Statistics and Research Agency. National Register figures from GRO (1944) *National Register, United Kingdom and Isle of Man: Statistics of Population on 29th September, 1939. By Sex, Age and Marital Condition.* London: HMSO, p. xi

---

** 2022 in Scotland.

Acknowledgements

Firstly, I would like to thank Richard Cracknell, now-former Head of Social and General Statistics at the House of Commons Library for supporting my writing ambitions and providing feedback on the first draft of this book. His much greater knowledge than mine on the UK statistics landscape has been a huge asset to me in writing this and many of the insights I've been able to provide here were ones I picked up from him. I'm also very grateful to Grant Hill-Cawthorne for approving the pitch for this book and reading the final draft manuscript.

Enormous thanks to my agent Kate Evans for believing in this idea – and seeing past what might, to some, seem a dry topic – and securing a wonderful publisher. Thank you to legend Holly Harley, my main editor at The Bridge Street Press, for shaping the drafts of this book into something infinitely better, and thanks to Sameer Rahim who saw it through to publication. I also very much appreciate the extremely thorough work of copy-editor Zoe Gullen.

It is thanks to the staff and resources of the actual Library of the House of Commons that I have been able to research these subjects in such depth. I'm very grateful to Greg Howard and Annabel Gladstone for locating materials in the main collection, and to Lydia Cowling for help finding some more obscure items in the archive. Many thanks to David in the Members' Library for helping carry census volumes to and from the archives for my use. I really appreciate the time and care Matthew Pentlow took to digitise items from the Library's archives for reproduction in these pages. Thanks also the staff at the National Archives for locating material for me on the National Register.

I am also indebted to experts who assisted me on specific topics. Thanks to David Torrance for input into the chapter on the 1920s and 1930s. Thanks to Professor Rob Dunbar at the University of Edinburgh for assistance with interpreting Scottish Gaelic. I owe a special mention and huge thanks to talented genealogist Dave Annal, who helped me locate Audrey Hepburn. Working together was also a lot of fun! I wish I could also have thanked Audrey Collins from the National Archives, who passed away in 2023, for how useful I found her work on censuses and the National Register.

I'd like to acknowledge Professor Edward Higgs at the University of Essex for his uniquely thorough work on censuses and pre-census data collection, the work of the General Register Office and William Farr, and the use of data by the modern state. I also found Andrew Whitby's book *The Sum of the People* (2020) particularly useful in understanding the evolution of the modern census. Many thanks to all others with whom I've had conversations about the book and who have given me food for thought, most notably Ed Humpherson at the Office for Statistics Regulation. And special thanks to George Eaton for giving me the initial idea for this book by asking, 'If that was the bad data, what about the good data?'

Finally, thank you to those who have given me personal support this year, especially my dear friends at Bunhill Row and to my English and Dutch families. And to Kyra, who counts more to me than anything in the world.

Notes

Introduction

1. Roger Hutchinson's *The Butcher, the Baker, the Candlestick Maker* (Little, Brown, 2017) is a comprehensive history of the UK census; *The Sum of the People* (Basic Books, 2020) by Andrew Whitby is a brilliant guide to the history of censuses around the world, from prehistory to the present day.
2. General Register Office [henceforth GRO], 1966 Sample Census Summary Report, table 11.
3. This is evident, for example, in the fact that many of the Sustainable Development Goals relate to privacy, equality and being able to enforce personal boundaries.
4. Thorvaldsen, G., *Censuses and Census Takers: A Global History*, Routledge, 2017/2019, p. 80.
5. Margolis, M., 'Latin American governments are gaming their numbers', *Washington Post* [online], 13 March 2023.
6. Booth, A., 'Census delay sparks deadly strikes in Bolivia's Santa Cruz region', *Al Jazeera* [online], 18 November 2022.

1. Starting from Zero

1. *Morning Chronicle*, 1 January 1801, p. 2; *General Evening Post*, 6 January 1801, p.3. Accessed via the British Newspaper Archive [BNA].
2. 'Debate in the Commons on the Population Bill', 19 November 1800, in Cobbett, W., *The parliamentary history of England, from the earliest period to the year 1803: from which last-mentioned epoch it is continued downwards in the work entitled, 'Hansard's parliamentary debates'*, T. C. Hansard, 1819, vol. 35, p. 598. Only ninety-two

out of 558 MPs were present for the debate prior to this one, so I have inferred that the chamber remained mostly empty.
3. Ibid., vol. 14.
4. Whitby, *The Sum of the People*, p. 38.
5. Ibid.
6. This relief appears on the Altar of Consul Domitius Ahenobarbus.
7. 1 Chronicles 21:1–6.
8. Luke 2:1.
9. Matthew 2:2–18.
10. Thorvaldsen, *Censuses and Census Takers*, p. 9.
11. Bannerman, J., *Studies in the History of Dalriada*, Scottish Academic Press, 1974.
12. The Statute of Winchester 1285 was a listing of men aged 15–60 for the purpose of assessing military strength. From the 1500s these military reserve lists came to be compiled frequently and referred to as muster rolls.
13. For this paragraph I relied on Chapman, C. R., *Pre-1841 Censuses & Population Listings in the British Isles*, 5th edn, Lochin, 1990/2002.
14. Winder, R., *Bloody Foreigners: The Story of Immigration to Britain*, Little, Brown, 2004/2013, p. 58.
15. Fleming, J. A., *The Flemish Influence in Britain, Volume I*, Jackson, Wylie & Co., 1930.
16. Winder, *Bloody Foreigners*, pp. 60–1.
17. Graunt, J., *London's dreadful visitation: or, a collection of all the Bills of Mortality for this present year: beginning the 27th of December 1664 and ending the 19th of December following: as also the general or whole years bill. According to the report made to the King's most excellent Majesty / by the Company of Parish-Clerks of London*, E. Cotes, 1665, p. 9.
18. Graunt, J., *Natural and political observations mentioned in a following index, and made upon the Bills of mortality / By Capt. John Graunt, fellow of the Royal society. With reference to the government, religion, trade, growth, air, diseases, and the several changes of the said city*, John Martyn, 1676, p. 16.
19. Ibid., p. 33.
20. One person died of a 'sore legge' in the week of 25 July to 1 August 1665 (Graunt, *London's dreadful visitation*); sixty-two people died 'suddenly' in 1632 (ibid., p. 9).
21. *The Diary of Samuel Pepys*, entry for 31 August 1665. The total death toll from the plague in 1665 is now estimated to have been around 100,000. At that time, thanks to Graunt's estimates, the total population of (inner) London was likely around 400,000.

22. Ibid., entry for 26 April 1668.
23. Graunt, *Natural and political observations*, p. 80.
24. Ibid. Initially he estimated the total population of London at 460,800 but in the 1665 edition of his book he revised this down to 403,000.
25. This was quite a way to exploit the aftermath of Cromwell's invasion of Ireland in 1649, which is estimated to have caused the deaths of between 15 and 50 per cent of the population and exiled a further fifty thousand Irish people to the Caribbean colonies.
26. Graunt, *Natural and political observations*, p. 33.
27. Maitland, W., *The History of London, from its Foundation by the Romans to the present time. Containing a faithful relation of the Publick Transations of the Citizens ... Parallels between London and other great cities; its Governments, Civil, Ecclesiastical and Military; Commerce, State of Learning ... with the several accounts of Westminster, Middlesex, Southwark, and other parts within the Bill of Mortality*, Samuel Richardson, 1739.
28. Browning, J., 'VII. Part of a letter from Mr John Browning, of Bristol, to Mr Henry Baker, F. R. S. dated Dec. 11. 1746. concerning the effect of electricity on vegetables', *Philosophical Transactions* (1747), pp. 373–5.

2. Population Problems

1. Hutchinson, *The Butcher, the Baker, the Candlestick Maker* [henceforth *The Butcher, the Baker*], p. 18.
2. The 1801 Census put the population of England, Wales, Scotland and Ireland and at over fifteen million.
3. *Commercial and Agricultural Magazine*, of which Rickman was the editor.
4. In a letter to his friend Robert Southey, reported in *The Butcher, the Baker*, p.37
5. Abstract, presented to the House of Commons of the Answers and Returns Made to the Population Act of 41st George III, 29 June 1801. Accessed via Histpop.org.
6. *The Butcher, the Baker*, p. 43.
7. *1821 Census of Great Britain*. 'Observations, enumeration and parish register abstracts', pp.vi–vii. Accessed via Histpop.org.
8. Spencer Perceval was shot and killed in 1812, and the palace burnt down in 1832.
9. *1831 Census of Great Britain*. Comparative account, p.3. Accessed via Histpop.org.
10. Ibid., p. 6.

11. Chapman, *Pre-1841 Censuses*, p. 48.
12. Goldman, L., *Victorians and Numbers*, Oxford University Press, 2022, pp. 24–7.
13. Even then, the records coming in were far from complete. It would take another law – the Registration of Births and Deaths Act 1874 – and, crucially, its threat of a fine for non-registration before compliance was fully achieved.
14. GRO, *1st Annual Report of the Registrar-General* [henceforth *ARRG*] *for the years 1837–8*, HMSO, 1839, p. 5.
15. Ibid., p. 17.
16. GRO, *2nd ARRG* (1938–9), HMSO, 1840, p. 5.
17. GRO, *3rd ARRG* (1939–40), HMSO, 1841, pp. 12–13.
18. Ibid., p. 13.
19. The hundred-year rule has been applied in a formal, though non-statutory, way since the early 2000s, when discussion of the release of the 1911 census data took place. Before this, censuses were generally opened up around eighty years after being taken, which reflects life expectancy being shorter in the past.
20. Entry for the Crapper household, Thorne Quay, Thorne, Yorkshire & Yorkshire (West Riding), England. Accessed via FindMyPast.co.uk [FMP].
21. Population growth in Great Britain was 14.5 per cent between 1831 and 1841 compared with 16 per cent in the decade before that.
22. *Illustrated London News*, 14 October 1843. Accessed via the BNA.
23. GRO, *1851 Census of Great Britain*. Population Tables I. Numbers of the inhabitants in the years 1801, 1811, 1821, 1831, 1841 and 1851. Vol. I, HMSO, p. xxv.
24. Ibid., p. xxxii.
25. Ibid., p. xliv.
26. GRO, *1851 Census of Great Britain*. Population Tables II. Vol. I. England and Wales. Divisions I–VI, p. ciii.
27. In 1860, London would host the International Statistics Conference, in Somerset House, marking what Lawrence Goldman has described as the 'zenith' of Victorian statistics. *Victorians and Numbers*, p. xliii.
28. *1851 Census of Ireland*. Part V. Tables of Deaths. Vol. I, HMSO, p. 245.
29. In 1851. Ibid., p. 243.
30. Brueton, A., 'An analysis of first names from the 1851 Glamorgan census', published online for Gen UKI, 2002. https://www.genuki.org.uk/big/wal/GLA/1851Names.
31. *1855 Census of the State of New York*, Charles van Benthuysen, p. xl.

32. 59,585 out of 96,486 New Yorkers who could neither read nor write (62 per cent). Ibid., p. xlviii.

3. Vital Signs

1. Johnson, S., *The Ghost Map*, Penguin, 2006/2008, p. 34.
2. Cholera Inquiry Committee, *Report on the Cholera Outbreak in the Parish of St James, Westminster, during the Autumn of 1854* [henceforth *CIC Report*], J. Churchill, 1855.
3. According to the appendix table, 199 residents died in the 'cholera area' on 1 and 2 September, although we do not know the exact time.
4. Johnson, *The Ghost Map*, p. 23.
5. One of the few treatments at the time which would have been somewhat effective was the administering of saline injections. We now know that, ironically, the treatment for this waterborne menace is to replenish the body's fluids by taking in plenty of clean water.
6. GRO, *17th ARRG* (1854), HMSO, 1856, p. 75.
7. Whitehead quoted in *CIC Report*, p. 20.
8. *CIC Report*, p. 62.
9. Ibid., p. 77.
10. Ibid., pp. 106–7. This woman is referred to as 'Mrs E—' but Snow's report refers to the name Eley.
11. Ibid., p. 105.
12. Ibid., p. 159.
13. Ibid., p. 53.
14. Johnson, *The Ghost Map*, p. 179.
15. *CIC Report*, p. 171.
16. Ibid., p. vii.
17. Ibid., p. v.
18. GRO, *19th ARRG* (1856), HMSO, 1858.
19. Quoted in Johnson, *The Ghost Map*, p. 114.
20. GRO, *20th ARRG* (1857), HMSO, 1859, p. 171.
21. GRO, *17th ARRG*, p. 65.
22. GRO, *20th ARRG*, p. 163.
23. GRO, *39th ARRG* (1876), HMSO, 1878, p. 251.
24. GRO, *27th ARRG* (1864), HMSO, 1866, pp. 180–1.
25. See GRO, *27th ARRG* (1864), HMSO, 1864, p. 181; also *Morning Chronicle*, 11 April 1849, p. 4 (accessed via the BNA).
26. This has been covered thoroughly by David Spiegelhalter, for example in *The Art of Statistics* (Pelican, 2019). See also the RSS's 2022 paper, 'Healthcare Serial Killer or Coincidence?'
27. GRO, *31st ARRG* (1867), HMSO, 1869, p. 209.

28. Ibid., p. 208.
29. GRO, *23rd ARRG* (1860), HMSO, 1862, p. 330.
30. GRO, *30th ARRG* (1867), HMSO, 1869, p. 176.
31. 'Report on the Social Sciences Congress at York 1854', *The Press*, 1 October 1864, p. 946. Accessed via the BNA.
32. Bostridge, M., *Florence Nightingale*, Penguin, 2008/2009, p. 319.
33. Office for National Statistics [ONS], Top 100 baby names in England and Wales: historical data. 1904–1994 edition (15 August 2014). Accessed online.
34. They appear in her *Notes on Matters Affecting the Health, Efficiency, and Hospital Administration of the British Army* (1858). Although biographers often refer to them as her 'coxcomb' diagrams, this may actually have been a name she gave to another collection of figures, according to Small, H., 'Florence Nightingale's statistical diagrams', research paper, 1998, available at https://www.york.ac.uk/depts/maths/histstat/small.htm.
35. Bostridge, *Florence Nightingale*, p. 314.
36. Harford, T., *How to Make the World Add Up: Ten Rules for Thinking Differently About Numbers*, The Bridge Street Press, 2020, p. 229.
37. British Library Add. MSS 43394, f210. 25/12/1857. Personal correspondence between Florence Nightingale and Sidney Herbert.
38. HC Deb vol. 151, col. 426, 'The State of The Thames', 25 June 1858.
39. HC Deb vol. 151, col. 28, question on 'the state of the Thames', 18 June 1858.
40. HC Deb vol. 151, col. 422, 'The State of The Thames', 25 June 1858.
41. HC Deb vol. 151, col. 1934, debate on the Metropolis Local Management Act Amendment Bill, 22 July 1858.
42. Collinson, A., 'How Bazalgette built London's first super-sewer', Museum of London [online], 26 March 2019.
43. GRO, *Annual summary of births, deaths and causes of death in London, and other great towns / published by authority of the Registrar-General* (1890), HMSO, 1891, p. xxx.

4. Life on the Line

1. GRO, *The Census of Great Britain in 1851 ... Reprinted, in a Condensed Form, from the Original Reports and Tables*, Longman, Brown, Green, and Longmans, 1854, p. 101 (Table XI); GRO, *Census of England and Wales, 1871: Population Abstracts*, HMSO, 1873, p. 449.
2. Bank of England, A millennium of macroeconomic data. Version 3.1,

April 2017, table A43. Accessible online at https://www.bankofengland.co.uk/statistics/research-datasets
3. Ibid., table A4.
4. *The Times*, 'Studies of England', 8 April 1846, p. 7. Accessed via The Times Archive online.
5. Mayhew, H., *London Labour and the London Poor*, Penguin, 1865/1985, pp. 66–7.
6. Ibid., p. 65.
7. Ibid., p. 430.
8. Ibid., p. 420.
9. Grant, J., *Sketches in London*, 1838; Gavin, H., *Sanitary Ramblings*, 1848; Beames, T., *The Rookeries of London*, 1850.
10. Harrison, B., *Peaceable Kingdom: Stability and Change in Modern Britain*, Clarendon Press, 1982, p. 307.
11. Goldman, *Victorians and Numbers*, p. 197.
12. House of Commons, *1831 Census of England and Wales*. Enumeration Abstract (Part 1), p. vii; Currency conversion using https://www.nationalarchives.gov.uk/currency-converter/.
13. Harrison, *Peaceable Kingdom*, p. 266.
14. Ibid., p. 265.
15. Goldman, *Victorians and Numbers*, p. 135.
16. '*"In the Clouds," or, Some Account of a Balloon Trip with Mr Green*, by Henry Mayhew', *Illustrated London News*, 18 September 1852. Accessed via the BNA.
17. Such as Henry Hyndman via the *Pall Mall Gazette* in 1885.
18. LSE Archive: BOOTH/B/361. 'George H. Duckworth's Notebook: Police District 28 [Kensington Town], District 29 [Fulham], District 30 [Hammersmith]' (1899). p. 221.
19. Booth, C., *Life and Labour of the People in London*. Vol. I, Macmillan, 1899/1902, p. 33.
20. LSE Archive: BOOTH/B/34. 'George H.Duckworth's Notebook: Police District 11 [Poplar and Limehouse], District 12 [Bow and Bromley] and District 13 [South Hackney and Hackney]' (1897), p. 61.
21. Rowntree, B. S., *Poverty: A Study of Town Life*, Policy Press, 1901/2000 p. 36 [House 32 in Class 'A'].
22. Ibid., p. 38 [House 46 in Class 'A'].
23. Ibid., p. 110.
24. Ibid., p. 299.
25. Ibid., p. 301.
26. The population of England and Wales in 1901 was 32,526,075 according to the census. Rowntree reports that around 77 per cent

of the population of York was classified as 'urban', and that his estimates indicate that up to 30 per cent of these urban-dwellers lived in poverty.
27. Rowntree, *Poverty*, p. 304.
28. Sims, G. R., *How the Poor Live*, 1883, p. 5. Quoted in Harrison, *Peaceable Kingdom*, p. 281.
29. Titmuss, R., *Birth, Poverty and Wealth*, Hamish Hamilton, 1943, p. 20.
30. Ibid., p. 269.
31. Ibid.
32. Booth, *Life and Labour of the People in London*, p. 20.
33. Goldman, *Victorians and Numbers*, p. 166. For example, Charles Babbage was given a 'most cordial welcome' by workers in Bradford when he came to study their manufacturing processes.

5. Rising Damp

1. *Caledonian Mercury*, 25 November 1861. p. 1 Accessed via the BNA.
2. *The Times*, 2 December 1861. Accessed via The Times Archive online.
3. *Lady's Newspaper and Pictorial Times*, 30 November 1861. Accessed via the BNA.
4. *Edinburgh Evening Courant*, 26 November 1861. Accessed via the BNA.
5. *Caledonian Mercury*, 28 November 1861. Accessed via the BNA. Quotation from a speech given by Reverend Dr Begg on 'Houses for the working classes', delivered in John Knox's Church, very near the scene of the collapse.
6. This phrase is used in GRO, *1851 Census of Great Britain*. Population Tables I. Numbers of the inhabitants in the years 1801, 1811, 1821, 1831, 1841 and 1851. Vol. I, p. xxxv. However, it may have been in use since 1604, when a version appears in the record of an English court ruling, or indeed before.
7. 'In enumerating the houses, some definition of the term was required. In the great majority of instances no difficulty is presented, yet, in certain exceptional Houses at previous cases, the difficulty of defining "what constitutes a distinct house" was considered insuperable by Mr Rickman; and in the earlier Censuses it was left to "those who made the Return," to decide "whether a college, or inn of court, or a town-house in Scotland, containing as many separate habitations as stories or 'flats,' was to be deemed one house or many." In the revision of the previous Censuses it appeared that "house," in different towns of Scotland, had been so variously understood, that the result

of the enumerations of houses is of little value.' *Eighth Decennial Census of the Population of Scotland, taken 3rd April 1871, with Report.* Vol. I, HMSO, p. xxxvii.
8. Ibid., p.xxxi
9. GRO, *1851 Census of Great Britain.* Population Tables I. Numbers of the inhabitants in the years 1801, 1811, 1821, 1831, 1841 and 1851. Vol. I, p. xxxvii.
10. *Eighth Decennial Census of the Population of Scotland.* Vol. I, p. xxix; *Ninth Decennial Census of the Population of Scotland, taken 4th April 1881, with Report.* Vol. I, HMSO, p. xx..
11. *Eighth Decennial Census of the Population of Scotland.* Vol. I, p. lix.
12. Ibid., p. xxiv.
13. Ibid., p. lix.
14. Ibid., pp. xxxii–xxxiii.
15. Ibid., p. xxxiv.
16. Ibid., p. xxxvi.
17. One with fewer than five rooms.
18. Plymouth is also an interesting one, with around a quarter of the population living more than two to a room. This was because of a large amount of one-room accommodation in the city. GRO, *Census of England and Wales 1891.* Vol. IV. General Report., HMSO, p. 119.
19. GRO, *Census of England and Wales for the Year 1871.* General Report. Vol. IV, p. 22.
20. Rowntree, *Poverty*, p. 167.
21. There had already been a lot of official interest in housing and sanitation as public policy issues. See for example, Chadwick's Inquiry into the Sanitary Conditions of the Labouring Population of Great Britain 1840, the Second Report of Commissioners of Inquiry into the State of Large Towns and Populous. Districts, 1842, [published in 1844], and the Report from the Select Committee on the Health of Towns 1840.
22. Rodger, R., *Housing in Urban Britain 1780–1914*, Macmillan Education, 1989, p. 46. Population of inner London during this time taken from 1871 Census (around 3.3 million people).
23. Song list found on The Gilbert and Sullivan Archive [online] although the music and lyrics are by Paul A. Rubens.
24. Booth, W., *In Darkest England and the Way Out*, 1890. Quoted in Boughton, J., *Municipal Dreams: The Rise and Fall of Council Housing,* Verso, 2018/2019, p. 12. A reference to accounts by the explorer Henry Morton Stanley of his expeditions in central Africa.
25. GRO, *25th ARRG* (1862), HMSO, 1865, pp. 180–1.

26. For example, in nearby Lamb Street. Accessed via FMP.
27. GRO, *30th ARRG* (1867), HMSO, 1869, p. 219.
28. Select Committee on the Health of Towns, Report of the Select Committee on the Health of Towns, together with the minutes of evidence taken before them and an appendix and index, House of Commons, 1840, p. viii.
29. Boughton, *Municipal Dreams*, p. 13.

6. Working Nine to Five

1. Gaskell, E., *North and South*, Penguin, 1855/1996, p. 60.
2. GRO, *Census of England and Wales and of Scotland 1841*. Occupation Abstract, MDCCCXL, Part I, HMSO, p. 8.
3. Ibid., p. 14
4. GRO, *Census of England and Wales for the year 1861*. General Report, HMSO, p. 27.
5. GRO, *Census of England and Wales for the Year 1881*. Vol. IV. General Report, HMSO, p. 25.
6. Ibid., p. 26.
7. Ibid., p. 27.
8. GRO, *The Census of Great Britain in 1851*, pp. 125–45.
9. GRO, *1831 Census of England and Wales*. Enumeration Abstract (Part 1), pp. 1044–51.
10. Collins family, Wild Court, St Giles in the Fields, St Giles, London & Middlesex, in the 1851 England, Wales & Scotland Census.
11. Spinoza, A., *Manchester Unspun: Pop, Property and Power in the Original Modern City. How a City Got High on Music*, Manchester University Press, 2003.
12. GRO, *Census of England and Wales and of Scotland 1841*. Occupation Abstract, MDCCCXL, Part I, p. 15.
13. Ibid., pp. 16 and 26. This is in Great Britain.
14. GRO, *Census of England and Wales 1901*. General Report, HMSO, p. 120.
15. GRO, *Census of England and Wales for the Year 1881*. Vol. IV. General Report, p. 30.
16. This refers to women over the age of twenty; 32 per cent in 1841 and 42 per cent in 1871. GRO, *Census of England and Wales and of Scotland 1841*. Occupation Abstract, MDCCCXL, Part I, p. 45; GRO, *Census of England and Wales for the Year 1871*. General Report. Vol. IV, pp. xiii and xlii.
17. ONS, Economic activity status by sex by age: Census 2021 variable RM024. Women over the age of twenty-one for comparison.

18. Such as the Elementary Education Act 1870, which made primary school attendance compulsory, and the 1881 Elementary Education Act, which made it free of charge, so as to make it possible for poorer families to comply.
19. GRO, *Census of England and Wales for the Year 1871*. General Report. Vol. IV, p. xlii.
20. GRO, *Census of England and Wales for the Year 1881*. Vol. IV. General Report, p. 60.
21. GRO, *Census of England and Wales and of Scotland 1841*. Occupation Abstract, MDCCCXL, Part I, p. 8.
22. GRO, *Census of England and Wales 1901*. General Report, p. 99.
23. Mayhew, *London Labour and the London Poor*, pp. 5–8.
24. Ibid., p. 45.
25. Ibid., p. 96.
26. Ibid., p. 209.
27. Ibid., p. 70.
28. Quoted in Winder, *Bloody Foreigners*, p. 168.
29. GRO, *20th ARRG*, p. 196, and GRO, *28th ARRG* (1865), HMSO, 1866, p. 180.
30. GRO, *24th ARRG* (1861), HMSO, 1863, p. 227.
31. GRO, *39th ARRG*, p. 223.
32. Letter: 'The dance of death', *The Times*, 1 February 1862.
33. Reported in Carr, H., *Our Domestic Poisons, or, The poisonous effects of certain dyes & colours used in domestic fabrics, second edition*, William Ridgway, 1879, pp. 17–19.
34. Letter: 'The dance of death'.
35. Her Majesty's Inspectors of Mines, *Mineral Statistics of the United Kingdom of Great Britain and Ireland, with the Isle of Man for the Year 1891*, HMSO, 1892, p. 20.
36. GRO, *Census of England and Wales for the Year 1891*. Vol. IV. General Report, HMSO, p. 103.
37. GRO, *47th ARRG* (1882), HMSO, 1884, p. 211; GRO, *40th ARRG* (1877), HMSO, 1879.
38. Some of the major pieces of legislation were the 1833 Factory Act, the 1844 Factories Act, the Factory Acts (Extension) Act of 1867, and Factory Acts in 1878, 1891 and 1895.
39. The Combination Act 1800 was repealed in 1820.
40. Booth, C., *Life and Labour of the People in London*, Vol. IX, 'Comparison, survey and conclusions', 1897, p. 175.
41. GRO, *The Census of Great Britain in 1851*, p. 122.
42. Ibid., p. 61.
43. Between 1851 and 1881.

44. GRO, *Census of England and Wales for the Year 1881*. Vol. IV. General Report, p. 32.

7. One In, One Out

1. This narrative is adapted from Craft, W., *Running a Thousand Miles for Freedom*, William Tweedie, 1860.
2. The National Archives [TNA], 'Slavery and the British transatlantic slave trade: How to look for records'. Accessed online.
3. Olusoga, D., *Black and British: A Forgotten History*, Macmillan, 2016, p. 223.
4. Ibid., p. 346.
5. Ibid.
6. This entry is in the 1881 census. The Harpur family, Lance Lane, Wavertree, West Derby, Lancashire, England. Accessed via FMP.
7. FMP: 1851 Census. Francis Mill, South Hill, Toxteth Park Extra Parochial, West Derby, Lancashire, England.
8. 'England's Immigrants 1330 – 1550', an Arts and Humanities Research Council-funded project by the University of York, The National Archives and the Humanities Research Institute, University of Sheffield, which ran from 2012 to 2015. Accessible at https://www.englandsimmigrants.com/
9. Royal Commission on Alien Immigration, *Report of the Royal Commission on Alien Immigration with minutes of evidence and appendix. Volume I: the report*, 1903.
10. GRO, *Census of England and Wales for the Year 1871*. General Report. Vol. IV. Appendix A, p. 78.
11. GRO, *Census of Great Britain*. Vol. I. Population tables II: Ages, civil condition, occupations and birth-place of the people, HMSO, 1854, p. clxxvi.
12. Ibid., p. cvii.
13. GRO, *Census of England and Wales for the Year 1861*. Population tables volume II: Ages, civil condition, occupations and birth-place of the people, pp. lxxv–lxxvi.
14. Ibid., p. lxxiv. Also remarked on in 1881, p. 51.
15. GRO, *Census of England and Wales 1881*. Vol. IV. General Report, HMSO, p. 56.
16. Royal Commission on Alien Immigration, *Report*, p. 14.
17. GRO, *Census of England and Wales 1901*. Summary tables. Area, houses and population, pp. 268–81.
18. Winder, *Bloody Foreigners*, p. 183.
19. Ibid., p. 197.

20. *Eighth Decennial Census of the Population of Scotland*. Vol. I, p. 19.
21. GRO, *Census of England and Wales 1881*. Vol. IV. General Report, p. 111.
22. Royal Commission on Alien Immigration, *Report*, p. 13.
23. GRO, *Census of Great Britain, 1851*. Religious Worship. England and Wales. Report and Tables, HMSO, p. cxv.
24. Booth, *Life and Labour of the People in London*, Vol. I, 'East London', p. 549.
25. Ibid., p. 551.
26. Refers to the proportion over ten years of age who were working in 'dress' manufacturing, out of the total number of working people. GRO, *Census of England and Wales 1901*. General Report, pp. 268–81.
27. Winder, *Bloody Foreigners*, p. 222.
28. Goldman, *Victorians and Numbers*, p. 280.
29. Royal Commission on Alien Immigration, *Report*, p. 5.
30. Ibid., p. 17; also GRO, *Census of England and Wales 1901*. General Report.
31. This quote is from the 1888 Select Committee on Restricting Immigration.
32. Winder, *Bloody Foreigners*, p. 264.
33. GRO, *Census of England and Wales 1901*. General Report, Table on 'Alien population in certain foreign countries and the United Kingdom'.
34. One rare counter-case was the 1709 General Naturalisation Act which welcomed all foreign Protestants to settle in England. It was, however, extremely short-lived and was repealed again in 1712 after complaints that an influx of new arrivals was bringing disease and that they were not fit to work.
35. Booth's notebooks for this area contain extensive references to opium dens and also show it to be a mixed area in terms of the classification.
36. FMP: 1861 Census. Strangers Home, Conant Place, Limehouse, Stepney, London & Middlesex, England.

8. The Second Sex

1. *Evening Standard*, 24 March 1911. Accessed via the BNA.
2. *Evening Mail*, 20 March 1911, p. 4. Accessed via the BNA.
3. *The Times*, 14 February 1911, p. 10. Accessed via The Times Archive online.
4. *The Times*, 17 March 1911, p. 9. Accessed via The Times Archive online.

5. *Spectator*, 18 February 1911, p. 6. Accessed via The Spectator Archive online.
6. *Evening Standard*, 24 March 1911. Accessed via the BNA.
7. Ibid.; and *The Times*, 17 March 1911, p. 9. Accessed via The Times Archive online.
8. *Westminster Gazette*, 24 March 1911. Accessed via the BNA.
9. Whitby, *The Sum of the People*, p. 75.
10. See, for example, Stafford, P., 'Women in Domesday', *Reading Medieval Studies*, XV (1989), pp. 75–94. If we did a census of the UK now that included livestock as well as humans, we would find that while women clearly outnumber pigs, there are roughly as many sheep as women (or, for that matter, men). We would also find that we, as humans, are outnumbered by chickens by around three to one. (Defra, 'Livestock populations in the United Kingdom at 1 June 2022').
11. Stafford, 'Women in Domesday'.
12. Levitan, K., *A Cultural History of the British Census*, Palgrave Macmillan, 2011, p. 124.
13. GRO, *The Census of Great Britain in 1851*, p. 64.
14. Ibid.
15. Quoted in Levitan, *A Cultural History of the British Census*, p. 132.
16. Ibid., p. 134.
17. Woolcock, H., *Rights of Passage: Emigration to Australia in the Nineteenth Century*, Tavistock, 1986.
18. *The Saturday Review*, 1862, in ibid., p.138
19. 1857 Matrimonial Causes Act; 1870 Married Women's Property Act.
20. *Evening Standard*, 29 June 1887, p. 8. Accessed via the BNA.
21. See for example *Pall Mall Gazette*, 7 July 1887.
22. *Dundee Evening Telegraph*, 11 July 1887, p. 2. Accessed via the BNA.
23. 1864 Contagious Diseases Act (extended in 1866 and 1869).
24. Smith, H. L., *The British Women's Suffrage Campaign 1866–1928*, 2nd edn, Pearson Education, 1998/2007, p. 17.
25. Pankhurst, C., *Unshackled: The Story of How We Won the Vote*, Hutchinson, 1959.
26. TNA: HO 144/1106/200455. Parliamentary Conciliation Committee for Woman Suffrage, 'Treatment of the Women's Deputations by the Police', 18 February 1911.
27. Harrison, *Peaceable Kingdom*, p. 26.
28. Richardson, M. R., *Laugh a Defiance*, Weidenfeld & Nicolson, 1953, p. 84.
29. Takayanagi, M. and Hallam Smith, E., *Necessary Women: The Untold Story of Parliament's Working Women*, The History Press, 2023, p. 129.

30. *Votes for Women*, 7 April 1911, p. 5. Accessed via the BNA.
31. Takayanagi and Hallam Smith, *Necessary Women*, p. 133.
32. Ibid., p. 139. Some reports include the presence of Baroness Helena Kennedy, KC in this story, but Parliamentary sources insist otherwise.
33. Iglikowski-Broad, V., '"No vote, no census": The 1911 suffrage census protests', The National Archives [online], 2 April 2020.
34. TNA: RG 14/1194. Entry for Aldwych skating rink, 1911 census.
35. TNA: MEPO 2/2023.
36. National Records of Scotland: GRO 6/380/16. Letter from R D Robertson, Registrar to the Registrar General for Scotland, 6 April 1911.
37. FMP: 1911 Census. Grace Annie Hepworth, 34 Vicarage St, Walsall, Staffordshire, England.
38. FMP: 1911 Census. Gertrude Pidoux, The Chalet, Bourne End, Wooburn, Buckinghamshire, England; FMP: 1911 Census. Ethel Lorena Bowen Burrows, 19 Marlborough Mans, Hampstead N W, Hampstead, London & Middlesex, England; FMP: 1911 census. Dorothea Hope, 55 Hamlet Garden Mansions, Hammersmith W, Hammersmith, London & Middlesex, England.
39. FMP: 1911 Census. Laura Bell, 2 Norton Way N, Letchworth, Hertfordshire, England
40. FMP: 1911 Census. Edith Schweder, Little Grange, The Quarter, Lamberhurst, Kent, England;
41. FMP: 1911 Census. Annie Packer, 4 Calais Gate, Cormont Road, Lambeth, London & Surrey, England.
42. Currency converter from https://www.nationalarchives.gov.uk/currency-converter/#currency-result.
43. FMP: 1911 Census. Emily Smith, 64 Bedford Gardens, Kensington, London & Middlesex, England.
44. FMP: 1911 Census. Jane Sbarbaro, 34 St Georges House, Whitechapel, London & Middlesex, England.
45. FMP: 1911 Census. Ada Twells, Grange Farm, South Kyme, Lincolnshire, England.
46. FMP: 1911 Census. Eleanora Maund, 8 Edith Road, Hammersmith W, Hammersmith, London & Middlesex, England.
47. FMP: 1881 Census. Elizabeth Blanch, 4 Sherwood Place, St James, Westminster, London & Middlesex, England; FMP: 1881 census. Ellen Eliza Harford, 93 Euston Road, St Pancras, London & Middlesex, England; FMP: 1881 census. Charlotte Niblett, 11 New Street, Barton St Mary, Gloucester, Gloucestershire, England.
48. FMP: 1911 Census. Abraham Stoker, 71 Beakes Road, Smethwick, Staffordshire, England. Stoker seems like a fascinating character: an

Irishman born in San Augustine, Texas, sharing a name with a very famous novelist.
49. Based on the male population in 1821 and that before this Act two-thirds of adult men had the vote. GRO, *Census of England and Wales 1921*. General Report with Appendices, HMSO, 1927, Table 33, p. 65.
50. GRO, *Census of England and Wales 1911*. Vol. XIII, Fertility of Marriage, part II, HMSO, 1923.
51. HC Deb vol. 17, debate on 'Census (Great Britain) Bill', 14 June 1910.
52. GRO, *Census of England and Wales 1911*. Vol. XIII, part II, p. lxxvi.
53. Ibid., p. lxxiv.
54. Ibid., pp. xxxvii–xxxix.
55. Sir Bernard Mallet, Registrar General in the years 1909 to 1920, was also a member of the committee of the Eugenics Society. Arguments as to whether the GRO was pro or anti eugenics are debated in Simon Szreter, 'Review by Simon Szreter of Edward Higgs, *Life, Death and Statistics . . .*', *Local Population Studies*, 75 (2005), pp. 75–81 and Edward Higgs, 'Life, death and statistics: a reply to Simon Szreter', *Local Population Studies*, 75 (2005), pp. 81–4.
56. The 'marriage bar', introduced in 1921, banned married women from working in the civil service. Non-statutory marriage bars were also in place in some other industries. In 1921, the Football Association banned women from playing on its members' pitches, saying 'the game of football is quite unsuitable for females and ought not to be encouraged'.
57. Higgs, E., *Life, Death and Statistics. Civil Registration, Censuses and the Work of the General Register Office, 1836–1952*, Local Population Studies, 2004.

9. A Downward Slope

1. Bank of England, A millennium of macroeconomic data Version 3.1, April 2017, dataset A1.
2. Ellis, J. and Cox, M., *The World War I Databook: The Essential Facts and Figures for all the Combatants*, Aurum Press, 1993/2001, table 6.1, p. 269.
3. GRO, *Census of England and Wales 1921*. General Report with Appendices, Diagrams H and J, between pp. 64–5.
4. HC Deb vol. 133, col. 138, 9 August 1920.
5. Northern Ireland Statistics and Research Agency, *Registrar General Northern Ireland Annual Report 2011*, 2012, 'Chapter 2 – A Brief History of the Census in Ireland/Northern Ireland' – written by Ian White, p. 50.

6. *Derry Journal*, 19 April 1926, p. 8. Accessed via the BNA.
7. Census of Ireland 1911: Preliminary report, p. 13.
8. Government of Northern Ireland, 'Census of Northern Ireland 1926: General report', HMSO, p. xxiv.
9. Ibid., p. xxvi.
10. BBC, 'Census lost: Historic 1926 NI records may be destroyed', 11 June 2013.
11. Thompson, F. M. L. (ed.), *Cambridge Social History of Britain 1750–1950, Volume 2: People and Their Environment*, Cambridge University Press, 1990, pp. 9–10.
12. Bank of England, A millennium of macroeconomic data Version 3.1, April 2017, dataset A20.
13. Thompson (ed.), *Cambridge Social History of Britain 1750–1950, Volume 2*, pp. 9–10.
14. Hatton, T. J., 'Emigration from the UK, 1870–1913 and 1950–1998', *European Review of Economic History*, 8:2 (2004), pp. 149–171.
15. Murdoch, A., *British Emigration, 1603–1914*, Palgrave Macmillan, 2004, pp. 85–98.
16. Aldcroft, D., *The Inter-War Economy: Britain 1919–1939*, B. T. Batsford, 1970, p. 153; GRO, *Census of England and Wales 1931*. General Report, HMSO, 1950, Section V.4.III, p. 132. There were 525,000 'hewers and getters' listed in 1921 and 439,000 in 1931. There was less of a drop in employment in more specialist and above-ground mining jobs.
17. Ibid., p. 155.
18. Ibid., p. 22.
19. Royal Commission on Unemployment Insurance, *First Report of Royal Commission on Unemployment Insurance*, HMSO, 1931, p. 13.
20. 'Transitional benefit', for the long-term unemployed, was introduced by the Unemployment Insurance Act 1927.
21. National Records of Scotland, *Census of Scotland 1931. Report on the Fourteenth Decennial Census of Scotland*. Vol. II, HMSO, pp. 130 and 141.
22. Stevenson, J. and Cook, C., *The Slump: Britain in the Great Depression*, 3rd edn, Routledge, 2009, p. 49.
23. Titmuss, *Birth, Poverty and Wealth*, p. 73.
24. GRO, *Census of England and Wales 1931*. General Report, pp. 158–9.
25. Titmuss, *Birth, Poverty and Wealth*, p. 73.
26. Lord Runciman, President of the Board of Trade, quoted in Wilkinson, E., *The Town that Was Murdered: The Life-story of Jarrow*, Left Book Club, 1939, p. 198.

27. Ibid., p. 199.
28. Ibid., p. 200.
29. *Sunderland Daily Echo and Shipping Gazette*, 5 October 1936. Accessed via the BNA.
30. *Daily News (London)*, 7 October 1936. Accessed via the BNA.
31. *Hull Daily Mail*, 14 October 1936, p. 12. Accessed via the BNA.
32. *Newcastle Journal*, 15 October 1936. Accessed via the BNA.
33. *Shields Daily Gazette*, 22 October 1936. Accessed via the BNA.
34. Wilkinson, *The Town that Was Murdered*, pp. 206–7.
35. *Shields Daily Gazette*, 22 October 1936. Accessed via the BNA.
36. Wilkinson, *The Town that Was Murdered*, p. 208.
37. Stevenson and Cook, *The Slump*, p. 184.
38. Ibid., p. 129.
39. ONS, 'The history of strikes in the UK' [online], 21 September 2015.
40. Some of the major studies of the time included a Social Survey of Merseyside from 1929 to 1934, a national study of Poverty and Public Health in 1937, a Social Survey of Bristol (which had suffered from the downturn in shipping) in 1939 and various pieces of research by the Pilgrim Trust which even looked into the psychological impact of unemployment. See Stevenson and Cook, *The Slump*, pp. 93–4.
41. Rowntree, B. S., *Poverty and Progress: A Second Social Survey of York*, Longmans, Green, 1941.
42. The 1934 Special Areas Act created two commissioners and an annual budget for four 'special', i.e. depressed, areas. By 1938, over £8 million had been spent, but only an estimated 14,900 new jobs had been created. It was acknowledged later to have had no real success in creating jobs, with Aneurin Bevin, MP describing it as 'an idle and empty farce'.
43. Bank of England, A millennium of macroeconomic data Version 3.1, April 2017, dataset A1.
44. Stevenson and Cook, *The Slump*, p. 18.
45. Aldcroft, *The Inter-War Economy*.
46. Stevenson and Cook, *The Slump*, p. 33.
47. Ibid., p. 34.
48. Gallup, G., *Gallup International Public Opinion Polls Great Britain, 1937–1975*. 2 vols, Greenwood Press, 1979, Vol. I, p. 1.
49. Ibid., February 1949 (p. 194), January 1938 (p. 7), March 1955 (p. 346).
50. Ibid., March 1958, p. 458.
51. *News Chronicle (Daily News)*, 17 October 1938, p. 10. Accessed via the BNA.

52. Calder, A. and Sheridan, D., *Speak for Yourself. A Mass-Observation Anthology, 1937–49*, Jonathan Cape, 1984, p. 58.
53. Ibid., p. 6.
54. One unforgettable image is of a woman 'who had been running' in a 'long coat, open, and an old leather motorbike crash helmet because of the rain' with 'long, bare muddy legs, shorts and a shirt, smoking a cigarette and pushing the pram'. Jennings, H. and Madge, C. (eds), *May the Twelfth: Mass-Observation Day-Surveys 1937 by Over Two Hundred Observers*, Faber & Faber, 1937/1987, p. 330.

10. All for One and One for All

1. BBC, 'Chamberlain announces Britain is at war with Germany, 3 September 1939'. Accessed online via History of the BBC.
2. TNA: RG 20/109. Destruction of the 1931 Census records.
3. TNA: RG 20/87. Correspondence between E. Batch and R. J. R. Farrow, December 1942–March 1943
4. HC Deb vol. 65, col. 1963, 5 August 1914.
5. Ellis and Cox, *The World War I Databook*, p. 272.
6. HC Deb vol. 1652, col. 72, 29 June 1915.
7. *The Nation*, 3 July 1915. Accessed via the BNA.
8. HC Deb vol. 1652, col. 72, 29 June 1915.
9. *The Nation*, 3 July 1915. Accessed via the BNA.
10. HC Deb vol. 73, col. 62, 5 July 1915.
11. TNA: RG 28/1. GRO, Memorandum on the National Registration Scheme.
12. Persons who were already members of the armed forces were exempt. Prisoners, prisoners of war, inmates of poor law institution hospitals and people with diagnosed mental disorders were also not to be included in the list.
13. TNA: RG 28/1. GRO, Memorandum on the National Register 1915–1919, 31 May 1919.
14. Ibid.
15. Ibid.
16. TNA: RG 28/1. Men Available for Military Service in England and Wales.
17. TNA: RG 28/1. GRO, Memorandum on the National Register 1915–1919.
18. TNA: RG 28/1. Correspondence between S. Vivian and V. Carruthers, May 1916.
19. TNA: CAB 103/396. 'History of National Registration by Sylvanus Vivian (narrative)', p. 79.

20. Elliot, R., 'An early experiment in national identity cards: The battle over registration in the First World War', *Twentieth Century British History*, 17:2 (2006), p. 173.
21. HC Deb vol. 351, col. 375, 4 September 1939.
22. Ibid., col. 376.
23. TNA: CAB 21/2068. Notes of Conference Held in Lord Privy Seal's Room on 28 August 1939.
24. TNA: RG 28/30. Letter from S. Vivian, 15 September 1939.
25. TNA: RG 28/30. S. Vivian. Notes on the Final Draft Report of the Sub-Committee on Manpower, 15 September 1938.
26. TNA: CAB 57/21. Report of the Sub-Committee on National Registration, March 1937, p. 11.
27. *Aberdeen People's Journal*, 30 September 1939, p. 12. Accessed via the BNA.
28. Manton, K., *Population Registers and Privacy in Britain, 1936–1984*, Palgrave Macmillan, 2019, p. 32.
29. Collins, A. 'Revisiting the 1939 Register with The National Archives' Audrey Collins' [a presentation]. Accessed via YouTube at https://www.youtube.com/watch?v=ujbjTxPqo_0&t=19s.
30. FMP: 1939 Register. Anna Eleanor Roosevelt, 3 Grosvenor Square, Knightsbridge, City of Westminster, Foreign Office Book 2, London, England.
31. Matzen, R., *Dutch Girl: Audrey Hepburn and World War II*, Mirror Books, 2020, p. 19.
32. Hinsley, F. H. and Stripp, A. (eds), *Codebreakers: The Inside Story of Bletchley Park*, Oxford University Press, 1992/1993.
33. This story comes from my granny, who worked on the Bombe machine at Bletchley. Like others from her generation, she took her vow of official secrecy very seriously and didn't talk about her work during the war for decades. It was only in the 1980s, when the story of Bletchley had become public, that she told her family anything about it.
34. Erskine, R. and Smith, M. (eds), *The Bletchley Park Codebreakers*, Biteback, 2011, pp. 79–92.
35. A monument at Westerbork, which was a transit camp in the Netherlands for the Jewish deportation, commemorates the 102,000 people who died, mainly in the concentration and extermination camps of Auschwitz and Sobibor, after passing through there.
36. Frank, A.; Frank, O. and Pressler, M. (eds), *Diary of a Young Girl*, Penguin, 1947/2019.
37. Whitby, *The Sum of the People*, p. 132.
38. Thorvaldsen, *Censuses and Census Takers*, pp. 213–17.
39. 464 Squadron RAAF.

40. Harrisson, T., *Living Through the Blitz*, Collins, 1976, p. 61.
41. Ibid., p. 65.
42. Calder and Sheridan, *Speak for Yourself*, p. 169.
43. Harrisson, *Living Through the Blitz*, p. 135.
44. Calder and Sheridan, *Speak for Yourself*, p. 89.
45. Harrisson, *Living Through the Blitz*, p. 212.
46. Ibid., pp. 217, 255.
47. Ibid., p. 217.
48. Imperial War Museum, 'The evacuated children of the Second World War' [online article], n.d..
49. TNA: RG 26/6. A Comparison of Abstract Book Figures and the 1931 Census for Certain London Boroughs.
50. GRO, *National Register, United Kingdom and Isle of Man: Statistics of Population on 29th September, 1939. By Sex, Age and Marital Condition*, HMSO, 1944, p. xx.
51. Details of the bomb census records can be found at The National Archives, 'How to look for records of the Bomb Census survey 1940–1945' [online article].
52. 'Somerset House (Bombed Buildings of London)', at https://www.layersoflondon.org/map/records/somerset-house-bombed-buildings-of-london.
53. TNA: RG 28/27. S. Vivian to E. N. de Normann, Office of Works, 28 October 1938.
54. TNA: RG 20/87. Resolution Passed by Members of the Civil Service Clerical Association, Sent to S. Vivian.
55. TNA: RG 20/87. Newspaper clipping: 'Bombshell for civil servants'.
56. Ellis, J., *The World War II Databook*, Aurum Press, 1993.
57. TNA: MH 55/978. GRO, History of National Registration, How Identity Cards Have Been Used, 21 February 1952.
58. Manton, *Population Registers and Privacy in Britain*, p. 36.
59. HC Deb vol. 351, col. 389, 4 September 1939.
60. Ibid., col. 394.
61. Bellamy, C. A., 'Why no population register in peacetime? Explaining Britain's difficult decisions, 1943–1969', *Contemporary British History*, 38:1 (2024), p. 14.
62. *Bradford Observer*, 22 February 1952, p. 3, and *Birmingham Daily Post*, 22 February 1952. Accessed via the BNA.

11. First Born

1. Beveridge, W., *Social Insurance and Allied Services*, HMSO, 1942.
2. Churchill used this phrase several times. The first version of it

appears in HC Deb vol. 26, col. 509, debate on the National Insurance Bill, 25 May 1911.
3. GRO, *5th ARRG* (1841), HMSO, 1843; GRO, *Supplement to the Registrar General's Seventy-fifth Annual Report*. Part II: Abridged Life Tables, Cmd. 1010, HMSO, 1919.
4. ONS, 'How has life expectancy changed over time?' [online article], 9 September 2015.
5. GRO, *1851 Census of Great Britain*. Population Tables I. Numbers of the inhabitants in the years 1801, 1811, 1821, 1831, 1841 and 1851. Vol. I, p. 77.
6. Harris, B., *The Origins of the British Welfare State: Social Welfare in England and Wales 1800–1945*, Palgrave Macmillan, 2004, p. 105.
7. The General Medical Act of 1858 formally established the medical profession, creating the General Medical Council and a medical register. The Medical Act 1866 established standards/qualification for the medical profession.
8. The 1867 Metropolitan Poor Act created the Metropolitan Asylums Board (asylum being a place for the sick poor). The Public Health Act 1872 created a single sanitary authority for each area, which should appoint its own Medical Officer of Health.
9. Harris, *The Origins of the British Welfare State*, p. 97.
10. Finlayson, *Citizen, State and Social Welfare*, p. 63. Quoted in ibid., p. 65. Figures from ibid., p. 67.
11. Ibid.
12. Ibid., p. 224.
13. Ibid., p. 113.
14. Titmuss, *Birth, Poverty and Wealth*, p. 21.
15. Ibid., p. 34.
16. The Pilgrim Trust, Enquiry into long-term unemployment 1936–1938, AST 7/255.
17. 1901 and 1931 Census reports. List of asylums taken from https://www.thetimechamber.co.uk/.
18. Nuffield Provincial Hospitals Trust, *The Hospital Surveys. The Domesday Book of the Hospital Services*, NPHT, 1945.
19. Rivett., G., 'Health care before the NHS', *The History of the NHS*, Nuffield Trust [online], n.d.. https://www.nuffieldtrust.org.uk/health-and-social-care-explained/the-history-of-the-nhs.
20. Collings J. S., 'General practice in England today: a reconnaissance', *Lancet*, 1950, pp. 555–85.
21. HC Deb vol. 388, col. 496, 6 April 1943.
22. Beveridge, *Social Insurance and Allied Services*, p. 7.

23. See for example, *The Times*, 13 January 1943, p. 2. Accessed via The Times Archive online.
24. Thomas, Mass Observation in WWII, 1988. Quoted in Fraser, D., *The Evolution of the British Welfare State*, 5th edn, Palgrave Macmillan, 1973/2017, p. 230.
25. British Institute for Public Opinion Survey commissioned by the Ministry of Information. TNA: PREM 4/89/2. Beveridge, *Social Insurance and Allied Services*. TNA: INF 1/292. Ministry of Information Home Intelligence Report, 10 December 1942.
26. *Sunday Mirror*, 13 December 1942. Accessed via the BNA.
27. *Daily Mirror*, 9 December 1942 p. 3. Accessed via the BNA.
28. *The Times*, 16 December 1942, p. 7. Accessed via The Times Archive online.
29. HL Deb vol. 126, col. 250, 24 February 1943.
30. HC Deb vol. 395, col. 1352, 10 December 1943.
31. HC Deb vol. 395, col. 779, 7 December 1943.
32. Beckett, F. and Beckett, C., *Bevan: Creator of the NHS*, Haus, 2004/2024.
33. *The Times*, 5 July 1948, p. 5. Accessed via The Times Archive online.
34. *Daily Mirror*, 5 July 1948, p. 5. Accessed via the BNA.
35. Fraser, *The Evolution of the British Welfare State*, p. 265.
36. ONS, Live births, 2022 edition; Deaths registered, 2021 edition.
37. Harris, J., *William Beveridge: A Biography*, Clarendon Press, 1997, p. 452.
38. Fraser, *The Evolution of the British Welfare State*, p. 265.
39. TNA: RG 28/27. Note by the Registrar General, n.d. (1936), p. 2.
40. Bellamy, 'Why no population register in peacetime?' p. 10.

12. Calculating Change

1. HL Deb vol. 254, col. 33, 16 December 1963.
2. Gallup, *Gallup International Public Opinion Polls Great Britain, 1937–1975*. Vol. I., p. 250.
3. GRO, *Census 1961 England and Wales*. Preliminary Report, HMSO, p. 11, table J.
4. 'A Plan for Plymouth' (1943), quoted in Boughton, *Municipal Dreams*, p. 62.
5. HC Deb vol. 650, col. 922–3922, 4 December 1961.
6. MOI: RG 23/37. Oatmeal and Potato Inquiry, March 1943.
7. HC Deb vol. 686, col. 852, 16 December 1963.
8. HC Deb vol. 671, col. 407–8, 5 February 1963.
9. HC Deb vol. 686, col. 850, 16 December 1963.

10. House of Commons Library archives [HOC]: 410.2. 'Sample Census 1966 and pre-test 1964: Forms, circulars and other printed papers'. GRO to the HoC Library, internal memo.
11. Royal Commission on Population, *Royal Commission on Population Final Report*, p. 25. Figures from the 1946 Family Census.
12. Ibid., p. 202.
13. HOC: 410.2. 'Sample Census 1966 and pre-test 1964: Forms, circulars and other printed papers'. 'Sample Census 1966 England and Wales. Background Note', p. 3.
14. HC Deb vol. 686, col. 850, 16 December 1963.
15. HOC: 410.2. 'Sample Census 1966 and pre-test 1964: Forms, circulars and other printed papers'. 'Sample Census 1966 England and Wales. Background Note', p. 3.
16. Ibid., p. 9.
17. Ibid., p. 7.
18. HC Deb vol. 708, col. 1628, 18 March 1965.
19. HOC: 410.2. Document 35. GRO, 'Five Million Seconds in Sunday's Census Moment'.
20. HOC: 410.2. Document 38. GRO, 'Census Publicity Campaign Report' [sent to all Census Officers 12/5/1966].
21. Ibid. The caption for this photo is 'Young ladies on the staff at the General Register Office, Somerset House, wear the styles of 1961 and 1966 as Britain's Ten Per Cent Census was launched. Joan Hunter of Highgate in the new 1966 short skirt (left) and June Masson of Croydon illustrate the transition and point out that many economic and social changes have made it necessary for the Census to break the ten-year cycle, the current one taking place only five years after that of 1961.'
22. HOC: 410.2. 'Sample Census 1966 and pre-test 1964: Forms, circulars and other printed papers'. 'Sample Census 1966 England and Wales. Background Note', p. 2; GRO, *Sample Census 1966 for England and Wales*, HMSO, 1967, Migration report vol. 1, table 1A.
23. Ibid., table 1B.
24. Ibid.
25. GRO, *Sample Census 1966*, Summary table 11.
26. Ibid., table 13.
27. HOC: 410.2. Department of Employment, 1966 Sample Census of Population: Paper no. 8 'Sub-Divisional Information'.
28. HOC: 410.2. Department of Employment, 1966 Sample Census of Population: Paper no. 6 'Females at work'.
29. HOC: 410.2. Department of Employment, 1966 Sample Census of Population: Paper no. 3 'Part-time work'.

30. HOC: 410.2. Department of Employment, 1966 Sample Census of Population: Paper no. 6 'Females at work'.

13. Divisions

1. *Nottingham Guardian*, 25 August 1958. Accessed via the BNA.
2. *Daily Herald*, 26 August 1958. Accessed via the BNA.
3. *Nottingham Evening News*, 25 August 1958; 26 August 1958. Accessed via the BNA.
4. Staveley-Wadham, R., 'Exploring the Notting Hill Race Riots of 1958.' Online article for the BNA, 2022.
5. Olusoga, *Black and British*, p. 491.
6. Ibid., p. 492.
7. Winder, *Bloody Foreigners*, p. 335.
8. Ibid., p. 338.
9. HC Deb vol. 649, col. 710, debate on the Commonwealth Immigrants Bill, 16 November 1961.
10. Ibid., col. 689.
11. *The Times*, 21 December 1962, p. 17. Accessed via The Times Archive online.
12. Winder, *Bloody Foreigners*, p. 371.
13. HC Deb vol. 649, col. 687, debate on the Commonwealth Immigrants Bill, 16 November 1961.
14. GRO, *Census of England and Wales 1981*. Preliminary Report, HMSO, 1981, p. 12.
15. Gallup, *Gallup International Public Opinion Polls Great Britain, 1937–1975*. Vol. I.
16. GRO, *Census of the British Empire 1901*. Report with Summary, HMSO, pp. 140, 161.
17. Ibid., pp. 251, 262.
18. Ibid., p. xlix.
19. Ibid., p. xlvii.
20. Ibid., p. 143.
21. Ibid., p. xlvii.
22. Bhagat, R. B., 'Census and caste enumeration: British legacy and contemporary practice in India', *Genus*, 62:2 (2006), pp. 119–34.
23. GRO, *Census of England and Wales 1971*. Country of Birth Tables, HMSO, table 1.
24. HOC: 1981 Census Miscellaneous Papers. Document 11. OPCS, 'Changing Britain: a census snapshot (OPCS Spotlight 6)'.
25. GRO, *Census of England and Wales 1971*. Country of Birth Tables, table 2.

26. Gallup, *Gallup International Public Opinion Polls Great Britain, 1937–1975*, Vol. II, p. 1032.
27. Ibid., p. 1026.
28. Williams, W., *Windrush Lessons Learned Review: Independent Review by Wendy Williams*. HC 93, HMSO, 2020.
29. Gallup, *Gallup International Public Opinion Polls Great Britain, 1937–1975*, Vol. II, p. 1199.
30. HM Government, 1981 Census of Population, Cmnd. 7146, HMSO, July 1978. p. 7.
31. Ibid.
32. HOC: 1981 Census Miscellaneous Papers. Document 11. OPCS, 'Changing Britain: a census snapshot (OPCS Spotlight 6)'.
33. HM Government, 1981 Census of Population, Cmnd. 7146, p. 7.
34. Select Committee on Race Relations and Immigration, *The Problems of Coloured School Leavers*, Paper 413-I, HMSO, 1969, p. 17.
35. Ibid., p. 13.
36. Select Committee on Race Relations and Immigration, *The West Indian Community*, Volume 1: Report. Paper HC 180-I, HMSO, 1977.
37. HOC: 1981 Census Miscellaneous Papers. CEN 78/4. OPCS, 'OPCS Monitor: 1981 Census. Developing a question on ethnic origin'.
38. HOC: 1981 Census Miscellaneous Papers. CEN 80/2. OPCS, 'OPCS Monitor: Tests of an ethnic question', p. 6.
39. Ibid., p. 2.
40. Ibid., p. 5.
41. Ibid.
42. GRO, *Census of England and Wales 1981*. General Report, HMSO, 1983, p. 9.
43. Ibid.
44. Ibid., p. 9.
45. Ibid., p. 10.
46. See the Select Committee on Race Relations and Immigration report on Police/Immigrant Relations, Vol. 1. Paper 471-I, HMSO, 1971.
47. Olusoga, *Black and British*, p. 517.
48. HOC: 1981 Census Miscellaneous Papers. CEN 80/2. OPCS, 'OPCS Monitor: Tests of an ethnic question', p. 2.
49. Ibid.
50. Ibid. The OPCS's report on 'Tests of an ethnicity question' says the following: 'Fieldwork had suggested that a large proportion of [West Indian] parents would prefer to describe their UK-born children as "black British", or something similar. This would be analogous to the use of the term "black" in the censuses of the USA and the countries

of the Caribbean, to describe people of African descent. But because of possible objections to any reference to colour in a census question for use in Britain, this possibility was not further explored.'
51. HOC: 1981 Census Miscellaneous Papers. CEN 80/3. OPCS, 'OPCS Monitor: The Government's decision on an ethnic question in the 1981 Census', p. 2.
52. HC vol. 983, 39 April 1980.
53. HOC: 1981 Census Miscellaneous Papers. CEN 78/4. 'OPCS Monitor: 1981 Census. Developing a question on ethnic origin', p. 9.
54. See the Home Affairs Select Committee's report on Racial Disadvantage, 1981. See also Lord Scarman's 1982 report on the Brixton riots.
55. Gov.uk, List of ethnic groups, accessed at https://www.ethnicity-facts-figures.service.gov.uk/style-guide/ethnic-groups/.
56. Thorvaldsen, *Censuses and Census Takers*, p. 95.
57. Whitby, *The Sum of the People*, p. 225.
58. Ibid., p. 226.
59. Statistics South Africa, *The People of South Africa. Population Census 1996*. Report number 03-01-11, Statistics South Africa, 1996.

14. All Equal

1. BBC News, 'Profile: Iqbal Sacranie', 10 June 2005.
2. These quotations from the letter are published in the MCB press release 'Identity – Faith not ethnicity', published online, 6 June 2000.
3. This comparison was made by Jamil Sherif, who has written the definitive summary of this episode and to whom I am thankful for being able to tell this story in detail at all. Sherif, J., 'A Census chronicle – reflections on the campaign for a religion question in the 2001 Census for England and Wales', *Journal of Beliefs & Values*, 32:1 (2001), pp. 1–18.
4. GRO, *Census of Great Britain, 1851*. Religious Worship. England and Wales. Report and Tables, p. cxv.
5. See, for example, GRO, *Census of the British Empire 1901*. Report with Summary, HMSO, p. 143.
6. Northern Ireland Statistics and Research Agency, *Registrar General Northern Ireland Annual Report 2011*, p. 46.
7. Cooley, L., '"It Will Do No More than Annoy the Protestants": The 1991 Northern Ireland Census and the Irish Language', *Nationalism and Ethnic Politics*, 28:3 (2022), pp. 269–89.
8. Or 'other'. HOC: 1981 Census Miscellaneous Papers. CEN 78/4. OPCS, 'OPCS Monitor: 1981 Census. Developing a question on ethnic origin'.

9. ONS, *Census 2001. General Report for England and Wales*, 2006, p. 249.
10. Sherif, 'A Census chronicle', p. 2.
11. ONS, The 1997 Census Test Advance Round and Information Leaflets: Assessment of Small Scale Testing, January 1997.
12. Sherif, 'A Census chronicle', p. 5.
13. Ibid., p. 8.
14. ONS, *Census 2001. National Report for England and Wales*, Table T53; General Register Office for Scotland, *Scotland's Census 2001: The Registrar General's 2001 Census Report to the Scottish Parliament*, table 9.
15. ONS, *Census 2001. Quality report for England and Wales*, p. 67.
16. ONS, *Census 2001 England and Wales. Classifications*, pp. 49–51.
17. ONS, *Census 2001* 'Summary theme figures and rankings – 390,000 Jedi There Are' [online article].
18. BBC News, 'Census returns of the Jedi', 13 February 2003.
19. ONS, *Census 2001 Scotland. Classifications*.
20. ICM Research, Muslim Poll – December 2002. Available online at https://www.bbc.co.uk/radio4/today/reports/archive/politics/muslim_poll.pdf
21. The CONTEST strategy, one facet of which was the anti-radicalisation scheme Prevent, was devised in 2003. In 2005, Hazel Blears, the minister responsible for counter-terrorism, told the Home Affairs Select Committee that it was inevitable that 'some of our counter-terrorism powers will be disproportionately experienced by the Muslim community'. Reported here: *Guardian*, 'Muslims face increased stop and search', 2 March 2005.
22. The Home Affairs Select Committee held a session specifically on Luton.
23. Sherif, 'A Census chronicle', pp. 11 and 15.
24. Weitz, E. D., *A Century of Genocide: Utopias of Race and Nation*, Princeton University Press, 2015.
25. 2001 Census, table UV93, accessed via Nomisweb. I asked the ONS whether an estimate was ever produced using the 1991 Census data and they could find no record of one. It would be a pity if the data has never been never analysed but, if the process in 2001 is anything to go by, it may have required a lot of data cleaning to make an accurate estimate.
26. The Equalities Review, *Fairness and Freedom: The Final Report of the Equalities Review*, HMSO, 2007, p. 30.
27. Home Office, *Criminal statistics England and Wales 1960. Statistics relating to crime and criminal proceedings for the year 1957*, Cmnd. 529.
28. Home Office, *Report of the Committee on Homosexual Offences and Prostitution*. Cmnd. 247, HMSO, 1957.

29. Home Office, *Criminal statistics England and Wales 1960. Statistics relating to crime and criminal proceedings for the year 1960*, Cmnd. 1437; Home Office, *Criminal statistics England and Wales 1966. Statistics relating to crime and criminal proceedings for the year 1966*, Cmnd. 3332.
30. Clery, E., 'A liberalisation in attitudes?', *British Social Attitudes*, 40 (2023), p. 53.
31. Ibid.
32. HC Deb vol. 492, col. 553, 11 May 2009.
33. See, for example, Benn, A., 'The big gap in discrimination law: class and the equality act 2010', *University of Oxford Human Rights Hub Journal*, 30 (2020). The case for including social class was also argued by some MPs at the time of the Equality Bill.
34. House of Commons Library, Bill Paper on the Equality Bill, 2009, p. 20.
35. Government Equalities Office, 'The Equality Bill – Government Response to the Consultation', CM 7454, July 2008, pp. 4–5; HC Deb vol. 492, col. 634 [see comments by Philip Davies MP near the end]; Mason, A. and Minerva, F., 'Should the Equality Act 2010 be extended to prohibit appearance discrimination?', *Political Studies*, 70:2 (2022), pp. 425-42; also Bi, S., 'Equality Act: 10 Years On', Equality Act Review, 2021.
36. ONS, Equalities data audit: March 2024 edition, 21 March 2024.
37. Government Equalities Office, *National LGBT Survey: Research Report*, July 2018.
38. ONS, 'Sex and gender identity question development for Census 2021' [accessed online], n.d..
39. Letter from the Director of Statistical Services at the NRS Peter Whitehouse to the Convenor of the Culture, Tourism, Europe and External Affairs Committee, 25 October 2019, Annex, p. 16.
40. It was not actually a finding of the testing in Scotland that including an 'other' option in the sex question was associated with a lower rate of response, although the argument was made that it was still not worth the risk. See https://kevinguyan.com/2019/04/30/a-non-binary-sex-question-in-scotlands-2021-census/.
41. ONS, 'Sex and gender identity question development for Census 2021'.
42. ONS, 'Quality of Census 2021 gender identity data' [accessed online], 8 November 2023.
43. ONS, 'Gender identity, England and Wales: Census 2021', 6 January 2023.
44. Office for Statistics Regulation, Final report: Review of statistics on

gender identity based on data collected as part of the 2021 England and Wales Census, 12 September 2024.
45. In testing in England and Wales, 71 per cent of participants found the question 'Do you consider yourself to be trans?' acceptable or very acceptable, whereas 90 per cent of participants found the question 'Is your gender the same as the sex you were registered at birth?' acceptable or very acceptable. From this the ONS concluded, in its article 'Sex and gender identity question development for Census 2021' that 'There was a significant difference in acceptability of the gender identity questions between the treatment types' and that '[the] question "Do you consider yourself to be trans?" was not suitable for use in England and Wales because of low public acceptability.'
46. ONS, 'Sexual orientation, England and Wales: Census 2021' and 'Gender identity, England and Wales: Census 2021', 6 January 2023. Without specifying means the respondent did not write in an identity such as 'trans man', 'trans woman' or 'non-binary'.
47. Scottish Government, 'Scotland's Census 2022 – Sexual orientation and trans status or history' [published online], 27 June 2024.
48. Government Equalities Office (2009) *Equality Bill Impact Assessment*, April 2009, Annex E.
49. Guyan, K., *Queer Data: Using Gender, Sex and Sexuality Data for Action*, Bloomsbury Academic, 2022, p. 57.
50. Law Commission, *Hate Crime Laws: Final Report*, HC 942, Law Com No. 402, 6 December 2021.
51. BBC News, 'Hate crime: Police record attacks on punks, emos and goths', 4 April 2013.

15. A New Order of Magnitude

1. *Guardian*, 'The Doughnut, the less secretive weapon in the fight against international terrorism', 10 June 2003.
2. *Guardian*, 'GCHQ taps fibre-optic cables for secret access to world's communications', 21 June 2013.
3. *Guardian*, 'UK gathering secret intelligence via covert NSA operation', 7 June 2013; *Guardian*, 'XKeyscore: NSA tool collects "nearly everything a user does on the internet"', 31 July 2013.
4. Higgs, E., *The Information State in England the Central Collection of Information on Citizens since 1500*, Palgrave Macmillan, 2004, p. 32.
5. T. H. Clancy, quoted in ibid., p. 31.
6. HL Deb vol. 172, col. 1343, 26 July 1951.
7. King, A. and Crewe, I., *The Blunders of our Governments*, Oneworld, 2013, p. 219.

NOTES

8. *Yorkshire Post and Leeds Intelligencer*, 13 December 1952, p. 1. Accessed via the BNA.
9. Bellamy, 'Why no population register in peacetime?' p. 16.
10. Ibid., p. 15.
11. Redfern, P., 'Population registers: Some administrative and statistical pros and cons', *Journal of the Royal Statistical Society Series A: Statistics in Society*, 152:1 (1989), pp. 1–28.
12. Higgs, *The Information State*, pp. 5–6.
13. Lindop, N., Report of the Committee on Data Protection. Cmnd 734, HMSO, 1978, p. 66.
14. The vice-president of the Royal Statistical Society, Jill Leyland, has drawn attention to a clause in the 2007 Statistics and Registration Service Act that has the potential to 'oblige the ONS under certain circumstances to hand over individual data for nonstatistical purposes to the police or security services' and has sought an explanation of how the ONS would handle requests for census information from the police or the security services (from Sherif, 'A Census chronicle').
15. Home Office, Entitlement Cards and Identity Fraud, Cm 5557, July 2002.
16. Bellamy, 'Why no population register in peacetime?' pp. 15–16.
17. King and Crewe, *The Blunders of our Governments*.
18. Grayling, A. C., *In Freedom's Name: The Case Against Identity Cards*, Liberty, 2005, pp. 8, 14.
19. Ibid., p. 7.
20. Ibid., p. 13.
21. Lilley, P., *Identity Crisis: The Case against ID Cards*, Bow Group, 2005.
22. Manwaring-White, S., *The Policing Revolution*, Harvester, 1983, p. 32.
23. King and Crewe, *The Blunders of our Governments*, p. 231.
24. LSE Department of Information Systems, The Identity Project: An Assessment of the UK Identity Cards Bill and its Implications, 27 June 2005.
25. HC Deb vol. 435, col. 1174, 28 June 2005.
26. Public Accounts Committee, Home Office: The Immigration and Nationality Directorate Casework Programme (HC 1999–2000, 130), p. 2.
27. King and Crewe, *The Blunders of our Governments*, pp. 182–98.
28. Wallis. N., *The Great Post Office Scandal*, Bath Publishing, 2021.
29. Higgs, *The Information State*, pp. 120–1.
30. ONS, '2011 Census and the Labour Force Survey' [online], 11 December 2012.

31. ONS, 'Labour Force Survey performance and quality monitoring report: April to June 2023' [online], 15 August 2023.
32. Francis-Devine, B., 'Has labour market data become less reliable?' House of Commons Library [online], 30 October 2023.
33. ONS, 'Exploring the use of external data to assess for observed bias in Labour Force Survey estimates: interim findings' [online], 20 September 2018.
34. Athow, J., 'Carry that weight: Reducing the effects of COVID-19 on the Labour Force Survey', *ONS National Statistical* [online], 8 July 2021.
35. The Rt Hon Francis Maude, MP to Sir Andrew Dilnot, CBE, 'Government's response to the National Statistician's recommendation', letter, 18 July 2014.
36. Treasury Select Committee, Eleventh Report of Session 2007–08, Counting the population, HC 183.
37. ONS, 'The future of population and migration statistics in England and Wales: A consultation on ONS proposals', 29 June 2023.
38. Comptroller and Auditor General, Challenges in using data across government, Session 2017–2019, HC 2220, National Audit Office, June 2019.
39. Listen and Learn, 'Most Common Last Names in the UK: Does Yours Make the List?' [online], 4 March 2014.
40. This was suggested in the 2023 consultation about the population statistics transformation. As of 2024, the ONS was doing work to assess the quality of ethnicity data gathered via various datasets from healthcare providers: for example, ONS, 'Quality of ethnicity data in health-related administrative data sources by sociodemographic characteristics, England: May 2024', 3 May 2024.
41. ONS, 'Population and migration statistics transformation in England and Wales, population characteristics update: 2023' [online], 26 June 2023.
42. Greenwell, B., 'Lost Lives', n.d., www.billgreenwell.com.
43. *Daily News (London)*, 10 April 1951. Accessed via the BNA.
44. *Sunday Mirror*, 'Susan's census strip', 18 April 1971. Accessed via the BNA.
45. *MailOnline*, 'The end of ID cards? Now Government reveals they WON'T be compulsory', 30 June 2009.
46. ONS, 'Unlocking Google COVID-19 data to analyse the impact of social distancing' [online], 8 April 2020.
47. Fitzgerald, F. S., *Tender is the Night*, Vintage, 1934/2010, p. 325.
48. Grayling, *In Freedom's Name*, p. 13.

List of Illustrations

25 Relief on the Altar of Consul Domitius Ahenobarbus in the Temple of Neptune on the Field of Mars (Campo Marzio), Rome. Peter Horree/Alamy Stock Photo

35 Title page of John Graunt's *Bills of Mortality* (1665). Photo by Oxford Science Archive/Print Collector/Getty Images

44 Somerset House, headquarters of the General Records Office from its establishment in 1836 until 1970. Cofiant Images/Alamy Stock Photo

59 John Snow's map showing deaths from cholera around Broad Street in Soho during the 1854 outbreak. Wikipedia

68 'Diagram of the Causes of Mortality in the Army in the East' from Florence Nightingale's *A Contribution to the Sanitary History of the British Army During the Late War with Russia* (1859). Wikipedia

84 Excerpt from Charles Booth, *Life and Labour of the People in London* (1899/1902) showing the Limehouse area. Wikipedia

90 'Immediate Causes of Poverty' from B. S. Rowntree, *Poverty: A Study of Town Life* (1901)

95 The collapse of an Edinburgh tenement, from *Illustrated London News*, 7 December 1861. Penta Springs Limited/Alamy Stock Photo

123 'Occupations of the People' from *The Census of Great Britain in 1851* (1854). Wellcome Collection

154 Household entry for the Houses of Parliament, 1911 census. The National Archives RG 14/489

156 Census return for Constance Tite of South Kensington. The National Archives RG 14/118

165 Total population diagrams from *Census of England and Wales 1921* (1927). Crown Copyright. Reproduced with permission of the House of Commons Library

175 The Jarrow March, October 1936. Smith Archive/Alamy Stock Photo
195 Completing the National Register, from *Nottingham Evening Post*, 29 September 1939
207 Shoppers queuing in Eltham. Fox Photos/Getty Images
240 Staff at the General Register Office at the launch of the Ten Per Cent Census (*left*). PA Images/Alamy Stock Photo. Official publicity material produced for the 1966 Ten Per Cent Census (*right*). Reproduced with permission of the House of Commons Library from the copy in their collection
261 'Tests of an Ethnic Question' from *OPCS Monitor*. Reproduced with permission of the House of Commons Library from the copy in their collection
275 Census awareness poster. Archives of the Muslim Council of Britain
287 Questions from the 2021 England and Wales census and the 2022 Scotland census. Source: Office for National Statistics licensed under the Open Government Licence v.1.0 / National Records of Scotland
299 Demonstration against the ID Card Bill, 28 June 2025. Jaime Turner/Shutterstock
309 British Housewives' League protest against continued rationing, April 1951. The photograph appeared in the *Daily News (London)* under the headline 'Westminster Flare-Up'. Mirrorpix/Getty Images
313 England's population centre of gravity by decade. Georgina Sturge, 2024, created using data from England and Wales censuses 1801–2021

Index

Abbey Mills pumping station 70
Abbot, Charles 22, 40
Abolition of the Slave Trade Act (1807) 128
Adelina (jester) 146
African-American troops 251n
age-at-death 46
Albert, Prince 47, 131
Albion Colliery 121
Aldwych Skating Rink 155
Aliens Act (1905) 138–40
Allen, Thomas 158
al-Qaeda 277
American Civil War 128
anarchists 137
Anderson, Benedict 323
Anderson shelters 203
Annal, Dave 197n
'ante-nuptial conception' 161
Annual Survey of Hours and Earnings 301
Armistead, Wilson and Mary 126–7
Arnold, Betsey 47
arsenic 119
Artizans', Labourers' and General Dwellings Company 101
Asquith, Herbert 186
Asylum for the Houseless Poor 78

atheists 45
Atkins, David 311–12
Attlee, Clement 182, 224
Australia 139, 148, 168, 250, 252, 318
Ayer's Cherry Pectoral 212

Babbage, Charles 66, 74, 132
baby boom, post-war 219
Baptists 45
Barbican Estate 231
Barbie dolls 231
Barrow-in-Furness 96–7
Basutoland 252
Bazalgette, Joseph 70–1
BBC 181, 185, 239, 254
Beatles, the 232
Bell, Laura 156
Bellamy, Christine 294
Benn, Tony 153
Bevan, Aneurin 209–10, 222–4
Beveridge, William 210, 218–22
bills of mortality 31–5
Bingham, John 48
biometric data 317–18
Birmingham 102, 170, 180, 190, 204, 241, 274
Black and White Minstrel Show 254
Black Death 55
Blair, Tony 267–8

Blanch, Elizabeth 158
Bletchley Park 198–200, 282, 290
Blitz 203, 205, 220, 227, 315
Blyton, Enid 254
Board of Health 62, 69
Boards of Guardians 178n
Boer War 215
Bolivia 17
Booth, Charles 81–8, 89n, 91, 122, 137, 316, 319, 320, 323
Booth, William 103
Boudicca 314
Bournville 102, 230
Bradford 102, 107–9, 133
Bristol 35, 41, 130, 176, 214, 251, 262
British Empire 15, 40, 79, 131, 139, 141, 178n, 252, 322
British Housewives' League 308
British Medical Association 65
British National Party (BNP) 278
British Nationality Act (1948) 249
British Social Attitudes Survey 281
Brontë, Emily 47
brothels 83
Brown, Henry 'Box' 127
Browning, John 35
Buckle, Henry Thomas 79
Burns, Lucy 155
Burrow, Ethel 156
Busby, Matt 112

Cadbury family 102
Canada 148, 168, 250, 252
canals 41, 74
cancer 224
Canterbury 31
car ownership 238, 242
Carroll, Lewis 47
Cass, Elizabeth 149

Catholics 30–1, 45, 268, 270
  priests and nuns 172
censuses 11, 15–17, 19, 22–30, 34, 39–43, 46–52
  biblical 25–6
  and country of origin 129–41
  future of 303–9
  and housing 96–100, 103
  intrusive questioning 160–3
  and occupations 110–16
  and race and ethnicity 252–3, 256–66
  and religion 267–78
  Roman 15, 23–7, 123–4
  and women 142–63
censuses (individual years)
  1801: 41–2, 97, 110, 145, 147
  1811: 43, 110, 308
  1821: 43n, 110
  1841: 47–8, 50, 110, 113–14, 129–30, 146
  1851: 49–51, 96, 112n, 122, 124, 130, 146, 211, 259, 324, 325
  1871: 98, 103, 114
  1881: 96, 111, 124, 158
  1891: 100
  1911: 142, 145, 151, 153–60, 322, 325
  1921: 164
  1931: 185–6, 243
  1961: 228, 235, 243
  1971: 308
  1966: 228, 235–44
  1991: 278–9, 322
  2001: 267–8, 270, 272, 274, 278–9
  2011: 304
  2021: 114, 304, 315
Central Statistical Office (CSO) 272n, 318n
Chadwick, Edwin 62, 69, 80, 95
Chakrabarti, Shami 297
Chamberlain, Neville 184–5

INDEX

Chartist movement 176
child benefit 224
children
   in employment 115–16
   'illegitimate' 49, 296, 322
   mortality rates 38, 161–2, 171–2, 211, 215–16
China 27, 141
cholera 51, 53–63, 65, 70–1, 134, 213, 230, 281, 316
Cholera Inquiry Committee 61–2
Church of England 269
Churchill, Winston 178n, 210
cinemas 180
civil liberties 38, 207–8, 292–4, 297, 300, 306, 308
Civil Registration Act (1836) 45
civil service 24, 50, 199, 218, 221–2, 244
coal mining 120–1, 123–4, 169, 172
Cohen, Jack 135–6
Cohen, Robbie 202
Cold War 282, 294, 301
Collins, Cornelia 112n
Commission for Racial Equality 257
Commonwealth Immigration Act (1962) 250
contraception 180, 233
Cooper, Duff 234
Cooper, Edmund 58
Corbyn, Jeremy 153
costermongers 117
cotton industry, *see* textile industries
Coventry 204, 242
Covid-19 pandemic 224, 314–16
Craft, Ellen and William 125–8, 140, 325
Crapper, Charles 48
Crapper, Sarah 47–8
Crapper, Thomas 48

Crime Survey 301
Crimean War 66–7
Cromwell, Oliver 34
Crystal Palace 49, 147, 178n

Dagenham car factory 244
Daily Mail 240
Daily Mirror 223
Dál Riata 28
Danelaw 42
Darwin, Charles 78, 136
Data Protection Act (1984) 296
David, King 26
Davison, Emily Wilding 144, 151–3
de Groot, Jan 31
death certificates 64–5
Defour, Judith 38n
democracy 11, 19, 136, 141, 182, 272, 282, 310
Denmark 202, 304–5, 320
Derby, Lord 189–90
Dickens, Charles 47, 78, 107–8
diet 86
digital data 309–10, 317
diphtheria 224, 234
Director magazine 239
disabilities 211, 284
disease
   industrial diseases 119–20
   miasma theory 55, 57, 62, 67, 97, 213
   transmission and control 62–72, 75, 103, 316
diversity monitoring 306–7
divorce 148, 243–4
DNA 318
dog tax 30
Domesday Book 29–30, 42, 107, 145–6, 194, 217, 314
domestic service 13, 15, 113–15, 129, 131
Dorling, Danny 311–12
Douglass, Frederick 127
drains 89
Druids 269

Dunadd Fort 28
Duncan, Dr William 104
dysentery 51

Easter Rising (1916) 165
Edinburgh 92–5, 97, 99, 105, 155
　tenement collapse 92–4, 101
Edinburgh City Improvement Act (1867) 95
Egyptians, ancient 27
electricity 179
Eley family 57–8
Elizabeth I, Queen 31, 45
Elizabeth II, Queen 232
emigration 167–8
enemy aliens 318
Engels, Friedrich 75–6
English Defence League (EDL) 278
environmental medicine 212–13
Epidemiological Society 58
Equal Pay Act (1970) 244
Equality Act (2010) 282–3, 288–9
'Essex poisonings' 64
ethnicity 14, 17, 256–60, 262–5, 270, 273, 285, 306–7, 319, 323
eugenics 136–7, 162, 253, 319
European Court of Human Rights 292
European Union 282
Evening Standard 142, 249

Factory Acts 115, 121
Family Expenditure Survey 234
Family Resources Survey 244, 301
Farr, William 56n, 62–3, 65–6, 71, 104, 118, 122, 211, 305, 316, 324
Faucher, Léon 75
Fee Grant Act (1891) 115
fertility rates 38, 162, 236

Festival of Britain 227–9
financial crisis (2008) 299, 303
Finland 320
First World War 162, 164, 167, 169, 179, 184, 194, 215, 218, 314–15, 318
　registration and conscription 186–91
fish-fryers 118
Fitzgerald, F. Scott 310
foreign nationals 50, 128, 138, 298
Foss, Hugh 198
France 22–3, 27, 39–40, 50, 121, 202, 320, 323
Franklin, Benjamin 38

Gallup polls 181–2, 228–9, 237, 251, 255
Galton, Francis 88–9, 136
Gambia 252
Gaskell, Elizabeth 106, 109
Gateshead 100, 308
GCHQ 290–3, 296
gender identity 19, 284–8, 307
Gender Reassignment Act (2004) 285
General Household Survey 244
General Post Office 88
General Register Office (GRO) 45, 48, 56, 62, 123, 158, 162, 190, 205–7, 225–6, 235–40, 295
General Strike 177
genetic factors 13, 88–9, 136, 264, 281, 283
genocide 272
George VI, King 232
Germany 184, 186, 197–8, 202, 205, 248, 253
　East Germany 294
Gestapo 202
Gin Craze 37
Glasgow 28, 98–9, 105, 204, 274
Gleeson, James 312

INDEX

Goldman, Lawrence 79
goths and emos 289
Government Code and Cypher School (GC&CS) 199
Graham, George 49
Graunt, John 32–5, 64
Grayling, A. C. 297, 306, 310
Great Depression 170, 216, 223
Great Exhibition 49, 227, 229n
Great National Hunger March 176
Great Ormond Street Hospital 213
Green, Charles 81
Green, Elizabeth 48
Guinness Trust 101
Gunn, George 94
Guy, Dr William 119–20
Guyan, Kevin 288–9

Hampstead 57–8
Harford, Ellen 158
Haringey census question 260, 262, 270, 319
Harrisson, Tom 182–3
Hart, Judith 235
Hastings, Battle of 29
Hastings, Sir Charles 65
healthcare charities 214
hearth tax 30
Henry VIII, King 30, 130
Hepburn, Audrey 197–8
Herbert, Sidney 68
Herod, King 26
Higgs, Edward 292, 301
Hill, Octavia 103, 135
Hindus 259, 271
Hitler, Adolf 197, 202
HIV/AIDS 281
HMRC 303
Hogarth, William 37
Holborn Viaduct 120
holidays 180
Hollerith tabulation machines 162
homelessness 78, 132, 283, 289

homosexuality 279–81, 283, 285, 323
  see also same-sex relationships
Hope, Dorothea 156
hot water 13, 241–2
housing 92–105, 179–80
  council housing 104–5, 236, 238, 316
  model villages 101–2
  overcrowding 60, 65–6, 75, 92–105, 168, 170–1
Housing of the Working Classes Act (1890) 105
Howden, Yorkshire 64
Howey, Mary 155
Huntington, Samuel P. 272
Hutchinson, Roger 38
hydrotherapy 113n

Iceland 22, 192
identity cards 16, 193, 195–6, 201–2, 207–8, 225, 293–4, 296–300, 308–9, 321
Identity Cards Act (2006) 296, 306
Illustrated London News 48
immigration
  Dutch and Flemish refugees 31
  immigration laws 138–40
  Polish refugees 247–8
  and race relations 247–66
  and taxation 129–30, 139–4
  'Windrush' migration 248–9, 255, 271
Immigration Act (1971) 255
imports 73–4
Improved Industrial Dwellings Company 101
Inca 27
India 131, 139, 141, 169, 255
industrial accidents and diseases 118–21
Industrial Revolution 11, 73
inequality 13–14, 46, 75, 85, 136, 150, 171, 242, 283–4
  see also Equality Act (2010)

infant mortality, *see* children, mortality rates
international dialling code 18
International Passenger Survey 234
Investigatory Powers Act (2016) 292
IRA 277
Ireland 34, 50–1, 75, 133, 165–7, 188, 270
Irish, in social surveys 83, 132–3
Irish Free State 165
iron and steel industries 121, 169, 176, 314, 314
IT systems 300
Italian barrel-organists 132

Jack the Ripper 149
Jarrow March 172–6, 314
Jedi 276, 325
Jenkin family 157
Jennings, Humphrey 182–3
Jewish Board of Guardians 214
Jews 77, 83, 133–8, 140, 201–3, 249, 251
Johnson, John 140
Judith, Countess 146

King, Martin Luther 254
kitchens, size of 238
Kleykamp bombing 201–2
Knox, Alfred Dillwyn ('Dilly') 198–200

Labour Force Survey 302–3
Labouring Classes Dwellings Act (1866) 104
Ladies' Sanitary Association 119
Lancashire 74, 100, 109–10, 128, 313
Land Acquisition Act (1946) 229
Lansbury Estate 228–9
lascars 45–6, 140–1
Le Bon, Gustave 136
Leeds 108, 126, 135, 174, 325
Leeds and Liverpool Canal 104

Lego 231
Leicester 174–5
Leofgeat 146
Lesslie, George 129
Leverhulme, Lord 102
Lewis family 60–1
Liberty 292, 297
life expectancy 210–11
Lilley, Peter 298
Limehouse 140–1
Lindop Committee 295
Lister, Thomas 45
literacy 46, 51, 116, 126, 257–8
Liverpool 43, 45–6, 73–4, 96, 104–5, 129, 133, 170, 204–5, 217, 248, 251, 262
Liverpool Sanitation Act (1846) 104
lodgers 48, 94, 99, 103, 129, 140–1
London
    air raids and evacuations 203–4, 315
    bills of mortality 31–3
    Booth's poverty survey 81–8
    Broad Street cholera outbreak 53–63, 72
    Bromley-by Bow cholera outbreak 70–1
    dock strike 122
    East End Germans 118
    East End Jews 137–8
    first council housing 105
    Great Stink 69–71, 75
    healthcare charities 214
    immigration 130–1
    Mayhew's survey 76–8, 117–18
    number of houses 35
    overcrowding 100–1, 170
    population size 33
    post-war rebuilding 227–9
    race relations 261–2
    sewers 70–1
Long, Walter 187
lunatic asylums 50

lustrum 23, 25
Luton 175, 278

McCulloch, John Ramsay 79
McIvor, Joseph 94
Macon, Georgia 125
Madge, Charles 182–3
mail coaches 41
Maitland, William 35
malaria 212
Malthus, Rev. Thomas 39–40
Manchester 46, 73–5, 109, 112, 128, 131, 150, 170, 241–2, 277, 299
Manchester City FC 112
Manchester Guardian 147
manufacturing, decline of 169–70, 314
Margaret, Princess 243–4
Marks and Spencer 135
marriage ceremonies 45–6
Marshall, Kitty 154–5
Marx, Karl 57, 220
Mass-Observation 182–3, 203–4, 218, 220, 239, 325
Maternity and Child Welfare Act (1918) 216
maternity leave 219
Mathers, Joanne 270
Maund, Edward 157
May, Mary 64
Mayhew, Henry 76–8, 81, 87, 112, 117–18, 132, 319
mental illness 211, 216, 317
Merseyside 42, 171, 313
Metropolitan Board of Works 70
Meysenburg, Malwida von 118
Middelburg 130
Military Service Act (1916) 191n
Mill, John Stuart 81, 316
Millennium Dome 227
Mongol Empire 27
Monroe, Marilyn 242
Moorfields Eye Hospital 213
Mormons 269
Morning Chronicle 76

Moser, Claus 318n
mud-larks 118
multiculturalism 272
Muslim Council of Britain 267, 274
Muslims 141, 252, 259, 267, 271–2, 274, 277–9
Mussolini, Benito 200

Napoleon Bonaparte 21
Nation 187
National Archives 197n
National Assistance Board 224
National Council for Civil Liberties (NCCL) 294
National Food Survey 234
National Front 261
National Identity Register 296–300, 305, 317–18
National Insurance 178, 214–15, 219, 223, 225–6, 306
National Record of Scotland 284
National Register (NR) 16, 187–9, 191, 193, 198–9, 204–7, 225–6, 241, 293–4, 299–300
and enemy aliens 318–19
National Registration Act (1915) 188
National Registration Act (1939) 192, 194
national service 206, 225, 232
National Service (Armed Forces) Act (1939) 193
National Survey of Hospitals 217
National Unemployed Workers' Movement (NUWM) 176
National Union of Women's Suffrage Societies (NUWSS) 150
Netherlands 22, 192, 197, 201–2, 304, 306, 320
New Commonwealth or Pakistan (NCP) 254–5
New Earnings Survey 244

New Lanark 101–2
new towns 230, 244
New York 51, 100
New Zealand 148, 168, 252
Newcastle upon Tyne 100, 171, 225, 241, 308
NHS 16, 209–10, 217–18, 223–4, 226, 229, 233, 306, 316
NHS numbers 226
Niblett, Charlotte 158
Nightingale, Florence 66–9, 316, 324
North, George 225, 293
Northern Ireland 11, 165–7, 269–70, 275, 279, 284n, 298, 315
Norway 310, 320
Notting Hill race riots 247, 249, 255
Nottingham race riots 246–7, 249, 255
nurses 124

Office for National Statistics (ONS) 272–3, 275, 284–6, 302, 304, 306, 309, 318n
Office of Population Censuses and Surveys (OPCS) 256–7, 264, 272n
Old Testament 26
Olusoga, David 262
opium 54, 140, 212
O'Reilly, Roseanne 200

Packer, Annie 157
Palace of Westminster 43, 152–3, 304
Pankhurst, Christabel 150
Pankhurst, Emmeline 142–3, 154
parish records 31, 35, 41–2, 45, 192
Peabody, George 101, 135
Peabody Trust 101, 103
Peel, Robert 80

pensions 122, 147, 224, 301
Pepys, Samuel 33
Petty, William 33–5, 300
Philadelphia 126
philanthropy 101, 103, 214
Pidoux, Gertrude 156
piemen 117
Pilgrim Trust 216–17
Pilrig Model Dwellings Company 101
Pitt Dundas, William 99
plague 32–3, 39, 55, 58
planning 229–31
Plymouth 204, 230–1
Poland 134, 135, 184
police constables 103
political arithmetic 34–5, 50, 61, 80, 300–1
poll taxes 30, 34, 130, 295, 300
Poor Census 30
Poor Law Commission 69
Poor Laws 79–80, 224
Poplar 227–8, 242
population
  centre of gravity 311–14
  decline 38–9
  density 65, 100
  estimates (nineteenth century) 42, 44, 49, 51, 75
  interwar boom 180
  rural to urban ratio 96
Population Act (1800) 22, 40
Port Sunlight 102
Porter, George 79
post-war consensus 210, 228, 236
poverty line 86, 177
Powell, Enoch 255
Presley, Elvis 232
Price, Rev. Dr Richard 38, 40
prisoners 306
privacy 16, 207, 292, 295–6, 309–10, 321–3
prostitutes 137, 149–50, 214
protected characteristics 283, 289

Public Assistance Committee 178
Public Health Acts 69, 213
public transport 87
Punch 76

Quakers 45, 90, 102, 127, 269

Race Relations Act (1965) 255–6
race riots 246–7, 249, 253–5
radicalism 277–8
radio 231–2
railways 41, 74, 116, 119
rationing 191, 196, 206, 220, 222, 225
rats 119
records and record players 233
Rees, Aneira 209–10
Reform Act (1884) 150
Regulation of Investigatory Powers Act (2000) 292
religion 14, 166, 259, 267–78, 283, 307, 317
and housing 102–3
Representation of the People Act (1918) 159
Rhondda Valley 121, 241
Richardson, Mary 151
Rickman, John 40–3, 46, 66, 324
Right to Privacy Bills 295
Robertson's marmalade 254
Roger, Earl 146
Romani people 253
Roosevelt, Eleanor 197
Roosevelt, Franklin D. 197, 218n
Round, Mary 158
Rowntree, Joseph 85
Rowntree, Seebohm 85–90, 100, 177–8, 316, 319, 323
Royal Commission on Army Medical and Sanitary Reforms 68
Royal Commission on India 68
Royal Commission on Population 236
Royal Commission on the Aged Poor 122
Royal Commission on the Health of Towns 69
Royal Commission on the Housing of the Working Classes 105
Royal Commission on the Poor Laws 79–80, 132–3
Royal Navy 191n
Royal Society 34
Runnymede Trust 257
Rushdie, Salman 272
Ruskin, John 103
Russia 67, 132, 134, 135, 170, 291

Sackville-West, Vita 280
Sacranie, Iqbal 267–8, 274
Sadler, Professor 143
St John's Wood 57
St Kilda 324
St Matthew's Gospel 26
Saltaire 102, 230
Salvation Army 103
same-sex relationships 278–9, 281–2
Sandwich 31
Sbarbaro, Jane 157
scarlet fever 63, 65
Scheele's green 119
schools, segregated by social class 87
Schweder, Edith 157
Scotland 11, 27–9, 31, 279, 304, 315
car ownership 242
child mortality 171
emigration 167–8
Irish immigration 133
overcrowding 97–8, 170–1
religious affiliations 273–4, 277, 317n
rural to urban population ratio 96

sexual orientation/gender identity 284–5, 287–8
shrinking population 241
'special study areas' 237n
Scottish Isles 242
Second World War 16, 167, 176, 184–6, 192–206, 210, 214, 217–18, 229, 241, 251n, 315, 318
Section 28: 281
Senchus fer n-Alban 28
September 11 attacks 277
Serbia 272, 278
servants, taxes on 30
Sexual Offences Act (1967) 279
sheep tax 30
Sherif, Jamil 272
Shetland Islands 98–9
Shields Daily Gazette 174
shipbuilding 169, 172, 314
Shipley 102
Shipman, Dr Harold 64–5
ships' passenger lists 129, 134–5
Sierra Leone 252
Sikhs 259, 271, 276
Skegness 180
slavery 40, 125–9, 262
smallpox 51, 69, 213
Smith, Emily 157
Snow, Dr John 55–62, 71, 316, 324
Snowden, Edward 291
soap operas 239
social class 84, 87–8, 122–3, 136, 145–6, 150, 161–2, 245, 283, 323
social science 81, 85, 237
Soho 55–6, 58, 71–2, 100
Somerset House 44–5, 71, 109, 205, 239
South Africa 15–16, 148, 265–6, 319
spa towns 113
Spain 22–3
Spitalfields 100–1, 103–4
SS *Empire Windrush* 248–9

SS *Ormonde* 248–9
Staffordshire potteries 111
Start, Mr and Mrs 197
Stationery Office 217–18
Statistical Account of the British Empire 79
Statistical Society of London 81
'sterile unions' 161
Stoker, Abraham 158
Stoney Stanton, Leicestershire 314
Strangers' Home for Asiatics, Africans and South Sea Islanders 140–1
suburbs 179–80, 230, 241–2, 244, 314
Sudan 139, 272
Sumerians 27
Sun, The 240
Sunday Mirror 221, 308
Sunderland 100
Sunshine Girl, The 102
surveillance 16, 203, 278, 292–3, 298, 301
Sweden 22, 304, 320, 321

taxation 12, 19, 23, 27, 29–30, 79, 91, 142, 145–6, 157, 219, 301, 303–4, 306
of aliens 129–30, 139–40
see also poll taxes; window tax
television 231–2
Tesco 136
textile industries 73–6, 107–10, 113–16, 123, 128, 169, 314
unemployment in 171–2
Thames, River 45, 62–3, 69–71, 205
Thames Embankment 71
Thornton, William 23, 26, 91
Tilbury Docks 135, 249
Times, The 143, 223
Titmuss, Richard 89
toilet facilities 13, 48, 63, 85, 95, 102, 242

Tower Hamlets 82
Town and Country Planning Act (1947) 229
Trade Disputes and Trade Unions Act (1927) 177
Trade Union Act (1871) 121
Trades Union Congress (TUC) 176, 177
tuberculosis 62
Tupperware 231
Turing, Alan 198–9, 282
Twells, Henry 157
typhoid fever 63, 65, 71, 213, 316
typhus 63, 65, 71

UK Statistics Authority 304
unemployment 170–8, 216–19, 223–5, 236, 307
Unemployment Assistance Board 173
unemployment insurance 162, 170, 214, 301
United Nations 282
United States 22, 100, 130, 134, 168, 170, 181, 232, 263, 320
  racist violence 253
  slavery 125–6, 128, 144–5

vaccination 69, 213, 224
van Heemstra, Baroness Ella 197
Victoria, Queen 47, 56n, 67, 122, 149
Vivian, Sylvanus 191–4, 208, 225, 305, 316, 324

Wall Street Crash 170
Wartime Social Survey 234
watercress girl 77, 112, 117
Watling Street 314
Watts, Charlie 308
welfare state 16, 91, 207, 210, 218, 222, 224, 229, 244

Welsh language 283
Whitby, Andrew 24
Whitehead, Rev. Henry 59–61
Wilde, Oscar 280
Wilkinson, Ellen 173–4
Willcock, Harry 208, 293–4
William the Conqueror 29
Wilson, Harold 295
Winder, Robert 250
window tax 30, 39
Wogan, Terry 277
Wolfenden Report 281
Wollstonecraft, Mary 38
Woman magazine 239
women 142–63
  'bare-headed' 83
  breadwinners 43n, 47–8
  and double standards 149–50
  emigration 148
  literacy 46
  and national insurance 219
  occupations 113–14
  participation in labour force 162, 242–4
  post-war 233
  and property ownership 148
Women's Royal Naval Service 199
Women's Social and Political Union (WSPU) 142–3, 150, 153, 155
women's suffrage 16, 142–4, 150–9, 176–7, 308, 325
wool industry, *see* textile industries
Woolf, Virginia 280
workers' rights 121–2
workhouses 80, 236
working hours 179

Yiddish 134
York 85–90, 100, 130, 177–8